# Parenting the
# EPHRAIM'S CHILD

# Parenting the
# EPHRAIM'S
# CHILD

Characteristics,
Capabilities, and
Challenges of
Children
who are
## INTENSELY
## MORE

DEBORAH TALMADGE and JAIME THELER

ISBN 13: 978-0-88290-773-4

Published by Horizon Publishers, an imprint of Cedar Fort, Inc.
2373 W. 700 S., Springville, UT 84663
Distributed by Cedar Fort, Inc., www.cedarfort.com

The Library of Congress cataloged the 2004 edition as follows:

Talmadge, Deborah.
    Parenting The Ephraim's child : characteristics, capabilities, and challenges of children who are intensely MORE / by Deborah Talmadge and Jaime Theler.
        p. cm.
    Includes bibliographical references.
    ISBN 0-88290-773-5
    1. Problem children. 2. Child psychology. 3. Temperament in children. 4. Child rearing.
    5. Parenting. 6. Parenting--Religious aspects--Christianity.
    I. Theler, Jaime. II. Title.
    HQ773.T34 2004
    649'.64--dc22
                                    2004022802

Cover design by Rebecca Greenwood
Cover design © 2012 by Lyle Mortimer
Typeset by Natalie Roach

Printed in the United States of America

10  9  8  7  6  5  4  3  2  1

Printed on acid-free paper

# ACKNOWLEDGMENTS

Many thanks to Jason for his support and input, Grammy for her unwavering belief, Christie Antczak for her encouragement, Robert LaBaron for the impetus to start, and to the publishing staff for all their hard work.

# Table of Contents

# PREFACE

*By Jaime Theler—*

My initiation into parenthood began on Father's Day with the birth of our first son just hours after giving a talk in sacrament meeting. He was a very alert baby who looked at everything and loved to be with people. My husband and I were amazed at how good-natured he was, despite the fact that he didn't sleep. From the first day, our son slept significantly less than the average infant. Naps were brief and completely gone by age two and a half.

When our son started to crawl (rather late), we saw a new personality emerging like a butterfly from a cocoon. We now had a very active, mobile baby who got into everything and let his wishes be known in no uncertain terms and at considerable volume. Gone was the mellow baby we had previously known. By one he was walking and talking and problem solving at a level that we did not expect. He noticed everything and followed adult conversations surprisingly well. He learned his numbers, colors, and letters with remarkable ease. We were excited by this bright, vivacious child. However, there were many times when we were alarmed by his intensity, the depth of his emotions, and how much he cared about every little thing.

Then we had our second son. He slept more than his brother, but from the first week showed a strong personality that was shocking in a newborn. This little spirit had amazing determination, as shown in the problems he had with eating. He refused to breast-feed. I was equally determined to do the best for my beloved baby so I consulted lactation specialists, read books, took herbs, and tried elimination diets to see if a specific food I was eating was the problem. I would try and try to feed my child, both of us fighting each other until I was exhausted and in tears. Finally I would give up after each feeding battle and give him a bottle of formula, which he heartily drank.

I also tried pumping milk for exclusive bottle feeding in case the problem wasn't the milk but the delivery system. One month later showed only a little letup in our son's cantankerous behavior, so we decided to switch to formula entirely. The change in our child was wonderful! He preferred formula. We think that he just didn't like the changing flavors of breast milk (a belief that has been validated as he's grown into the most selective eater I know). In those two months, I learned that a seven-pound baby could beat me in a battle of wills, and I began to worry.

I had always thought that I could be a decent parent. I am a patient, understanding, and confident adult. I believed that with time, practice, and prayer I could do it. I felt that it wouldn't be too difficult to figure out what to do. My two children were giving me a different view.

Maybe it was when every instruction resulted in a lengthy debate that caused me to worry. I'm sure the hysterical fits over seemingly inconsequential matters—like which plate we served dinner on—contributed to my alarm. The fact that my children never obeyed my instructions definitely worried me. I had many people watch my children, turn to me and sympathetically say, "You are in for it." I began to think they were right.

Some people probably thought that we were too permissive and that was the reason for our problems. After all, if you don't enforce your rules and authority, then how do you expect children to obey? That was the one thing that we sure we were doing. I always felt like the meanest mom on the block. My husband has been both a teacher and administrator at an elementary school, and he was even stricter than I was. But, as he did not take care of the kids every day, he felt more lost, exasperated, and frustrated than even I did. What were we doing wrong?

I decided that I needed to figure out how to parent my kids while they were young. I needed to develop some effective tools because I didn't feel that what I was doing was working. A big step was to finally admit that my children were more of a parenting challenge than many other kids I saw and knew. I had felt the truth of it deep inside, but I was afraid that I was just being a wimp. Most importantly, I didn't want to exchange my kids, I just wanted to do a better job guiding them.

My mother started a quest to discover the best ways to handle my kids. Together we read any books we could find that seemed pertinent. We noticed a pattern: the difficult child, the challenging child, the strong-willed child, the high-need child, (and other names) were all profiles of the same kind of child! Apparently I wasn't alone in my concerns and challenges with my children. The many books we read discussed certain temperamental traits that made parenting this child more difficult. The different authors suggested various solutions, many of which were the same from book to book. We began to compile the suggestions for our own use.

Our first goal was to understand my children. Next, we wanted to know how to work with each child so that we could raise him with less frustration and anger. Last, we wanted to look beyond the difficulties and see the strengths in my children so that we could help them develop those strengths. We turned to the scriptures and words of the prophets and apostles to try to understand why these spirits were sent to us at this time. Obviously, the Lord thought that we could prepare our children for whatever He planned for them. I just wasn't sure how to do that when every day seemed like an uphill battle, and I was ready for bed before my children were.

My mother and I began to think that other parents would benefit from the same information and perspective that we was gathering. There must be other LDS parents having similar struggles with their children. This book is the result of much research and prayer in our own search to be the best parents possible to our Ephraim's Children. Most of the content is not our own spectacular insight, but the combined wisdom of psychologists, teachers, educators, and scholars, presented from an LDS point of view. This book is for all of those who are tired of pulling their hair out and want to understand, raise, and, above all, enjoy their own Ephraim's Child.

*By Deborah Talmadge, Jaime's Mother—*

I had heard some interesting stories over the phone about clashes of will between my daughter and her children, but when I came for a week-long visit at Christmas one year, I was witnessing them firsthand. And sympathetically listening to a story was much different than living it. One day Jamie looked like she wanted to cry and strangle her son at the same time. She was stumped, overwhelmed and completely at a loss over what to do. The two-and-a-half-year-old was practically hysterical with anger and frustration. He had been screaming and crying for the past fifteen minutes, upset over what to eat for dinner.

He wanted a hotdog. Jamie gave it to him. No, he didn't want to eat it. So she took it away. "No!!! Don't take it away!" he screamed.

"Are you going to eat it?"

"No!"

"Then, I'm putting it away."

"No!"

"Make up your mind."

"I don't want to!"

Over and over, back and forth, the battle waged. The child screamed and cried over everything, wanting and not wanting at the same time. The mother tried to be calm and reasonable, but grew overwhelmingly frustrated as the difficult child refused to be placated or eat. She had heard that feeding toddlers could be a chore, but had not expected World War III over a hot dog.

This behavior appeared a few days before; an isolated incident that became two incidents, and then three incidents, which quickly escalated into an all-day-long ordeal that became three very long, difficult, days. This child had turned into a creature from outer space. His bewildered and frustrated parent tried to cope with this new problem, but nothing she did calmed the storm.

I felt powerless to help. I was afraid that anything I did would just make matters worse. My grandson did not need somebody else telling him what to do. My daughter did not need that coming from me either, so I retreated and resorted to prayer. A statement by Brigham Young kept going through my mind. "The sons of Ephraim are wild and uncultivated, unruly, ungovernable. The spirit in them is turbulent."[1]

I had felt for almost two years now that my daughter had what I was beginning to think of as an Ephraim's Child. Brigham Young had other things to say about the present day blood of Ephraim. "No hardship will discourage these men . . ." and "there is no hardship that this people would not face and overcome."[2]

So I listened to the struggle between my daughter and her husband and their son, feeling troubled about the outcome of the situation. I completely understood Jaime's bewilderment. My grandson was bright and articulate; he could communicate far beyond his two-and-a-half years. His memory was remarkable, and he could grasp concepts of a four- or five-year-old. But this out-of-control emotion was new, and beyond normal "terrible two" behavior. We were all concerned.

However, concern was not the only thing that was on my mind that day. I felt that I was seeing the presence of a certain kind of child, one who would stretch us adults to the limits. Since then I have seen these children everywhere—in church, at the store, and in parks and schools—children remarkably different from what mine were like at that age, but who are very similar to each other. I call them Ephraim's Children.

# 1

# Why ANOTHER Parenting Book

*One morning during that same visit to my daughter's family, I went downstairs early and found Jaime pouring through a parenting book. Her mother-in-law had given her two for Christmas. I had also given her one. Everyone in the family knew that her two children were going to be a challenge to raise.*

*During the remainder of my visit she devoured the first two books and was working on the third when I left. Her comments to me were: "They're not talking about my kids. The children they are describing are not like mine. If I did the things they say to do I would be in eternal negotiation. These kinds of techniques do not work with my children!"*

After that fateful visit, we searched to find the parenting books that *would* apply. We discarded much of what we found. Can you realistically ignore the temper tantrum of a child that screams for 30 minutes because you unlocked the car door when he wanted to do it? The books never mention what to do if your child rips apart her room during time out. (Do you then put her in a different time out?) What do good parents do when you tell your child, "No," firmly, calmly, and with a clear explanation for your reasoning, and the result is a ten minute debate that finally ends with you both unhappy? How about when your small child refuses to stay in her bed despite repeatedly returning her to it for an hour, or despite pleading, threats, yells, and spankings? What do you do when your child challenges you through reason, sometimes with reasoning so logical that you have to stop and think about it?

After exhausting the normal parenting resources, we turned to the ones dedicated to more challenging children. These books are written about the "difficult child," the "strong-willed child," the "high need child," or the "problem child." Even though these books do address some of the issues that frustrate you, for some reason they don't seem to fit your child. Yes, she can be difficult, but some days she is not, and is a joy to be around. There is no doubt that she is strong-willed, but the daily battles are not merely to rebel or challenge your authority—it is just part of her personality. However, we did not find any books about the "sometimes-difficult child," the "forever-debating child," or "the cares-a-whole-lot-about-everything child."

We then unearthed a much smaller selection of books that came close to identifying with the little boy that our family knows, loves, and occasionally wants to lock in a room to get ten minutes of peace. These books used names like the "active-alert child" and the "spirited child." We were overjoyed to find that we were not alone. There is profound relief in admitting that yes, this child is different from others and that we truly did have a child on our hands that makes parenting more difficult. It was enlightening and uplifting to read of other parents and their experiences.

In her book, *Raising the Spirited Child,* Mary Sheedy Kurcinka states that according to the personality research, 10 to 15 percent of all children living in the United States fit the description of this kind of a child.[1] You are not alone. Your child is not alone; there are a lot of these children out there right now.

Once we calmed our fears that these children really were more challenging, we were able to step back from the situation. We began to realize that the solutions were not going to be found in most of the parenting books in libraries and book stores. We watched numerous mothers struggling with their children, trying to do what the conventional wisdom said to do with an active, wiggly, emotional child—only to have their efforts fail. We saw the frustration on parents' faces and the displeasure (or disapproval) on the faces of the people around who were watching the little dramas unfold. What do you do when all the "tried and true" methods simply do not work?

After searching through several books written by psychologists, teachers, educators, and scholars, and coming up relatively empty-handed, we remembered the Lord's promise of help given through James. In James 1:5 it states: "If any of you lack wisdom, let him ask of God, that giveth to all men liberally, and upbraideth not; and it shall be given him."[2] We decided that we were lacking wisdom. At this point we extended our search to include the scriptures and words of modern-day prophets together with secular resources.

Quickly we began to realize that these extraordinary children, these wondrous spirits, these gifted children of God, are some of Heavenly Father's strongest. They are His "mighty nation." In Spencer W. Kimball's book, *Faith Precedes the Miracle*, he talks about babies and armies. He quoted F. M. Bareham as saying that while the men of the world are thinking of battles to make a difference in the world, Heavenly Father is sending babies to do the same. His illustration was that in 1809, while the world was waiting for news of Napoleon and his wars, a very young child was in the world whose name was Joseph Smith.[3] At the tender age of fourteen, young Joseph changed the world more profoundly than an army ever could have. Surely we can understand the significance.

These spirits are the "little ones" the Lord foretold would "confound the wise," "become a strong nation," and "thrash the nations by the power of his Spirit."[4] This is the Lord's army. Is it any surprise that they are as strong-willed as they are? "No hardship will discourage [them]; they will penetrate the deepest wilds and overcome almost insurmountable difficulties."[5]

Hugh B. Brown tells us that these children are angels that the Lord has sent down for us to teach and prepare. Only a short time ago they were with Him. We should not shrink from the responsibility to teach them.[6] Great is our responsibility, but it is very challenging also. How do you change contrariness, obstinacy, willfulness, and strong-headedness into steadfastness? Is it possible to transform a stubborn child into an unwavering servant of God? The answer is *yes*. It *is* possible, or the Lord would not have asked it of us. It is as Nephi wrote so many years ago, "I know that the Lord giveth no commandments unto the children of men, save he shall prepare a way for them that they may accomplish the thing which he commandeth them."[7] What was true for Nephi is also true for us. In this we can have absolute faith.

We know that we have a challenge. It is for all of us: mothers, fathers, grandparents, neighbors, teachers, and Church leaders. "And they shall also teach their children to pray, and to walk uprightly before the Lord."[8] But how do we teach the Ephraim's Children being sent to earth, when conventional methods and wisdom don't work? The books available now do not help us understand why these children have been reserved until now to come to Earth. Why has Heavenly Father held back the "difficult child" until now and then started sending them here by the millions? How do we need to parent them so they are spiritually prepared for their missions on Earth?

The spiritual aspect of these children needs to be addressed. We decided that we needed to handle these issues ourselves. We started searching for our own solutions. Thus began this book. We searched parenting books, the scriptures, writings of prophets and apostles, and the experiences of others.

Our goal is to help us all magnify our callings in raising Heavenly Father's latter-day army. We hope to help you identify, understand, teach, and enjoy the Ephraim's Child.

# 2
# What is an Ephraim's Child?

**What's In a Name?**

*Names are verbal symbols: they announce existence, herald one's reputation, and express character; they are, in some instances, a scepter of authority or even a crown of glory. Biblical names generally were descriptive of the one bearing them. They might identify position, memorialize a significant event in someone's life, express a hope entertained by those giving the name, or even represent a prophesied destiny. . . . In modern usage, names are convenient labels by which we differentiate one thing from another, one person from another. But in the ancient world Shakespeare's question 'What's in a name?' would have been taken very seriously. For a person's self was expressed and contained in his name.[1]*

Why have we added yet another name with which to label children? The fact that you are reading this book probably means that you have a child some call active, difficult, strong-willed, stubborn, or a problem. This chapter will explain why we have chosen a different name—Ephraim's Child—over other labels already in existence. Let's look at some of those names and why we rejected them.

## The Problem/Difficult Child

When you label someone as a problem or as difficult, then you are likely to have made a self-fulfilling prophecy. These names are intrinsically negative. They merely focus on the challenges of parenting these special spirits. These two names completely disregard the positive strengths of these kids.

## The Strong-Willed Child

Dr. James Dobson was the first child psychologist to introduce the term "strong-willed child" in 1978.[2] He and other psychologists had noticed an increase in children being referred for challenging behavior. Dr. Dobson deduced that these challenging behaviors were often the result of these children's naturally headstrong personalities.

The term "strong-willed" is often used to refer to a child who is stubborn, argumentative, and defiant. They can be difficult, frustrating, aggravating, loud, opinionated, and stubborn. However, they can also be witty, funny, loving, creative, bright, insightful, exciting, and a joy to be around. You vacillate between laughter and tears when dealing with them.

The name "strong-willed child" also tends to focus on the difficult aspects of the child's personality. When calling your child strong-willed, you and he are both more likely to think of negative traits such as stubborn and defiant behavior, and power struggles. When we name a child "strong-willed," then most likely that will be what we see. The name does not bring to mind the wonderful and enjoyable personality traits of the child.

## The Active Alert Child

The next name we investigated was the "active alert child." Dr. Linda S. Budd, a practicing psychologist specializing in working with children and their parents, created this name after years of working with parents who came to her for help. She writes, "What emerged from my work with those families was an image of a child who doesn't fit the 'norm,' who slips through the cracks of what 'experts' know about child rearing, who has *more* energy, *more* creativity, *more* intensity—*more everything*."[3]

Dr. Budd discussed eleven different characteristics of

this type of child. However, the name "active alert child" only refers to two of the traits: active and alert. What about the nine other personality traits that were discovered? And although many of these children are very active, not all of them have high energy. This name also does not address the spiritual side of these strong kids.

### The Spirited Child

The next name we tried out was "spirited child." This is a more positive label. When you think of someone being spirited, you think of enthusiasm, effervescence, and energy. A spirited horse is one that is difficult when young, but is often more desirable for that extra flash of spirit. Much good information about these children is containted in Mary Sheedy Kurcinka's book, *Raising Your Spirited Child*. This name is more comfortable, but ironically enough, the "spirited child" label still has no spiritual moorings.

### The Ephraim's Child

We wanted to take our name further. We wanted a name that would not only describe some of your child's personality traits, but also bring to mind some promises that the Lord has given His children for these latter days. When we have finished, we hope that the name "Ephraim's Child" will remind you of the divine worth of your child and the fact that she will have an important role in building the kingdom of God. Not only that, but her ability to fulfill that role greatly depends on the personality aspects which are right now driving you nuts. These are the children of the final days when strength of character will be so crucial.

To understand the Ephraim's Child, we need to understand her inheritance. The people of the tribe of Ephraim were turbulent and headstrong. Joseph Fielding Smith, Jr. wrote extensively about the tribe of Ephraim. He said: "We learn from the Bible that Ephraim played no small part in the history of Israel. It is definitely shown that he was quarrelsome and rebellious."4 However, in another book, *Doctrines of Salvation*, Joseph Fielding Smith, Jr. talks about Ephraim in the latter days. "We have very good reason to believe . . . that it was the tribe of Ephraim, rebellious, proud, and headstrong, which was scattered more than any other among the people of other nations. The chief reason is that it is Ephraim who is now being gathered from among the nations. In these last days the Lord said that Ephraim should not be rebellious as he was formerly, and that now, the rebellious were not of Ephraim and should be 'plucked out.'"[5]

Archibald F. Bennett, author of *Saviours on Mount Zion,* wrote:

> The tribe of Ephraim, rebellious, proud, and headstrong, was carried into captivity with the others of the ten tribes. There was a divine purpose in this dispersal of the blood of Ephraim. Not only was it a punishment to a rebellious people, but a blessing to all those nations amid whom Ephraim "mixed himself" and intermingled his believing blood with theirs. As predicted "wanderers among the nations" (Hosea 9:17), their scattering has been most thorough, until the children of Ephraim today can be found among all nations.[6]

In the Bible Dictionary we read: "Ephraim was given the birthright in Israel (1 Chr. 5:1-2; Jer. 31:9), and in the last days it has been the tribe of Ephraim's privilege first to bear the message of the restoration of the gospel to the world and to gather scattered Israel (Deut. 33:13-17; D&C 133:26-34; 64:36)."[7]

Joseph Fielding Smith, Jr. also said:

> It is essential in this dispensation that Ephraim stand in his place at the head, exercising the birthright in Israel which was given to him by direct revelation. Therefore, Ephraim must be gathered first to prepare the way, through the gospel and the priesthood, for the rest of the tribes of Israel when the time comes for them to be gathered to Zion. The great majority of those who have come

into the Church are Ephraimites. It is the exception to find one of any other tribe, unless it is of Manasseh.

It is Ephraim, today, who holds the priesthood. It is with Ephraim that the Lord has made covenant and has revealed the fulness of the everlasting gospel. It is Ephraim who is building temples and performing the ordinances in them for both the living and for the dead. When the "lost tribes" come . . . in fulfillment of the promises made through Isaiah and Jeremiah, they will have to receive the crowning blessings from their brother Ephraim, the "firstborn" in Israel.[8]

Through many generations, the traits that have typified the tribe of Ephraim have been passed down. What we call Ephraim's Children are people who exhibit the traits of Ephraim—most especially the headstrong nature. This does not mean that someone who is adopted into the tribe of Ephraim, versus direct blood lineage, cannot be considered an "Ephraim's Child." John A. Widtsoe said:

In giving a blessing the patriarch may declare our lineage—that is, that we are of Israel, therefore of the family of Abraham and of a specific tribe of Jacob. In the great majority of cases, Latter-day Saints are of the tribe of Ephraim, the tribe to which has been committed the leadership of Latter-day work. Whether this lineage is of blood or adoption does not matter (Abr. 2:10).[9]

We believe that in large measure, Ezra Taft Benson was referring to the lineage of Ephraim when he stated:

For nearly six thousand years, God has held you in reserve to make your appearance in the final days before the second coming of the Lord. Some individuals will fall away, but the kingdom of God will remain intact to welcome the return of its head—even Jesus Christ. While our generation will be comparable in wickedness to the days of Noah, when the Lord cleansed the earth by flood, there is a major difference this time. It is that God has saved for the final inning some of His strongest children, who will help bear off the kingdom triumphantly. That is where you come in, for you are the generation that must be prepared to meet your God. In all ages prophets have looked down through the corridors of time to our day. Billions of the deceased and those yet to be born have their eyes on us. Make no mistake about it—you are a marked generation.[10]

In 1929 Hyrum G. Smith said:

"Today" is the day of Ephraim. It is the day which the Lord has set to fulfil his promises made in the times of the ancient patriarchs, when he said that he would scatter Israel to the four corners of the world, and that Ephraim should be scattered in all the nations, and then in the "last days" be gathered out again. . . . This is why so many of us are declared to be of Ephraim.[11]

Today, as much as it was seventy years ago, is the day of Ephraim, and the day of Ephraim's Children. We like the name "Ephraim's Child," as opposed to the other labels, because the name Ephraim still engenders images of determination, energy, and strong will, which are all characteristics of this tribe. It also helps us remember that Ephraim is a covenant people with special traits and promises.

Accordingly, Ephraim's Children do not always exhibit the character traits that you might expect from a well-behaved child of God. They still have some of the qualities of their ancestors in ancient Israel. Life with an Ephraim's child is often a chain of battles. These battles cover everything from getting dressed, to eating, to simply leaving the house, to basic concepts like obedience. The winner is often determined by who is the most stubborn at that particular time—the parent or the child. The amazing thing is that the family can be battle-scarred before the child ever reaches the Terrible Two's.

*A young mother and her family were sitting in front of me during sacrament meeting. I soon began to ignore the talks from the pulpit because I was engrossed in the drama unfolding between the mother and her little girl. The child had a stack of books to keep her occupied and quiet. It sounds like a quiet activity, right? Wrong! The little girl was not simply standing and looking at books, she was wiggling, climbing, kneeling, standing, sitting, and changing positions every 30 seconds while looking at books. She was constantly moving.*

*The child put the book on the floor. Her mother pulled her up to put the book on the seat again. The little girl then climbed onto the pew to sit on her knees while looking at the book. Her mother made her stand on the floor and use the seat as a table. The little girl then tried to put the book on her mother's lap where the baby was; her mom put the book back on the seat. The little girl whined a protest and tried to put the book back on her mother's lap. The mother said, "No. Sit down," and tried to make her daughter sit up on the pew.*

*The child tugged out of her mother's grasp and dropped to the floor on her knees, protesting louder. The mother pulled her back up and said, "Sit down."*

*The little girl said "No!" in a voice signaling she was getting upset. The mother, while juggling the sleeping baby, tried to pick up the child and physically put her on the pew. The little girl objected loudly with a grunt.*

*Her mother said in a loud whisper, "Stop it!"*

*The girl shot back, "You stop it!" At this point the mother tried ignoring her, but the little girl was not satisfied. "You stop it, Mommy! You stop!" Eventually, this escalated into the child being taken out of sacrament meeting wailing. Soon Mom, looking tired and exasperated, returned with her child. Then came round two.*

If you are the parent of an Ephraim's Child, you probably do not have any trouble relating to this scenario. In fact, you are probably thinking, "Been there, done that!" You have fought dozens of battles like this with your own child. You have likely noticed other children the same age as yours behaving. You know that it is possible for a child to do it. So why won't yours? The answer begins with a better relationship between you and your Ephraim's Child.

## Everyday Names

A better relationship with your Ephraim's Child starts with you. You need to improve how you view your child every day. There is the overarching name or label for your child (we suggest Ephraim's Child), and there are the names you use on a daily basis. Everyday names can be nicknames or terms of affection—like *sweetie, honey,* or *cutie.* Everyday names can also be the names you call your child as you interact with him—whether out loud or simply in your head. These interaction names are what we are going to address next.

Everyone faces an array of everyday names that are spoken or unspoken. These names affect the way that we think, feel, and act towards ourselves and others, including our children. The power of words is significant. Would you rather spend time with someone who is described as touchy, or as tender-hearted? The word *stubborn* evokes a more negative feeling than the words *determined* or *persistent.* If we use more negative everyday names for our children, then we feel more negatively towards them, and the children pick up on our emotions and how we view them.

How do you describe your Ephraim's Child? In *Raising Your Spirited Child*, Mary Sheedy Kurcinka suggests an exercise to start redesigning your everyday names. She suggests that you write down all the words you can think of to describe the behavior of your child that drives you crazy, including all the worst names. Include words you have heard others use to describe your child "that made you flare in anger or shrink in embarrassment."[12] As you make your list, be assured that you are not the first and only one to have some dreadful names. Ephraim's Children can bring out the worst in us. Now stop reading and go make your list.

How did you do? Here is a list we made one day: *argumentative, stubborn, obstinate, unpredictable, demanding, noisy, whiny, difficult, controlling, wild, disruptive, angry, explosive, obnoxious, extreme, picky, melodramatic, know-it-all, manipulative, temperamental, bossy, resistant,* and *attention-hungry.*

These negative everyday names can be destructive to the child. How easy is it for a child to build a healthy self-esteem with the everyday names *obnoxious, demanding,* or *stubborn* looming over him? Others react to everyday names as well. How does the mother feel when her neighbors consider her child *argumentative*? What is the new teacher going to think when you forewarn her that your son is *bossy*? What do your other children think when their sibling is called *whiny*?

Mary then advises you to pull your favorite image of your child from your memory—a memory on one of the good days when you couldn't help but laugh and squeeze your child because of the joy you felt from being in her company. Keep that image in your mind as you redesign the negative names. If you look closely, you will discover that these words often reflect strengths that are in extremes. For example, *stubbornness* can be changed slightly into *perseverance. Overly sensitive* can be *tenderhearted. Wild* can be *energetic* or *enthusiastic. Manipulative* can be refined into *charisma. Picky* may become *selective.* List the new everyday name opposite your old negative ones.

Now look at your new and improved list. Make an effort to use the more positive everyday names when you talk to and about your Ephraim's Child, even when you discipline him. You can affect how you view your child simply by changing your vocabulary. The new everyday names stimulate different feelings than the old names. It feels much better to have an enthusiastic, charismatic, tenderhearted child that is persevering than one who is wild, manipulative, overly sensitive, and stubborn. Your new names will help others see your child in a new light too. And they will help your child see himself more positively as well. It may be difficult to change your everyday names right now, especially if it has been "one of those days." But it is often your child's most trying traits that can become something quite extraordinary.

Cynthia Tobias, author of the book *You Can't Make Me,* talked about one of the main traits of Ephraim's Children that drive adults nuts: their strong wills. She said:

> Being strong-willed does not have to be a negative trait! I often remind parents . . . that their children may change the world—after all, it's not likely that the world is going to change them! Your [child] may be God's instrument for making the world a better place. It is a great gift to have a child with firm convictions, a high spirit, and a sense of adventure. Think about some of the great leaders and innovators in our past—Thomas Jefferson, Marie Curie, Albert Einstein, Joan of Arc, Thomas Edison, and others. Each of these people held up under adversity, stood for his or her convictions, and persisted against all odds. They refused to believe their dreams were hopeless.[13]

And their parents probably thought of them as stubborn and overzealous from time to time.

# 3

# Do You Have an Ephraim's Child?

How do you know if you have an Ephraim's Child? Since you have read this far, chances are that you suspect you have one of these special children. The best gauge may be your gut reaction to this list from parents of Ephraim's Children:

*You Might Have an Ephraim's Child If:*
• Upcoming family vacations involving eating out, amusement parks, condos with balconies, plane rides, or car rides give you nightmares.
• Silence is a foreshadowing of disaster.
• Your child doesn't cry—he wails.
• Taking your child to a movie is more of a workout than going to the gym.
• You are already exhausted by the end of breakfast.
• You are afraid to program your phone's memory dial because you know your child will call Grandma at 5:30 a.m. when he bounds out of bed.
• Your list of instructions to your child takes five minutes. For example: do not hit your brother, or punch him, or kick him, or push him, or head-butt him, or tackle him; do not get off your bed, take off the blankets, throw pillows, toys, or books into your brother's crib; do not climb on the dresser, pull the clothes out of the drawers, jump on the bed, yell, kick the wall, open the blinds, or take all your clothes off.
• Your child's whole world crashes because you cut her waffle into bite-size pieces and she wanted it whole.
• During your child's 30-minute TV show he has managed

to climb all over every piece of furniture in the room—multiple times.
• Others look at you, shake their heads and say, "You are in for it."
• You receive parenting books for Christmas.

If you find that you can relate to some or all of these situations, you probably have an Ephraim's Child. If you still are unsure, here are some questions:

1. Is your child on the go all day?
2. Is it possible (not that he does it often) for your child to sit for long periods of time when doing something he is interested in?
3. Does/did your child have difficulty going to sleep? From infancy did your child sleep very little, i.e. take very short naps, or have difficulty sleeping through the night?
4. Is your child emotional, with no moderate moods?
5. Does your child remember things for long periods of time?
6. Does your child have areas where his ability to learn is astounding?
7. Is your child's imagination constantly at work? Does he have a never-ending stream of ideas and projects?
8. Does you child have difficulty with not getting his way? Does telling him "no" bring on abnormal crises or long negotiations?
9. Is your child bossy? Do you have to remind him that you are the parent?
10. Does your child have difficulty transitioning from one activity to another?
11. Do others surprisingly have little or no difficulty with your child?
12. Does your child's intensity seem to build through the day?

## Temperament

*We can't form our children on our own concepts; we must take them and love them as God gives them to us.*[1]

"Temperament generally refers to a child's inborn behavioral style or innate tendencies to act a certain way. Temperament is reflected in how a child typically approaches, interacts in, and experiences social relationships."[2] There are distinct differences in how each child responds to the world around him/her. These differences are often due to temperament. There are numerous temperamental traits. A child's overall temperament is the combination of these individual traits.

Temperament is generally considered to be inborn. Many believe that a child's temperament can be seen in early infancy. You did not do anything to make your Ephraim's Child a higher maintenance child; it is a result of her temperament. When your child acts in a way that seems completely foreign to you, you might wonder if your child is normal. Ephraim's Children are normal. They just exhibit certain temperamental traits to a more extreme degree than most people.

However, temperament is not rigid or unchanging; it is not fixed. Temperament can be changed and modified depending on how it is managed. Your child's actual behavior is a function of *both* her temperament and your parenting. Our job as parents is to work with the plan—our child's temperament—that nature provided us. You can help your Ephraim's Child understand his temperament, his strengths, and the potential rough spots. You can emphasize the strengths of your child's temperament and help him learn to express himself appropriately. For example, your intense child will always care deeply about many things, but with your guidance that intensity can be refined and channeled into motivation and zeal.

Two general aspects of temperament inherent in everyone require some discussion: reactivity and mood. These are not characteristics in which Ephraim's Children are different from others, but are important nevertheless in gaining a complete picture of your child's temperament. Reactivity refers to how someone responds to new situations. Mood is someone's general disposition.

There are basic temperamental differences in how people initially respond to new situations. Some react without hesitation and are very open to trying new things, while others hold back and prefer to watch and assess a new situation before joining. Ephraim's Children can fall into either category.

Those who jump into new situations without looking ahead can scare us by their tendency to leap before the thought ever occurs to look first. You may spend a lot of time at the doctor or emergency room patching up active go-getters. Other people hesitate when faced with a new situation, and often refuse to participate at all. They may cry, kick, and scream whenever they are faced with anything new. They look, and take another look, and look again just to be on the safe side before ever considering leaping. Those children that react cautiously are often the most challenging to parents because our society tends to support fearless go-getters.

Many Ephraim's Children will insist they don't like something and will not try it whenever they are approached with anything new: a new food, a new school, a new Primary teacher, new clothes, or a new activity. It is important to realize that this is a first reaction, not a final decision. These children take time to warm up to things. After enough time, they will most likely give it a try. Forcing cautious children into new things before they are ready will likely result in another battle. As a parent, you need to discover the difference between encouraging and pushing a reluctant child.

The second aspect of temperament we will discuss is mood. This is what people usually mean when they use the word "temperament." Some children are generally happy, cheerful, positive, and friendly. Others are generally more serious, cry and whine more, and are more critical. These are the children that are more challenging for parents because they always seem to dwell on the negative and see the flaws in everything and everyone. It can be aggravating to have a small child constantly telling you what you are doing wrong.

Serious children may seem overly critical, but what they are is analytical. They analyze situations and pick things apart to obtain a logical picture. Rather than enthusiastically expressing joy over the great family vacation you just finished, the analytical Ephraim's Child will more likely tell you what he didn't like about it. He may even offer suggestions on how to improve the next vacation. This child will need to learn how to be more diplomatic when dealing with others.

By understanding your child's innate temperament, and adapting your parenting style accordingly, you can help her grow and live with others. The Lord has said, " . . . I have commanded you to bring up your children in light and truth."3 It will be much easier to teach light and truth if we are not locked in a constant war with our challenging Ephraim's Child. "For verily, verily I say unto you, he that hath the spirit of contention is not of me, but is of the devil, who is the father of contention, and he stirreth up the hearts of men to contend with anger, one with another."4

It is vital that you understand your child's temperament. Once you realize that the things he does that drive you nuts are a product of his temperament, you can begin to work with it. It is liberating to know that your child isn't acting this way just to get under your skin. He isn't shrieking to cause a scene; he isn't acting stubborn to question your authority. There is a reason for some of his baffling behavior. If you know what that reason is, you can begin to parent your child more effectively.

## Characteristics of the Ephraim's Child

The defining characteristic of an Ephraim's Child is *more*. He is like other children, only more so.

You might have known since pregnancy that this child was different from other kids—normal but different. . . .

Or it might not have been until birth, when the nurses in the nursery shook their heads in dismay and wished you luck. It could have been years later. At first you might have thought all kids were like this. Your 'awakening' might have come with the birth of a [milder] second child. . . . Or it could have been the birth of your sister-in-law's child. . . . Your intuition has fought the stares and the indictments brought against you, knowing, believing that this child was tougher to parent, but not quite sure if you were right, and if you were, you didn't know why.[5]

In our research, we found that several authors created nearly the same list of characteristics that a "strong-willed," "spirited," or "difficult" child would probably possess. Our experiences with Ephraim's Children have yielded a very similar list. The first trait—intensity—is present in all Ephraim's Children. The next four of these characteristics (persistence, adaptability, awareness, and sensitivity) an Ephraim's Child will almost assuredly exhibit. One or more of another four characteristics (activity, intelligence, control, and independence) are likely to manifest themselves. For each of the nine characteristics there is a varying degree to which they can be displayed. While an Ephraim's Child will probably not be off the charts in every characteristic she has, she will display enough of them to distinguish her from the average child. Remember, it is not that these traits are in and of themselves extraordinary, it is the degree to which they are demonstrated that sets these kids apart. We will briefly introduce each characteristic, which will then be covered in greater depth in later chapters.

## 1. Intensity

Intensity is the degree to which your child is consumed by feelings and situations. This is the "more" we were talking about. Intensity is the defining trait of an Ephraim's Child because it sets the emotional parameters for anything he/she engages in. These children feel deeply. They experience every emotion and sensation powerfully. Ephraim's Children are not merely angry; they are livid. They don't cheer for their team; they're fanatical. They don't watch TV; they are completely engrossed in it. They're not sad; they are inconsolable. They don't study; they scrutinize. Some Ephraim's Children demonstrate their intensity overtly with all kinds of fanfare. Others do it quietly and internally.

To put it bluntly, there would be no Ephraim's Child if it weren't for intensity. If your child wasn't intensely sensitive, active, or persistent, you probably wouldn't be looking for help from parenting books. But if you can channel your child's intensity to righteous and good goals, then you can have someone who is intensely righteous and serves others intensely.

## 2. Persistence

Persistence refers to how long a child stays with an activity. Ephraim's Children are often quite persistent. If they have an idea or activity that they want, they want it and they want it now! They do not give up easily, and you can just forget trying to distract them from their idea. Persistence is an admired quality in an adult, but often a frustrating one in a young child. These children will refuse to let go of their own ideas, but couldn't care less about yours. Many times these children will are so persistent that it drives their parents crazy. It takes more energy and effort to parent a persistent child, but think of what your child can do if he never, never, gives up.

## 3. Adaptability

Some people take little notice of changes or transitions in their lives. Others find even minor change stressful. Adaptability refers to how well a child adapts to changes in situations and events. Ephraim's Children usually adapt very slowly. They need forewarning of upcoming transitions, especially difficult ones like stopping a fun activity or starting something they don't want to do. These slow-to-adapt children dislike surprises.

If you are quick to adapt, you may not have noticed that your child has a hard time with it. Chances are that a problem with change is an underlying factor in many of the daily battles with your Ephraim's Child. Meal time, nap time, running errands, visiting at other houses, dropping your child off at school, and picking her up from school are normal transitions that are difficult. Switching plans suddenly can cause a crisis, such as fixing spaghetti for dinner instead of the soup your child was expecting. Moving to a new house can be disastrous. A new sibling can cause major repercussions above and completely beyond the norm. You need to be aware of your child's slow adaptability so you can help her prepare for changes.

## 4. Awareness

Ephraim's Children often have a heightened awareness of their surroundings; they notice *everything*. One time we were visiting some friends and the whole time our young Ephraim's Child was exclaiming, "Train! Train!" None of the adults could find a train anywhere in the room. Finally, just before leaving someone noticed a picture of a train on a mug in the next room. It was hanging on a hook under a kitchen cupboard, surrounded by at least eight other mugs. It took a roomful of adults thirty minutes to find the train that an observant one-year-old spotted within one minute of walking in the door.

An Ephraim's Child is so mindful of her surroundings that she doesn't miss much. She hears the conversations from across the room or notices the candy that you sneak into your mouth so you don't have to give her some. She will notice what you are watching on TV even if she is involved in something else. An observant Ephraim's Child will notice the penny in the middle of the parking lot, or the plane almost out of sight in the sky. She may also have noticed where you left the car keys or where you put your coat.

Being so aware and observant, though a desirable trait when you are trying to find a misplaced item, can also be frustrating. If you are trying to hurry your child down the sidewalk it can be exasperating when he stops every three steps to watch the ant, or pick up a rock, or listen to the plane passing by. If you send your Ephraim's Child to get something from his room you may storm up the stairs ten minutes later to find that your child became distracted by something before ever getting to his room. There is just so much to see and investigate in the world of an Ephraim's Child, more than half of which many people would never even notice. This is the trait that leads to your child being easily distracted. You will need to help your child learn how to tune in to the most important messages.

### 5. Sensitivity

Not only are Ephraim's Children very aware of their surroundings, but they often react intensely to the stimuli they receive from their senses. This is what we mean by sensitivity. For example, you and I may be irritated by a scratchy tag on the collar of our shirt. An Ephraim's Child may very well have a tantrum until every particle of the tag has been removed. Loud noises, chaotic activity, bumpy socks, or funny smells may not make any difference to others, but usually affect Ephraim's Children. Because of their heightened awareness, every experience is a sensual bombardment as these children see, hear, feel, and smell things that others might miss.

Chances are the sensitive Ephraim's Child will not be able to fall asleep in a room full of people, although all other children present are sleeping. Changes in environment can throw him off; things feel different or sound weird. These sensitive children absorb all the sounds, smells, bright lights, and textures around them, and react intensely to them. Ephraim's Children also respond to emotions. They are a good indicator of family stress or emotion level. When you are the most stressed, their antennae pick up on it and they act the worst.

It is not unusual for the sensitive child to become over-stimulated because she is so much more aware of sensual things. Certain situations such as crowds and noisy celebrations can overload your child after a short time. Your Ephraim's Child is usually not acting out to embarrass you in front of all the relatives gathered in your house. She probably has had all the noise, movement, and commotion that she can take. This is a natural reaction for a temperamentally sensitive person, and you can help your child learn how to manage it.

## 6. Activity

Many Ephraim's Children seem to possess incredible amounts of energy. They are busy from the minute they leap out of bed at dawn until you finally manage to get them into bed at night. They prefer to run instead of walk. They like to climb over something instead of going around it. They wiggle constantly and fall off chairs, spill food, and run into people and things. Children with high energy have an obviously active temperament that requires them to move their bodies in order to feel good. They don't just like to move, they NEED to move.

Some Ephraim's Children do not loudly ping around the room all the time, but can still be active. These children are just as busy, but are much more quiet about it. They don't screech or talk incessantly or make ear-piercing sound effects. Even though they don't bombard your senses as they move from activity to activity, they still manage to accomplish a lot. They are constantly on the move as well, but you may not notice it until you survey the room in shambles. Ephraim's Children often move from activity to activity to activity, making boredom a constant threat.

## 7. Intelligence

Ephraim's Children are often very bright. They can be wonderfully alternative thinkers and may learn differently than other children. Many of these children have high verbal skills and excellent memories. Balancing above-average intelligence with average emotional maturity can be challenging. The bright three-year-old may talk and often reason like a five-year-old, but still has the emotions of a three-year-old.

An important dimension of intelligence is emotional intelligence. This is the ability to understand feelings, manage them, and see and work with the emotions of others. Because Ephraim's Children have such strong and intense feelings, it is important that they learn how to handle them. When they understand their own emotions, children will be in a better position to use their heart, rather than ignoring it or being ruled by it.

## 8. Control

Don't all children want their own way? Yes, but in our experience, most average children do not attempt to dictate to their parents which route to drive to grandma's house or tell the babysitter how to do everything. Many Ephraim's Children have an intense need for control. Often a controlling Ephraim's Child will try to discipline siblings or friends. They always want to be "in charge." Ephraim's Children are often verbally skilled, and use this to their advantage. They negotiate, argue, debate, or charm to get their way. And those children who are unable to verbally express themselves may resort to hitting or other actions to physically enforce their wants. We need to refine this potentially manipulative trait into leadership, using the Savior's example.

Many parents find themselves locked into daily power struggles with their Ephraim's Child. How do we allow our children some measure of control, while not relinquishing it ourselves? Through understanding temperament and addressing the emotional need behind issues, we can help our Ephraim's Child grow and develop without so many battles. Then we can be on the same side instead of opposing each other.

## 9. Independence

The independent Ephraim's Child has a strong desire to do things herself, even if she can't. She wants to feed herself, buckle her car seat herself, walk by herself, or figure things out herself. Not only does she want to be independent, but she wants it intensely. Sometimes this ends with the parent and child frustrated when tasks take a really long time. Sometimes the parent just does it anyway, and the child wails at the top of her lungs for half an hour. It is important to teach the independent child about dependence, independence, and interdependence. Interdependence will be a necessary skill in developing healthy relationships, and eventually this strongly independent individual will need to see her dependence on God—an idea which may not come naturally to the Ephraim's Child.

## The Extrovert/Introvert

There is another aspect to personality and temperament that is important to address, and that is extroversion and introversion. An Ephraim's Child can be either an extrovert or an introvert. However, you need to find out which one he is because your child will approach life and relationships with others in a vastly different manner as an introvert than an extrovert.

Extroverts are predominantly concerned with external things and people. Extrovert Ephraim's Children are easy to pick out. These kids are usually intensely noisy when they do anything. They shout and yell when playing. They are ear-splitting when upset. They don't cry, they howl. They don't laugh, they roar. Trying to get them to talk in quiet voices is almost a physical impossibility.

There are quiet Ephraim's Children too. These are the introverts. Introverts are predominantly concerned with their own thoughts and feelings. These children usually observe situations intently before entering. They are more cautious and look before they leap. They are just as intense as the noisy Ephraim's Children, but their intensity is more internal. Do something to upset them and they can be as loud, if not louder, than their more outgoing counterparts. Many times the quiet Ephraim's Child's reactions last longer.

In *Raising Your Spirited Child*, Mary Sheedy Kurcinka describes extroversion and introversion as ways that we get our energy. The following paragraphs are a summary of her ideas as stated in her book. Kurcinka comments that these children need energy to manage their strong temperament. It takes a great deal of effort to refine and modify these character traits—to express intensity as assertiveness rather than aggressiveness, or to make transitions smoothly, or to stay calm in a noisy room full of people. When energy levels are low, these children have difficulty coping and just don't have the strength to refine their behavior.[6] Your Ephraim's Child will get his energy in different ways if he is an extrovert than if he is introverted. You can help your Ephraim's Child be more successful by helping him keep his energy bank full. Understanding your child's preference will help you teach him how to recharge his batteries before they get too low, and you will have a happier and calmer Ephraim's Child.

Extroverts draw their energy from others. They prefer to interact with the world around them and through other people. They are the babies that love being with other people and talk incessantly even before they have intelligible words. Extroverts want to share ideas and tell you what happened as soon as it happens. If extroverts do not have the opportunity to talk immediately, they become more grumpy and demanding because they are running out of energy. When allowed to recharge by being with other people they are able to cope much better.

Extroverts get their energy from the outside; they not only like other people, they need them. Expecting them to entertain themselves and stay at home may be unrealistic. If given the opportunity, they will gladly play with friends for hours. If friends are unavailable, then it falls to you to help them recharge. Extroverts think best by talking, and allowing them to talk gives them energy. From the second he bounds out of bed he has something to say. Other children may feel that it is difficult to get a word in edgewise, or to grab mom's and dad's attention. The extrovert Ephraim's Child can wear parents out.

Introverts get their energy by being alone, or with one or two special people. They prefer to deal with the world by reflecting on their thoughts and feelings inside before sharing them. They recharge by spending time alone. If they have some alone time first, then they can play well with other kids and be more cooperative. If they are not allowed it, they can be disagreeable and difficult.

*Sometimes one young Ephraim's Child would remove himself from situations to recharge. At these times he would reject anyone who wanted to interact with him. He played with his cars on the couch, totally ignoring everyone for a little while until he was ready to be with people again. Other times he would go to his room and play with his keyboard or look at his books. We learned that during these times, he did not want to be bugged by anybody—not even Mom or Dad. If anyone tried to talk to him or play with him, they were rebuffed. It was not a personal rejection, he just needed some alone time. When he was ready he would play again.*

Introvert babies often become overwhelmed at family gatherings. As these children grow, they continue to be worn out after being with a lot of people, especially those who are not close friends. Give them time to recharge after school or church. They need a break, a chance to be alone. You can teach them appropriate ways to pull out of a group. As a parent, you may need to create opportunities for your child to "take five." Watching television, playing video games, or reading are favorite energizers.

Pressure to be part of a group can be tough if the introverted child has not recharged. These children will be ready to share their thoughts and experiences with you after they have recharged, but you usually have to initiate it through questions. They share things in small amounts, and you have to listen or you might miss them. Sometimes you must wait days to find out what is happening in their lives. Introverts like to think about things first, and then talk about them. Demanding immediate answers from them pulls their energy.

It is important to realize that neither extrovert nor introvert is better than the other. Both introverts and extroverts have their strengths and weaknesses. However, introverts are more often misunderstood. They can be pressured to become more outgoing and to quit "escaping" into their room. It is nice for the introvert to realize that he is not weird because he likes to be alone. It is important for the extroverted family and friends to recognize the differences between their personalities and allow for those differences. Your child may demonstrate both extrovert and introvert tendencies, but if you watch carefully you can determine which one is dominant.

Once you understand your child's method of refueling, take a look at your own methods. If your preference is different from your child's, then you may clash. Once you understand yourself better, you can work together with your child to keep both of you charged. Just as being an Ephraim's Child takes a lot of energy, being the parent of an Ephraim's Child takes energy too. You will be more effective at teaching your child how to keep her batteries at full power if yours are charged up as well.

## The Big Picture

It is our hope that after you finish this book you will have a better understanding of your Ephraim's Child. A greater look at her temperament will help you know what makes her tick, and know that she is not doing what she is doing just to drive you crazy. Each chapter can be one piece of the puzzle. Once you understand that often irritating and grating behaviors are a large result of natural temperament, you can adjust yourself and situations to build on your child's strengths and not exacerbate her weaknesses. Then you can help your child understand herself, and work together to refine these strengths. Remember, the

Ephraim's Child will always be MORE. Our mission is to help her capitalize on these characteristics to become MORE righteous, MORE steadfast, MORE zealous, MORE charitable . . . MORE like our Savior.

# 4

# Intensity

Imagine for a moment that you are thirsty. You open the refrigerator door and are faced with numerous choices. Perhaps cold bottled water would be the most refreshing. Or you could choose something with more flavor—like tomato juice, milk, or lemonade. Or would a soft drink hit the spot? No matter what you choose, the fact is that all of the choices are drinks. The water is not any less a beverage than the soft drink. Tomato juice will have more kick than water, but less flavor than a can of 7-Up. The main difference between the drinks is the intensity of the flavor.

Intensity is often used in the world of color. There are several dimensions to color. *Hue* is the color we see, such as red, yellow, or blue. *Intensity* is the brightness or dullness of a hue. Therefore, intensity is an integral part of every green, red, or purple that you see. Neon green is more intense than wintergreen. The more intense the color, the *more* of it there is.

As with beverages and colors, people also exhibit a range of intensity. The person who is more mellow is no less a person than someone who is very intense, just as water is no less a beverage than lemonade. The defining characteristic of the Ephraim's Child is intensity. He is the carbonated beverage and the neon green. He possesses the same qualities and characteristics as other children, but to a greater extent. He feels and does everything with more vehemence than most people and because of this intensity the Ephraim's Child is *more.*

Many times it is the high intensity of Ephraim's Children that makes life more difficult for you and for them. You may ask, Isn't every young child intense? Don't they all get upset? The answer is yes, but if you have experienced the reactions of an Ephraim's Child, you can tell the difference. While other children may become upset, the Ephraim's Child is devastated. Instead of being merely happy, the Ephraim's Child is ecstatic. Life is black and white, with few gray areas. His emotions are huge—whether sad, happy, or angry—with rare gradations or in-betweens. Everything is a BIG DEAL, whether it's meals, playtime, going to the store, taking a nap, or trying something new.

An Ephraim's Child's reactions can sweep up everyone nearby, so that they all feel tossed about by the waves of deep emotion. Take any normal quality or reaction and multiply it, and you can see why adults are thoroughly drained at the end of the day. One parent of an Ephraim's Child forlornly asked, "Will he ever learn how to be in between sleep and hysterical?" Even if your child is happy, he is *intensely* happy, which can be tiring to others. And when the Ephraim's Child is sad or upset, he acts as if his life is ending.

Then you have the numerous daily crises in any normal child's life. The reaction of the Ephraim's Child to life's normal disappointments is catastrophic. You try to explain that it is not a life-and-death situation whether your child eats off the blue or the black plate. You try to convince her that she is not dying from a scraped knee. When most children make mistakes they shrug their shoulders and move on, but common mistakes are major events that can ruin the entire day for an Ephraim's Child. Trying to teach perspective to a young Ephraim's Child is frustrating, because no matter how hard you try to persuade her to not care so much about every little thing, the fact is *she does*. She cares intensely about EVERYTHING.

The loud, extroverted Ephraim's Child is the easiest to find. Many times chaos reigns wherever she goes. She is surrounded by a whirlwind of intensity; intense sound, movement, and general upheaval that doesn't seem to abate until she leaves. In her wake the loud Ephraim's Child can leave frazzled nerves. But quiet, intently observant children who assess each situation before joining are also intense. They merely focus their intensity internally, rather than externally. Don't let the quiet Ephraim's Children fool you. They are as intense as their noisy counterparts.

Being the parent of an Ephraim's Child can be lonely. When the advice of family and friends simply does not work, you may wonder if something is wrong with you or your child. The answer is that there is nothing wrong with either of you. Because your child is *more*, much of the counsel that works for parenting other children is ineffective for your child, a fact which we discovered ourselves. However, remember that these are not "difficult" children. Parenting them is difficult. You have a child who is intense in everything: intensely persistent, intensely sensitive, intensely independent, intensely controlling, etc. The normal ups and downs of life become mountains and chasms, and it is challenging to navigate such rugged terrain.

Let us confirm a possible suspicion: it does take more to parent, teach, and guide the Ephraim's Child. Take a deep breath and feel the relief. You are not a worse parent than others. You will have days when the people in the grocery store disapprovingly watch you try to deal with a screaming, inconsolable child who acts like you are in the process of cutting off an arm or leg, all because you went down aisle three instead of aisle four. But you will also have the days where you and your child laugh together until tears come out of your eyes. So, buckle up. It is a bumpy road, but it is worth it!

*I watched a primary teacher enter the primary room looking tired and bewildered. She is an experienced teacher both in the public schools and at church. It was the second lesson in January, her second week of having three of these marvelous Ephraim's Children in a class of four. I couldn't help laughing when she said, "I think I need some help." My heart went out to her because I knew that she had her hands full.*

## Handling the "Flip Out"

The Ephraim's Child is usually *intensely emotional.* This aspect of their personality can be spotted quickly. Mary Sheedy Kurcinka quotes Daniel Goldman in the *New York Times* in 1987:

> Some people find themselves in emotional tumult even in reaction to mundane events, while others remain unperturbed under the most trying of circumstances. These levels of feeling characterize a person's entire emotional life: those with the deepest lows also have the loftiest highs, the research shows. And differences between people seem to emerge early in childhood, if not from birth, and remain a major mark of character.[1]

One of the great challenges of life is learning to handle our emotions. The goal is not to completely ignore, hide, or conceal our emotions. We do not want to be logical, rational automatons, or become a Mr. Spock who cannot access his feelings. Neither is it wise to let our emotions run rampant and completely rule our lives. The ultimate goal is to have a synergistic relationship between our emotions and our intellect. After all, it is the combination of mind and heart that makes our soul.

Ephraim's Children have an extremely difficult time with their emotions, simply because their feelings are so intense. They experience emotions and sensations powerfully and deeply and usually express themselves at incredible volume. These kids wail when they are sad; they yell when they are excited; they scream when they are mad. It is vital that you understand that the Ephraim's Child is not acting this way to frustrate, irritate, or manipulate you; she really does feel *that much* emotion.

It is not easy to know what to do when a child is in the grip of intense emotion, especially when it is not a happy emotion. It can be extremely uncomfortable, and above all we usually want the child to just calm down. Emotion raging out of control is scary to those caught in the crossfire. Sometimes adults can forget that the child is just a child, and is probably scared of the intense emotion herself. She doesn't know how to deal with her rampaging feelings, and may be frightened by the magnitude of them. Ephraim's Children often do not understand their own intensity. They don't know why they howl when they cry, or why they lose it over seemingly minor things. They just do. It is our job to help these children come to terms with their emotions and not bury them or be a slave to them. (More will be said about managing emotions in chapters 11 and 12.)

We have a term for when our Ephraim's Child completely loses control of his emotions: "Flipping Out." But "going berserk," "wacko," and "losing it" are just as appropriate. If you deal with an Ephraim's Child, you know exactly what we mean by "flipping out." It's what happens when your child's favorite shirt is dirty and he can't wear it. It is often the reaction you get when you change plans suddenly. The intense Ephraim's Child may "flip out" over a change in bedding. His reaction to seemingly inconsequential things can rock the household on a daily basis. And because the child is above all intense, no matter what the cause, the reaction will be explosive.

The most important rule of thumb in dealing with your intense child when she flips out is to avoid getting sucked in. But flip outs are like a black hole, and they are easy to fall into. If you do, or should we say *when* you do, you will probably get angry and yell or scream. You might also resort to sarcasm or hurtful words directed at your child. You may take the logical route and debate with your child about why his emotions don't make sense. Some get physically sucked in and enter a wrestling match to drag the child into his room. These tangles often resemble a cartoon where a character is holding onto the doorway with hands and feet while someone tries to push or pull him through against his will. Soon his arms and legs start stretching like elastic, and finally the cartoon uses fingernails and toenails to maintain his grip. This amount of resistance is amusing until you experience it firsthand.

If you are naturally of a mellow disposition, it is probably easy to remain cool and step back from the situation. If, however, you are also rather intense by nature, it takes incredible forbearance to keep calm. Our advice: do it anyway. Even if you have to lock yourself in the bathroom for a self-inflicted time out, do it. Dueling with your intensely reacting child while you are reacting intensely rarely does anything but exacerbate the situation. All you've done is create a vicious cycle in which you and your child are feeding off of each other's emotions.

The best way to handle a "flip out" is to avoid having one in the first place. The trick is to step in and diffuse the situation before it becomes a crisis. There are subtle, usually nonverbal cues that signal your child's intensity is building. No two children will have the same cues, but all of them will give off some indication that they are on their way to a blow up. Your job is to notice the cues of your Ephraim's Child and take preventive action. Don't ignore them because you are tired or busy or are sick of stepping in all the time. By understanding and acting on your child's flip-out cues, you can avoid a major crisis that would end up taking more of your time or energy anyway.

It will take a conscious effort on your part to discover your child's cues. Some parents may even know their child's cues already as merely a gut feeling. Several common cues are gritting teeth, clenching fists, increased volume, and growing aggression or taunting. Once you know what the cues are, you can not only intervene but also teach your Ephraim's Child to notice them herself. As you catch the cues, tell your child what you see. "When you start running around wild I can tell that your feelings are getting out of control." "You are getting more and more aggressive, and that shows me that you need some time to calm down." The goal is to eventually have her avoid a flip out on her own, using her own volition.

However, you cannot teach your Ephraim's Child how to verbalize and recognize his own cues when he is in the middle of a "flip out." Wait until he is calmer to point it out. By giving names to his feelings, your child can learn how to use words to meet his needs before he is overwhelmed. It is important for your child to be able to express his intense emotions, one way or another. Using words will acknowledge what he is feeling, without him having to physically show you. It has been said that one of the reasons that two-year-olds have so many temper tantrums is because they do not yet possess the verbal skills to express themselves and they get frustrated. Two-year-olds then express their feelings through hitting, kicking, and screaming. Talk about your child's intensity until your child is able to control it himself. Don't forget to use your new and improved everyday names when you do it!

### Now What?

You know your child's cues. You have recognized a situation and jumped in to avoid the "flip out." Now what do you do with your Ephraim's Child who is still reacting intensely? In *Raising Your Spirited Child,* Mary Sheedy Kurcinka suggests soothing and calming activities to help diffuse the child's intensity. Many of the following ideas are taken from her book.[2] You may find that you are already using some of these ideas through trial and error. Try different activities and note the ones that work. It is even a good idea to incorporate some of them into your bedtime routine to help your Ephraim's Child calm down and better fall asleep. Some of the suggested activities are: water activities, imagination, sensory activities, reading, humor, and taking a break.

### *Water Activities*

Water can be a soothing entity to intense children. You can give your child a bath, fill up a wading pool in the backyard, let your child play in the sink, turn on the hose, or let your child paint with water. One of our Ephraim's Children loves to fill buckets of water to make rivers, lakes, or simply mud in the backyard. Another one in our family will stop and splash in any puddle or sink. If your child is having a really bad day, maybe tossing him in the tub with a bunch of cups will be the only thing preserving your sanity. Since our Ephraim's Children were infants, we began the bedtime routine with a bath, no matter the dirt level of the child. Though it may seem a little extreme, this habit has been a saving practice in getting our children to calm down enough to go to sleep. When the bath has been skipped, we often have a more difficult night.

## Imagination

Most of these Ephraim's Children have a wonderful sense of imagination that you can use to help them moderate their intensity. Not only does it get their attention, but it can distract them from the whirlwind of emotions that are entangling them. Kurcinka gives the example of pretending that your child is dressing up to go to a fancy party.[3] You help her brush her hair, put on earrings, pull on socks, put on perfume, etc. For boys, you can pretend to shave or trim sideburns or tie a necktie. Use touch to help the child calm down. Run your fingers through your child's hair to "brush" it, lightly touch places to dab on perfume, or run your fingers over your child's feet and up her legs to simulate pulling on long stockings.

Another way to use imagination is through creative dramatics. For example, you could help a hyper child release her energy by pretending she is a flower in the middle of a windstorm. First she is blown all over in a frenzy of activity. Then the storm dissipates, and gradually the flower is no longer tossed to and fro, but is able to be still and take deep breaths. These kinds of activities help your child to visualize her energy and creatively release any excess energy.

## Sensory Activities

These children have very keen senses of touch, taste, smell, hearing, and sight. Certain activities, because they focus heavily on one sense, can help an Ephraim's Child channel his energy and diffuse some intensity. Some favorite tactile activities are playing with Play Dough and Silly Putty (see Appendix for recipes of these and more). You can also fill a container with things like rice or beans and let your child experience different textures. Sometimes favorite musical selections or books on tape can help your child calm down by focusing on sound. Activities that involve sight, like computer games or TV (in limited quantities) can also help. Head scratches, tummy rubs, and drawing with your finger-tip on your child's back are always good ways to help diffuse intensity. You can also sit outside on the porch and feel the breeze, bask in the sun, or watch the patterns of light shining through trees. Use your imagination to find other activities to let your child use her senses to diffuse intense emotion.

### Reading

When all else fails or is unavailable, try reading. Pull out a book, invite your child to sit on your lap or next to you, and use the written word to help diffuse an intense situation. This also helps your child see the importance and attraction of books. Studies show that children who have been read to usually read better themselves. Take advantage of the local library and garage sales to build up a collection of books in your home that you can use any time it is needed.

### Humor

It has been said that—*laughter is the shortest distance between two people.*4

Sometimes when the Ephraim's Child is reacting intensely, reason does not work. Many times humor can help your child manage her intensity as well. Crack a joke, start a tickling war, or find some way to make your child laugh. Once the emotion is diffused, you can approach the situation with your child more calmly. Humor can also help avoid power struggles. Don't over-look the power of laughter.

### Taking a Break

When adults are stressed or overwhelmed, they often try to take a break—whether a set break at work, down time in front of the TV, or a planned vacation. However, when children need to calm down, adults often put them in "time out" as a punishment. Yet what these children sometimes need is time to calm down. We decided to use the term "taking a break" for when our Ephraim's Child needs to remove himself from a situation to calm down. Taking a break is not a punishment, but an invitation to regain control. When your child is on the road to "flipping out," remind your child of the cues that indicate that his intensity is spiraling out of control and then have him take a break. Many times simply telling the Ephraim's Child that he needs a break will let him know that he needs to calm himself. Through time your child can learn how to tell when he needs to take a break himself, without you needing to intervene.

Children need your help to learn how to relax and calm down. You can stay with them during their break and do some soothing activities or talk things out. Others will prefer some time alone first. When they are ready to have you near, then you can work on calming down together. Be prepared that an Ephraim's Child that is still in the grip of intense emotion may need a considerable amount of time to calm down. We have had break times last an hour in our house, during most of which we were not welcome in our child's presence. If it takes that long for your child's emotion to dissipate, don't worry. But after the storm has passed, involve your child in a discussion about better ways to handle these kinds of situations before he needs an hour to calm down.

## About Competition

Competition can bring out the intensity of the Ephraim's Child in all its glory. Often these children care enormously about winning. It isn't restricted to sports either. Your child may argue and debate until she is blue in the face, just so that she can "win" a discussion. Getting your child to admit that she was wrong about something may be like pulling teeth.

You will most likely see traumatic reactions at those times when your child is not the winner.

Many times Ephraim's Children have perfectionist tendencies. They have their view of how things should be done. When their expectations are not met or they are misunderstood, these kids can go off the deep end. When your child wants you to cut a square instead of a rectangle as you help him with his art project, he may very well get so angry that he refuses to even look at or touch the offending artwork ever again. When reality is different from their inner vision, these children can get very frustrated, which can lead to a "flip out."

However, competition can be a great motivator for these kids as well. The Ephraim's Child who does not want to brush his teeth just because he is supposed to may not mind racing to see who can finish brushing teeth first. A young child who is reluctant to eat may not realize he is doing it by competing to see who can get the most noodles on the fork. Being competitive is good as long as it does not get out of control.

You can help your Ephraim's Child with her intense competitiveness by helping her understand the end goal. Perhaps playing soccer at the family reunion is for exercise rather than World Cup level athletic competition. A family game of Monopoly is for fun and togetherness rather than to fiercely take over the real estate market. And a friendly race to the bathroom is not intended to turn into a knock-down wrestling match to keep the others from getting there first. If the Ephraim's Child understands the desired end product, then she will have more information to help her express her intense competition more appropriately.

### Intense Examples

The most effective teaching tool that you possess is yourself. Children learn the most through your example. Therefore, it is imperative that you handle the intensity of the Ephraim's Child in a positive and productive way. If her intensity makes you uncomfortable or angry or impatient, then she is likely to feel the same about herself. Tell your child how much you value her energy, enthusiasm, passion, commitment, and zeal. Show her you appreciate her deep feelings and meaningful interactions with others. And then show her appropriate outlets for her feelings. They are not going to just go away, and your child needs your help to know what to do with them.

If you are intense yourself, you may need to work on becoming comfortable with your own intensity. Perhaps you need to look at the everyday names that were used when you grew up. If they are negative, you will need to redo the names you use with yourself. If you are uncomfortable with your own immediate and strong reactions, or if you feel negatively about them, your Ephraim's Child will pick up on it. Sometimes you may need to take your own break before you "flip out." Your child will observe how you handle yourself, so make sure it is the way you want your Ephraim's Child to behave.

Intensity is not a bad thing. Even though some days you wish that your Ephraim's Child would just chill out, intensity can add extra depth, dimension, and excitement to life. Intensity channeled in a productive direction can be an advantage. It provides your child with drive and passion that can propel him to accomplish and succeed. In the world of sports, for example, athletes who play with intensity (different than anger) are highly valued. Often it is the level of intensity that makes an excellent rather than an average athlete. One college athlete wrote, "Playing with intensity is creating a sharper focus in the game and building a determination that one would sacrifice personal benefits for the team's sake."[5]

## Refining Intensity Into Zeal

Intensity can become a powerful tool when it is refined from rampant emotions into a sharper focus. Christ said, "Thou shalt love the Lord thy God with all thy heart, and with all thy soul, and with all thy mind."[6] Sounds like intense devotion, doesn't it? Our experience has been that Ephraim's Children cannot do anything without throwing their "heart, might, mind, and strength"[7] into it; such is their nature. It is important to remember that intense, internal motivation is a highly valued characteristic in adults. This child who is anxiously engaged in throwing mud all over the sliding glass door so that you cannot see through it (a true story) could some day be completely immersed in building the kingdom of God.

Not only do we want to help the Ephraim's Child focus his intensity, but he needs to learn to put the greater good ahead of himself. His passion needs to be focused in the right direction: towards helping others instead of helping himself. Intensity is most sought after when those around know that the intensity is focused towards a shared, common goal. When someone is moving toward a goal with determination and passion, he is considered zealous and motivated (more everyday names to add to your list).

The scriptures tell us that those who embark in the service of God are commanded to "serve him with all . . . [their] heart, might, mind and strength,"[8] and that it is the will of the Father that "men should be anxiously engaged in a good cause, and do many things of their own free will, and bring to pass much righteousness."[9] "For the power is in them, wherein they are agents unto themselves."[10]

Neal A. Maxwell wrote, the "rising generation [is] seemingly determined to be 'anxiously engaged.'"[11] Ephraim's Children seem to be born with a deep inclination to be "anxiously engaged." Is it possible that these children may feel a sense of purpose brought from the presence of their Father? From the scriptures, we know of some who were sensitive to their purpose and began their missions in life from a very early age. Nephi was one such person and had a strong desire to follow God from his youth: "I, Nephi, being exceedingly young . . . and also having great desires to know of the mysteries of God, wherefore, I did cry unto the Lord; and behold he did visit me."[12]

Nephi's younger brother Jacob was also someone who had great spiritual stature from an early age. "Jacob was a powerful personal witness of the anticipated Redeemer, which was his most prominent theme. Nephi noted that "Jacob also has seen him [the premortal Christ] as I have seen him" (2 Ne. 11:3), and Lehi indicated that it was *in his youth* [italics added] that Jacob had beheld the glory of the Lord" (2 Ne. 2:4)."[13]

Mormon was another such purposeful young man. In Mormon 1:2-4 he wrote:

> And about the time that Ammaron hid up the records unto the Lord, he came unto me, (I being about ten years of age, and I began to be learned somewhat after the manner of the learning of my people) and Ammaron said unto me: I perceive that thou art a sober child, and art quick to observe; . . . And behold, ye shall take the plates of Nephi unto yourself, and the remainder shall ye leave in the place where they are; and ye shall engrave on the plates of Nephi all the things that ye have observed concerning this people.

At the age of ten Mormon began his work as the major abridger-writer of the Book of Mormon. In the *Encyclopedia of Mormonism* it states: "[Mormon] was prepared by the experiences of his youth to become a prophet . . . and in his fifteenth year was 'visited of the Lord' (Mormon 1:2, 15). At sixteen he became the general of all the Nephite armies and largely succeeded in preserving his people from destruction until A.D. 385, when virtually all of them but his son Moroni were destroyed in battles with the Lamanites (6:8-15; 8:1-3)."[14]

At the young age of fourteen, Joseph Smith prayed with enough faith to receive a personal visitation from Heavenly Father and Jesus Christ. Joseph subsequently told religious leaders about his vision and they reviled him. As Joseph put it:

> I soon found, however, that my telling the story had excited a great deal of prejudice against me among professors

of religion, and was the cause of great persecution, which continued to increase; and though I was an obscure boy, only between fourteen and fifteen years of age, and my circumstances in life such as to make a boy of no consequence in the world, yet men of high standing would take notice sufficient to excite the public mind against me, and create a bitter persecution; and this was common among all sects—all united to persecute me.[15]

Talk about peer pressure! Nevertheless, Joseph Smith never denied what he saw, and the Prophet of the Restoration was stalwart and true to the end of his life.

The Savior himself exhibited the knowledge of a mission in life at a very early age. "When at Jerusalem, about twelve years of age, He began to be conscious of the suggestions of the Spirit within Him, that he had a work to do in the world for His Father."[16] "And he said unto them, Why is it that ye sought me? Knew ye not that I must be about my Father's business?"[17] Joseph F. Smith wrote that the Savior is our example:

He possessed a foreknowledge of all the vicissitudes through which he would have to pass in the mortal tabernacle. When he conversed with the brother of Jared, on the Mount, in his spiritual body, he understood his mission, and knew the work he had to do, and if Christ knew beforehand, so did we . . . By the power of the Spirit . . . we [can, in some measure, as the Savior did] catch a spark from the awakened memories of the immortal soul.[18]

Not only are we to be "anxiously engaged," but we are told to "be zealous."[19] The word *zeal* means great energy or enthusiasm for a cause or objective. Some of the greatest role models in the scriptures were set apart by their zeal. The people of Ammon "were zealous for keeping the commandments of God"[20] and were "distinguished for their zeal towards God, and also towards men . . . and they were firm in the faith of Christ, even unto the end."[21] These people were so zealous that they willingly died by the sword rather than break their covenants. "And thus they were a zealous and beloved people, a highly favored people of the Lord."[22]

In *Mormon Doctrine*, Bruce R. McConkie writes, "True zeal is an attribute of godliness which men acquire through participation in the cause of righteousness. It consists in being earnestly, *intensely* [italics added], and 'anxiously engaged in a good cause' (D&C 58:27; Gal. 4:18) . . . Members of the Church are obligated to 'be zealous' in the cause of Christ (Rev. 3:19)."[23] A strong amount of passion and intensity is what is required of those who are to love and serve God with everything they possess. Every Ephraim's Child has the intensity. It is our job to help her control, refine, and direct that intensity into righteous zeal.

# 5

# Persistence

*After a long day, the adults were sitting down on the couch to enjoy a moment of quiet and inactivity after the children were in bed. Suddenly, the sound of little footsteps interrupted the parents' solitude. A small face peeked at them from the head of the stairs. "Come rest with me?" the two-year old asked. Patiently his mother gave him a hug and a kiss and tucked him back in bed. Scarcely had she sat down on the couch when once again the little face appeared and the query was heard again. "Come rest with me?" Mother gently picked her angel up and once again resolutely put him to bed.*

*"Mom, I want you to rest with me." This time she had not even fully sat down. Her patience starting to wane, she put her child in bed and sang him another lullaby along with the instruction that he was to remain in bed. Two minutes passed and she stopped watching the stairs. "Mommy, I want you to rest with me." Gathering the threads of her patience she picked him up, a little less gently this time, and swiftly deposited her son back in his bed and told him, "No." She left with the promise she would rest with him on his bed tomorrow.*

*The mother was unable to relax for the next 45 minutes as the battle waged on. Nothing could convince her son to remain in his bed. She tried everything she had read about or even heard in passing on how to train your children to stay in bed. She even got mad, yelled some, and tried spanking. At the end of her rope, she sent in Dad, who usually could get their son to obey. Dad's threats worked for five minutes before the next intent request. "Mommy, rest with me!" After an hour of frustration on the parents' part, and dogged determination and persistence on the two year-old's part, the mother laid down with her child, who fell immediately asleep.*

One word that strikes dread into the heart of a parent is the word "stubborn," which is often equated with disobedience. The Ephraim's Child can be stubborn. Usually this child will not do something simply because you tell her to. Very often she will *refuse* to do something just because someone else wants her to. From the scriptures, we are able to form the picture that the tribe of Ephraim was obstinate and stubborn and often disobedient to God's commands. Ephraim's Children come by this trait honestly.

The Ephraim's Child is frequently called stubborn, strong-willed, contrary, willful, rebellious, and even defiant. Your child's stubborn streak may regularly conflict with what you, as his parent, believe is best. This temperamental trait plays a large role in power struggles, and is often a major source of frustration for parents who feel that they must forcefully and physically compel their stubborn child to obey any instruction.

You know what we mean. You too have had times like our "Battle of the Silverware"—when your Ephraim's child decides that he wants the big fork. Not just any big fork but a specific big fork, and he could be starving to death and would still refuse to eat until he gets the correct big fork. You are trying to see the importance of a piece of stainless steel and refuse to be dictated to over such a trivial matter. He should be grateful that he gets any food at all! There was no way you could have gotten away with this behavior when *you* were a child. And yet your kid sits at the table like a thirty-pound chunk of immovable granite. After twenty minutes of war you swallow your pride, dig the dirty fork out of the dishwasher and clean it by hand. You present it to "His Majesty", who then complains that his food is cold.

The inevitable and constant struggle with a persistent child creates the threat of establishing rebellious behavior patterns that may propel your child away from you in the future. You do not want to first realize when your son is a teenager that you have dealt with him the wrong way and actually driven him away from you. Not long ago we heard a new catch-phrase: "force conformity." We know that sometimes it would be appealing to have a child who obeys just because you say so. Do we really want to force our Ephraim's Child to conform? A war was fought before we came to Earth with Lucifer who wanted to "force conformity" to his plan.

However, the Ephraim's Child needs to learn obedience. The Lord said, "We will prove them herewith, to see if they will do all things whatsoever the Lord their God will command them."[1] The third Article of Faith states, "We believe that through the Atonement of Christ, all mankind may be saved, by obedience to the laws and ordinances of the Gospel." We can be saved, but only through our own obedience. If we don't obey we have been told, "Behold, I, the Lord, command; and he that will not obey shall be cut off in mine own due time."[2] It is necessary to learn obedience in this life. The challenge lies in teaching the vital principle of obedience without going to extremes like forcing conformity or forcing our child away from our protection.

During "The Battle of the Silverware," it is natural to use everyday terms like stubborn, obstinate, immovable, headstrong, willful, inflexible, and bullheaded. It is harder to think of your child as persistent, resolute, determined, persevering, steadfast, unfailing, and resolved. Yet the second set of names are positive qualities that are actually admirable and good. From now on we will use the new everyday name of persistent, instead of stubborn.

We know that living with a persistent Ephraim's Child is not easy. You know that this quality can be a valuable asset throughout your child's life, but persistence in the raw is challenging. Even as infants, these kids are tremendously determined and strong. When you oppose their will, these children let you feel their wrath with all its intensity. They push and demand more than other kids. They never give up, and they are always ready to do battle. Ephraim's Children do not behave this way on purpose to drive you into an early grave. They are simply born this way.

Many times the first and very strong reaction of the Ephraim's Child is to resist when told what to do. But is natural resistance a good or a bad thing? Let's look at a couple of stories of resistance in the scriptures. The first is the story of Pharaoh and Moses. In this case, Pharaoh resisted instructions from God as given him by the prophet Moses. Pharaoh stubbornly refused to obey, despite the many testimonies and signs from God Himself. As a result, Pharaoh lost not only the wealth of his kingdom but his firstborn son.

Then there is the story of Joseph and Potiphar's wife. Potiphar's wife tried hard to convince Joseph to commit a grievous sin. The scriptures say that "she spake to Joseph day by day . . . [but] he hearkened not unto her."[3] One day Potiphar's wife was alone in the house with Joseph. She "caught [Joseph] by his garment" to physically compel him to her wishes, "and he left his garment in her hand, and fled, and got him out."[4] Both of these men showed resistance, but Pharaoh refused to obey God, while Joseph withstood temptation to do evil. Resistance can be both good and bad, depending on the path you are traveling.

## Turning Stubborn Into Steadfast

The difference between perseverance and stubbornness is that one often comes from a strong *will*, and the other from a strong *won't*.[5] In this case the strong will means—I *will* do, I *will* succeed, I *will* obtain.

The other side of stubborn is persistence. Napoleon said, "Victory belongs to the most persevering."[6] We all know that if it weren't for perseverance, many things would never have been accomplished. If Thomas Edison had given up the first few hundred times that his experiment failed, we wouldn't have the light bulb. In a speech given in the Grant Oratorical Contest at Brigham Young University, Roderick L. Cameron and Lawrence R. Flack talked about how a great deal can be accomplished in this life if one is willing to pay the price of persistence. But, they ask, how many are willing to pay that price? Most of us are good starters but poor finishers of everything we begin. Moreover, we are prone to give up at the first signs of defeat. Most people are willing to attempt something once, a few will do it a hundred times, but how many will keep on doing the same thing a thousand times, if necessary, until they have succeeded?[7] The Ephraim's Child will keep on trying, and drive us nuts doing it.

Consider the child who absolutely refuses to accept "no" for an answer. She persists long after many would give up, and is not discouraged even when she doesn't hear a yes. However, if occasionally her parents give in, is this child stubborn or persistent? If an adult refuses to accept defeat in his career and eventually succeeds, he is praised for his determination. Is this persistence a trait to be stamped out as parents may be tempted to do, or one to be directed?

Whether we like it or not, Heavenly Father is sending these personalities to the world today. We can help them work with what they are—spirits with this trait that the Lord finds valuable—or we can try to destroy their natural persistence in an effort to mold them into totally compliant offspring. If we do not help channel their determination, we run the risk that their persistence will be used against righteousness.

The phrase *"Never, never, never give up"* has been used in talks by several General Authorities over the past few years. It was Elder Boyd K. Packer who first used it in a spiritual context,[8] but it was Winston Churchill who coined the phrase. In his Conference talk "Never Give Up," Elder Joseph B. Wirthlin tells the story of Winston Churchill returning to the school where he studied as a boy. "Before he arrived, the headmaster told the students, 'The greatest Britisher of our time is going to come to this school, and I want every one of you to be here with your notebooks. I want you to write down what he says, because his speech will be something for you to remember all your lives . . .' Churchill stood and delivered the following words from an immortal speech that he once gave in Parliament. He said, 'Never, never, never give up.' Then he sat down. That was the speech. It was unmatched."9

Elder Wirthlin then said, "Perseverance is a positive, active characteristic. It is not idly, passively waiting and hoping for some good thing to happen."10 Persistence can be a positive trait. These overwhelmingly, intensely persistent children need to know that we approve and value their persistence. Someone who will stand firm and steadfast despite opposition is a valuable commodity in society and in the kingdom of God.

## Dealing With Persistence

"If anybody says someone is 'stubborn as a mule,' he doesn't know anything about mules. . . . If you can't make a mule do what you want him to do, he's not being stubborn, he's just outsmarting you."11 How do we manage persistence and avoid being outsmarted?

### Choose the Trees that You Focus On

Ephraim's Children will frequently view any instructions contrary to their desires as a chafing restriction of their freedom. They want to do things for themselves, they want to make their own choices, they do not want to be compelled to do anything. Some days you probably feel like a drill sergeant. You snap at your Ephraim's Child every five minutes. Every sentence begins with "No," "Stop," or "Don't." When confronted with the daily reality of a persistent Ephraim's Child, even the best-intentioned parent finds himself backed into the "No, you can't" corner. This is when the automatic reply to every interaction with your child is negative.

In his book *Don't Leap With The Sheep*, author S. Michael Wilcox discusses the attitudinal differences between "No, you can't" and "Yes, you may." In the Garden of Eden we are introduced to how Satan uses freedom—or the lack of it—to lead away the children of men. "[The tempter's] . . . first words to Eve reflect his desire to cast a mist over all the good things we can freely enjoy and focus our attention on the things that are forbidden: 'Yea, hath God said—Ye shall *not* eat of *every tree* of the garden?' (Moses 4:7) . . . He wanted Eve to concentrate only on the tree that had been forbidden. Lucifer desires us to focus on the things we do not have and cannot do."[12]

Lucifer's choice of words implied that Eve was not totally free; she was being denied something desirable. Satan uses the suggestion that rules, commandments, policies, counsels, laws, and so on are a limit to our freedom and that we therefore have a right to rebel against them.

Wilcox contrasts this with God's approach to the same situation. In the Garden of Eden the Lord explained: "'Of *every* tree of the garden *thou mayest freely eat*, but of the tree of the knowledge of good and evil, thou shalt not eat of it, nevertheless, thou mayest choose for thyself, for it is given unto thee; but, remember that I forbid it, for in the day thou eatest thereof thou shalt surely die.'[13] Notice that the Lord started his commandment in a positive manner. Adam and Eve could eat from dozens of trees. Only one was forbidden, and for good reason. The key word in the Lord's instructions is *every*. In light of the many trees they could partake of, one single tree that was forbidden did not seem so restrictive (emphasis added)."[14]

The first way to deal with persistence is to help your Ephraim's Child focus on the correct trees. Naturally he will concentrate on the "forbidden tree," but help him see that there are dozens of other trees that are allowed. This will also help you maneuver out of your "No, you can't" corner as your own focus shifts to a "Yes, you can" mentality. Instead of automatically telling your child "no" all the time, you can help him discover the things he can do. Don't expect your child to always agree with you and stop testing you, but it is good to point out to him that there are many things that he can do.

### Begin With the End in Mind

When you find yourself about to enter the ring with your persistent child, take a minute before jumping into the fight.

Do not butt heads with your child simply because she has dared to challenge your authority. The Ephraim's Child is not being obstinate to irritate or manipulate you—that is simply the way she is. You need to begin with the end in mind; where do you eventually want to be?

Elder Dallin H. Oaks talked about this when he elaborated on the difference between ultimate, eternal goals versus the short-term objectives and methods used to pursue them:

> "If we concentrate too intently on our obvious earthly methods or objectives, we can lose sight of our eternal goals. . . . If we do this, we can forget where we should be headed and in eternal terms go nowhere. We do not improve our position in eternity just by flying farther and faster in mortality, but only by moving knowledgeably in the right direction."[15]

The Lord Himself has given us the same advice. "That which the spirit testifies unto you even so I would that ye should do in all holiness of heart, walking uprightly before me, *considering the end of your salvation*" (emphasis added).[16] If we are to reach the end goal, we need to begin with that goal in mind; we need to *consider the end*. We will not achieve our goal simply by frantically expending energy randomly. We must use our energy in the right direction.

It is the same when you are faced with a potential power struggle with your Ephraim's Child. Many times we wildly enter the fray just because we want our way as much as our child wants his way. It becomes a battle of wills, where winning matters more than the outcome. Don't let the power struggle overshadow the final goal. Begin with the end in mind. In other words, what is the point? What is the end product or final goal that you want to achieve in this situation?

For example, it is the end of a long and busy day and you have finally rounded up the children to get them into pajamas. Your Ephraim's Child flatly refuses to get into her pajamas. For your sake and the children's health, they need to go to bed and they need to go now. You try coaxing your child into pajamas. No luck. She wants to sleep in what she is wearing . . . period. You have two choices. You could grab the child, wrestle her to the ground and forcefully change her clothes while she kicks and screams, then try to put her to bed with both you and her in a rotten mood, or you could give in and let her sleep in the clothes she is wearing. Neither feels like a good solution.

What is the desired end product in this situation? Is the ultimate goal to have your child wear pajamas or is it for her to go to bed? Is it really imperative that she wear fabric that has been labeled as "pajamas?" If the desired result is to get your child in bed and asleep, then does it really matter what is on her body as long as she does it? If you begin with the end in mind, then you could let your child sleep in her clothes, or pick out different clothes that might be more comfortable. You avoid a power struggle and wrestling match, and your child goes to sleep. Was that really so bad?

What about when teaching a class in church? You have an Ephraim's Child that simply will not stay in his chair. Is the object of the class to have the child sit in a chair, or learn the gospel and feel the Spirit? As a teacher, perhaps your students sit on the floor that day instead of watching you engage in a power struggle with the immovable Ephraim's Child. This would be keeping the end in mind.

Beginning with the end in mind does not mean that you simply give in all the time. There will be times when you become the immovable one because your stance is the one that will promote the final goal. We are just trying to show you that sometimes it is perfectly acceptable to say "yes." Sometimes it is good to encourage the persistence of the Ephraim's Child. Once in a while it is okay for you to bend. In so doing, you show your child that flexibility is important. Your child learns by watching you. Do you want the end product of raising this Ephraim's Child to be an adult that must always have his way because that is what he learned from his parents? We must be examples of cooperation as well as authority.

## The Problems with Ignoring or Distraction

Conventional parenting wisdom advises to ignore or try to distract a child when they get frustrated and angry or don't accept your answer to something they want to do. This may work with other kids, but the persistent Ephraim's Child won't let you ignore him. For example, when your young child repeatedly wakes in the night, numerous authorities suggest that you leave him in bed to cry himself back to sleep. The theory is that he will cry less each time and eventually learn to soothe himself to sleep. This is under the assumption that the child will actually stop crying. A persistent Ephraim's Child may cry harder and harder until he works himself into hysteria. One mother we know tried this and gave up after a continuous string of rough nights when her son cried for two hours straight.

These children are also difficult, if not impossible, to distract. They lock on an idea and, like a crocodile, refuse to let go. The futility of trying to divert an Ephraim's Child can be shown from this story of a toddler bent on climbing a rocking chair. At this time his grandmother was already sitting in the chair, but that did not deter him. He merely used her legs to clamber into her lap, not to be held, but to use her as a ladder to climb to the top of the chair. She repeatedly set him down on the floor, only to have him climb up her legs again. Eventually the grandmother left her seat, thinking that he would stop when his human ladder was gone. That tactic didn't work. He immediately darted to the chair. Each time she removed him he instantly returned. He never gave up. A couple of times the adults got distracted by other things happening in the room. In the seconds it took for them to return their attention to the climber he had reached his goal and was diving head first over the back of the chair. The adults were unable to distract this Ephraim's Child from his goal, despite repeated efforts.

The Ephraim's Child knows what he wants and is not about to give up on it until he either gets his way or finds something better. Ignoring persistent kids until they give up or distracting them from their goal is not effective. Adults become frustrated when nothing works and sometimes give in simply because they do not know what else to do. Battling with a child who never, never, never gives up is draining.

Sometimes the first step in stopping these battles is taking the time to actually listen to our kids. That does not mean being quiet until it is your turn to debate, but actively and physically paying attention to what your child says. Listen with the intent to understand, and tell your child that you are attentive to her position on the subject.

Okay, so you stop what you're doing and actively listen to your child. Now do you stick to your guns, or do you give in? Parents are advised to hang tough and not back down, or else your child will know that he can manipulate you. However, this stance is not necessarily true when faced with the immovable Ephraim's Child. Sometimes the better response is negotiation.

### Negotiation

Wait a minute! As the responsible adult, you don't negotiate with kids, right? Most of us grew up with the idea that trying to negotiate with parents was talking back. Mom said to do something and because she was the authority, you did it, despite your feelings on the issue. However, the persistent Ephraim's Child will not do something just because the authority says so. This child will argue and try to negotiate to get his way.

*The Random House Dictionary* defines the word "negotiate" as: to reach an agreement or compromise by discussion, to find a way over or through (an obstacle or difficult path) in a satisfactory manner.[17] Everyone is a negotiator; everyone negotiates something every day. We negotiate when we make family vacation plans. We negotiate when we discuss with our spouse where to eat for dinner, or what movie to go see. You may not view this as negotiating, but it is. Not all negotiation involves grappling for position in a power struggle between wily opponents.

In *Getting to Yes, Negotiating Agreement Without Giving In,* authors Roger Fisher, William Ury, and Bruce Patton examine the traditional methods of negotiation. In the era we grew up there were two ways to negotiate: soft and hard. Soft negotiators want to avoid conflict and usually concede a lot and with little fuss. Their goal is agreement. Hard negotiators are the stiff-necked negotiators who demand one-sided gains. Their goal is victory. Traditional negotiation generally produces a winner and a loser.[18]

"I won't eat my green beans," your child states at dinner one night. "You *will* eat them or you will go to your room until you are ready to eat them," you reply. These statements immediately lock you and your child into a position. And the more you try to convince each other that you are going to stick to your position and won't change, the more difficult it becomes to do so. It has now moved beyond the question of nutrition into a contest of will. If you don't force your child to eat the green beans, she wins and you lose. If she goes to her room, you win and she loses. But a more important thing than a few vegetables has been affected: your relationship. Fisher, Ury, and Patton introduce us to a new kind of negotiation called "principled negotiation."[19] This method decides issues on merit rather than through a haggling process focused on what each side says it will and won't do. You focus on the issue rather than on each other's position.

Principled negotiation changes the game. You no longer state positions and view each other as opponents. In principled negotiation you battle with the issue instead of your opponent and decide to problem-solve together. The goal is to reach a satisfactory outcome together. Together you focus on interests, not positions. Together you look for options toward mutual gain using objective criteria. You focus on common interests and ideas so you can develop a relationship with your child that involves teamwork and finding win-win solutions.

Whenever you lock yourself into a position, there is a reason; an interest or need you are trying to meet. What may be difficult to remember is that the persistent child challenging you locks herself into positions for a reason as well. In principled negotiation, we try to resolve the underlying cause rather than the resulting effect. In other words, we need to focus on the interests rather than the positions.

The easiest way to clarify interests is to ask. "Why don't you want to eat your green beans?" After your child responds, tell her why you want her to eat the green beans. Finding out the why's will uncover the interests or needs at issue. If your child is too young to express herself clearly, you may have to do a little detective work to discover her reason. Ask some yes or no questions and try to guess for her. "Do you not like green beans? Is your tummy full? Do you want a drink first? Do you want corn instead?" Clarifying interests takes time and is not easy, but you will also be teaching your Ephraim's Child how to use words to express herself. Once you understand the underlying interests at stake, you can begin working towards a solution.

However, before negotiating a solution, we need to address the difference between expectations and rules. Rules are usually serious guidelines involving safety or unacceptable behavior, whereas expectations are often preferences or routines. Expectations, such as "green beans are always served with spaghetti," or "you must eat your vegetables before being excused from the table," may be negotiable. On the other hand, rules are those guidelines that are firmly set and non-negotiable, such as "we do not hit siblings" or "you do not cross the street without an adult." Remind your child of the existing rules and expectations before finding a solution. Perhaps the solution will be found in the rules and you will not need to continue looking for an answer.

It does take time for people to move out of their position, especially for persistent children. Many power struggles occur when we are in a rush and do not allow extra time for our child to unlock gradually. At these times we need to somehow give them the time they need. Our experience has shown that you end up wasting more time in battle with your persistent child anyway.

Talk to your child at times when you unlock out of your position. Walk him through it with you and show him how you solve problems. Almost as important as showing him that it can be done is showing him that although you are disappointed, you will live through it. The persistent Ephraim's Child who intensely cares about his position needs to know that it is okay to be flexible.

After you have allowed time to maneuver out of your positions, brainstorm solutions with your child. Find ways to address both of your interests. Part of the nature of brainstorming is the fact that anything goes. No idea is stupid or gets thrown out until after the brainstorming is over. This will allow your child to see that there are actually several solutions available that allow you both to be winners. Choose a solution and try it. In our green bean example, a possible solution would be that your child can pick the vegetable she wants before dinner is prepared, every other day.

The last step in principled negotiation is to evaluate the solution you choose at a later time. You may find that your new solution is worse than the old problem. Talk about it and see if it is a solution that works. If not, brainstorm again. Choose a different solution, try it for a while, then evaluate again. Keep making adjustments until you find the best answer.

"It is not abdicating our parental authority to sometimes say yes and to allow our . . . children to try a new idea or come up with the solution to a problem. In fact, realizing that they are good problem solvers is a major breakthrough for persistent kids. It helps them to stop the struggles before they ever start."[20] Finding ways together to say "Yes, you can" teaches persistent children to consider the needs of others, to solve problems amicably, and to make decisions that everyone can live with. Even better, negotiating this way does not sacrifice your relationship over a contest of will. Our kids are worth more than green beans.

Many adults, including relatives, may not be familiar with "principled negotiation" and might comment or throw shocked glances or disapproving "tut tuts" in your direction. Ignore most of them, but let your closest friends and relatives know that you are not giving up your authority and letting your Ephraim's Child walk all over you. Explain to them that you are intentionally deciding when and how you involve your children. You are teaching important life skills. You are recognizing your children's natural persistence and teaching them how to use it well. You are helping them, and yourself, feel better about persistence.

## Persistent Parents

Often persistent Ephraim's Children have persistent parents. We all know adults that are immovable, unyielding, and downright stubborn themselves. Maybe you even include yourself on that list, and sparks will fly when a persistent parent meets head on with an equally immovable three-year-old Ephraim's Child. Sometimes we must be the one who is flexible in order to avoid a battle. We have more years and experience to help us keep proper perspective. But when you are in the thick of the Battle of the Silverware or the Pajama Skirmish, it is hard to remember that sometimes we are the ones who need to yield.

Pray that you can have wisdom in the heat of the moment. Enlist the Lord's help in avoiding the "wrestle your child to the ground and forcefully make him brush his teeth to prove that you are in charge" moments. The Lord knows your child. He knows you. He knows you both more than you do, and He knows the best way for you to grow together. Ask Him.

## We Need Persistence

John Calvin Coolidge, the thirtieth president of the United States, stated:

Nothing in the world can take the place of persistence. Talent will not; nothing is more common than unsuccessful men with talent. Genius will not; unrewarded genius is almost a proverb. Education alone will not; the world is full of educated derelicts. Persistence and determination alone are omnipotent. The slogan "press on" has solved and always will solve the problems of the human race.[21]

The world needs people with conviction; people with purpose. Even more importantly we need people who will stand fast despite the buffetings of wickedness against them. In a talk at a Regional Representatives Seminar, Ezra Taft Benson said, "Many years before the coming of the Savior to this earth, the prophet Enoch saw the latter days. He observed the great wickedness that would prevail on the earth at this time and foretold the great tribulations that would result from such wickedness."[22] In the times that are upon us and the difficult things that we've been told are still before us, a persevering spirit is going to be immensely valuable.

Elder Wirthlin reminds us of the following:

"The ultimate example of perseverance is our Lord and Savior, Jesus Christ, who has and will overcome every obstacle in doing the will of our Heavenly Father. Indeed, Jesus is perfect in perseverance and has taught us to be perfect, even as he and his Father are perfect (see 3 Ne. 12:48). . . . He completely overcame every temptation that the cunning Satan could devise (see Matt. 4:1-11). This is the type of perseverance in the face of temptation that each of us can and must exercise if we are to avoid the misery of sin."[23]

We know that these children are not fence sitters. It is not their nature. They are going to get into the thick of things, simply because they are not content to just sit. We want a child who, once his feet are set on the right road, will not turn aside no matter the obstacles, difficulties, or temptations. The Ephraim's Child is blessed to already possess a large measure of persistence, perseverance, and determination. It will be easier to "endure to the end" when one is already steadfast, unfailing, and resolved. We are told that those who endure to the end shall be saved at the last day.[24] Isn't that the ultimate end goal for us all?

Perhaps the most profound thing Elder Wirthlin says in his talk is: "Satan seldom gives up."[25] This is another major reason we do not want to stamp out persistence in the Ephraim's Child. This is why we need righteous people who will likewise "never, never, never give up."

# 6

# Adaptability

*One grandmother stayed the summer with her daughter who was on "bed rest" for the last few weeks of a pregnancy. Grandma was there to help with the numerous things mom couldn't do, the most important of which was to take care of her two-year-old son. This toddler had his own set way of doing things, and if the routine was tampered with he went out of control. This summer, the one major constant in the toddler's life changed: his mother was no longer able to care for him. Every time Grandma helped do anything, her grandson screamed. Insisting that he stop screeching, kicking, hitting, or crying only made the reactions worse. Many times Grandma felt rejected. Then she realized that she was dealing with a slow-to-adapt Ephraim's Child whose world had suddenly and completely changed.*

We live in a world of change. Your activities and environment constantly change. In a typical day you begin by changing from sleep to wakefulness. Then you take a shower, change clothes, eat breakfast, and leave the house, etc. Each of these changes is considered a transition, and you do it multiple times a day. Transitions are a part of life, and unfortunately the Ephraim's Child does not adapt well to transitions.

When your child must leave a friend's house to come home you can understand why she cries and fights you. But why does getting in the car, coming to the table for meals, or getting dressed elicit equally strong reactions? Why is going to a different bank than usual a matter of tears? Is your new sofa really that life threatening? Why is your child heartbroken when your neighbor clears out the flowers in their front yard? Why do you have to drag your kid out of bed, wrestle him into his clothes, prod and push him to the table for breakfast, haul him to the bathroom to brush his teeth, and then threaten him into the car every morning? No wonder you are ready for a nap by 9 a.m.!

You need to understand that all of these situations involve change and transition. Ephraim's Children often have an unbelievably difficult time with change—any change. A normal day involves a chain of transitions, and if you have to fight your child through every one of them, then you are in for an exhausting day for both of you. These children *require* time and space to prepare for change.

More than other kids, Ephraim's Children need smooth transitions. Your child is not misbehaving or trying to rebel. Your slow-to-adapt Ephraim's Child is having a difficult time dealing with the changes that seem to bombard him at lightning speed. You can see this problem with change more clearly at the times when you know your child actually *wants* to do the new activity, but still balks with all his strength. He wants to go to Grandpa's house and enjoys going to school, yet you still have to enter the wrestling ring to get his cooperation. Transitions may never be a piece of cake for your child, but you can learn to make them easier.

## Routine

Most children thrive on predictability and routine. However, routine is *essential* for children who are slow to adapt. With a specific time to wake up, eat meals, nap, play with friends, and go to bed, Ephraim's Children can predict what is going to happen and then prepare for the change. Surprises trigger intense reactions, even if they are pleasant surprises. When these children know what to expect, they feel more in control and can transition easier. Ephraim's Children feel more secure in a consistent routine. Establishing a routine will reduce many of the transition problems that you have with your child, but don't expect automatic smooth sailing. You will have fewer fights, but the Ephraim's Child will still test you.

Some people do not believe in establishing a regular routine. They may feel that it is too strict to "force" their child to follow a schedule. However, our world runs on schedules. Society would be chaotic if we couldn't count on businesses, public transportation, or shipping companies adhering to predictable time schedules. Some things must be predictable to run smoothly. And in order for your child to be successful in society he must learn how to live within a schedule as well. For example, the child who is not accustomed to a consistent bedtime, waking time, or mealtimes will likely find adjusting to school difficult. School starts the same time every day, it finishes at the same time, and has set lunch and recess times. This applies to the work force as well. An adult that cannot make it to work on time on a consistent basis will find it more challenging to remain employed in most jobs.

Another argument against routine is that you lose flexibility. How many people want to have to stop in the middle of something just so their child can have a nap? Some parents may feel resentful having their entire lives structured around their child's schedule, but having a consistent routine does not mean that you become a slave to your child's schedule; that you can never be spontaneous again. Simply respect your Ephraim's Child's need to have a predictable schedule. There will be routine days and exceptional days. On routine days, try your best to organize your activities around a schedule. Be reasonably consistent about when you do things. You do not have to have lunch exactly at noon; a few minutes variation is okay. On exceptional days, such as special events, your routine may fly out the window, but there are still things that you can do to help your child feel in control.

Realize that there are no absolute or rigid schedules because every day is going to be somewhat different. The goal is not to have absolute regularity in your schedule, where every event occurs at exactly the same time every day, but reasonable regularity and consistency, which gives you reasonable flexibility. Once you have experienced the peace of keeping your child on a predictable schedule, however, the days when you deviate will feel a little like a tornado. You will probably voluntarily choose to limit those "tornado" days.

## If Your Child Has an Inconsistent Nature

Having a routine is easy if your child naturally follows a regular schedule. It is much more difficult if she is never hungry at the same time or is tired at different times from day to day. Some children are more regular than others in terms of their body needs and functions. What if your child is not naturally a "schedule person?"

Some Ephraim's Children just don't automatically fall into a predictable schedule. One day they may nap four hours and the next day they may not sleep at all. It is hard to predict when they will be hungry, how much food they will eat, or what time they will get up in the morning. You don't know what to expect because your child's body rhythms seem to be all over the place. It may take years for a child like this to finally sleep through the night, which is exhausting and frustrating for the sleep-deprived parents.

Children who are not regular by nature are not trying to upset family life; they are not intentionally being difficult. Their bodies just do not easily find a predictable rhythm. You don't need to worry that if you only did something different in your parenting that your child would then be more predictable. You are not a worse parent because your child will not automatically fall asleep at the same time every night like his cousins. Together you can find ways to help him adapt to schedules, something he will need to figure out in order to survive in our world of regular schedules. Inconsistency requires extra patience and creative problem solving for parents, especially from those who are consistent themselves.

Believe it or not, a regular routine can help these children too. When you have a predictable routine for bedtime, for example, every night the same cues are given to help your child adapt to the family schedule. Understand that moving to some sort of schedule is probably not going to be easy. The irregular child can eventually adapt to routines, but it is doubtful that she will become regular. She will sit at the table with the family during dinner, but sometimes she will simply not be hungry even though everyone has eaten and all the dishes are finished. She may go to bed at the same time every night, but she will not always fall asleep at the same time.

If you are like this yourself, your child's sporadic nature may not be a problem. Just make sure that you provide enough regularity to help your child adapt to school schedules. Your child will need enough routine to get the rest and nutrition needed to be successful in school. And realize that a slow-to-adapt child, even one who is irregular, will respond better to some sort of predictability. If you are feeling frustrated with the inconsistent body of your Ephraim's Child, remember to use positive everyday names. These kinds of people may be the ones who thrive in jobs requiring odd hours or swing shifts. Doctors, nurses, fire fighters, police officers, pilots, and night watchmen certainly have irregular schedules.

## Forewarning

Realtors say that the biggest factor in selling a house is "location, location, location." Likewise, the biggest factor in helping your slow-to-adapt child deal with transitions is "forewarning, forewarning, forewarning." Your child needs time to adjust to transitions, whether it is going to bed, going to the store, sending friends home, eating lunch, having a babysitter for the evening, or the changing of bedding with the onset of winter. You give him time by forewarning him. Letting your child know what is going to happen will give him a head start on the change. It helps to give him a clear idea of what to expect: that you are going somewhere, how long you will be there, who will be there, what you will be doing, etc.

Each Ephraim's Child is different, so try different ways of forewarning. Big changes, like an upcoming vacation, moving to a new house, or a new sibling, require some finesse. Some children will do best with days or weeks of advanced warning. Others will just worry themselves into hysteria if given too much time. For the normal daily transitions we use a five-minute warning, followed by a two-minute and then a one-minute warning. This gives our Ephraim's Child a count down to when the change is actually going to take place. You can also use a clock to help your child keep track of the time until a transition. For example, "When the big hand is on the six, we will leave." Here are some more examples of ways to forewarn:

In five more minutes it will be time to . . .
After this show is over we will . . .
Two more swings and then it is Jenny's turn . . .
After this song we need to . . .
When Dad comes home . . .
You can play with the toy for two more minutes, then
    John gets it for two minutes . . .
After school today we will be going . . .
Friends need to go home in two minutes . . .
Wednesday you have a doctor's appointment . . .

Look at the day and try to pinpoint where the transitions will be, then forewarn your Ephraim's Child about what is to come. This tactic can make such a difference that it may soon become second nature to you, and over time your child will feel secure that you will warn her of transitions. However, don't expect your child to always gracefully stop what she is doing just because you have forewarned her of an upcoming transition. She is still an intense and persistent Ephraim's Child.

You may feel like your entire day is spent counting down to your slow-to-adapt child. What you may not realize is that we as adults do this as well. How many times during a day do you check your watch or a clock to see how much time until you have to do something? Although it is not as deliberate and obvious as what you do with your child, in essence you think to yourself, "five minutes until I need to start dinner," or "one more hour until my appointment." Ephraim's Children just can't do this for themselves yet.

The grandma in the first story was not accustomed to forewarning her grandson. She just picked him up to go to the car or cleared his plate when it appeared he was finished eating, without giving him a clue what was coming. Intense battles were the result. Finally, she realized that she needed to forewarn him of transitions, and although it was a hassle at first, the child's behavior and cooperation improved. It wasn't always his grandma that he was fighting, but rather the changes that came without warning.

## Give Your Child the Time He Needs

Your routine may be clear and you may forewarn your child, but you need to allow enough time for your slow-to-adapt child. These kids are not wasting time when they take forever to get dressed or get into the car. They are merely warming up and allowing themselves time to adapt to the change. Even more time is needed for transitions that are not part of your normal routine. Although it may sound paradoxical, if you want more time in a day, allow more time for your child to transition. That may require getting up ten minutes earlier so that you will feel less rushed. If you try to rush your Ephraim's Child, then expect him to dig in his heels with all his persistent nature.

You may need to advocate for your child with other people who may not understand that she requires warm-up time. Suggest that the doctor talk with your child for a few minutes before beginning an examination. Explain to relatives that your child will give them a hug in a few minutes, but for now she needs to get used to the situation. Arrive to school a few minutes early to give your child time to adjust. When your child is at a friend's house, call ahead to tell her that you are coming to get her.

One time a nurse needed a blood sample from the finger of a young Ephraim's Child. Knowing that he was nervous, she decided to prick his finger quickly before he knew what was happening. This did not give the child time to deal with the surprise, and he ripped himself from her arms and was out the door and down the hall before anyone could react. The boy's mother had to chase her hysterical child through the office to drag him back. In this situation, the nurse probably would have been wiser to allow the child time to warm up first, maybe through showing him the different tools or explaining what would happen. The boy's mother could also have been a better advocate on behalf of her son.

## Find a Stopping Point

Part of allowing your Ephraim's Child time to adapt to change is helping him find a stopping point. What kids are doing is important to them, and it can be extremely frustrating if they are not allowed to finish. Imagine that you were constantly being stopped before finishing things you start. For example, you are talking on the phone when you are forced to hang up in mid-sentence and go eat lunch. Perhaps you are reading a book and it is snatched from you in the middle of the climax and you are herded into the car. Or what if you are in the middle of watching a television show when the set is turned off and you are marched up to bed. Wouldn't you feel a little upset too? Yet we continually do this to our Ephraim's Child. Remember, what your child is doing is just as important to him as the things you are doing are to you. Respect that, and plan time for your child to somehow wrap up his activities.

Often, simply forewarning your child of upcoming transitions will provide a finishing point. After three more catches, your child's friend must go home; that is the end of the game. However, when you need to get in the car and go, despite the unfinished Lego masterpiece, you will need to find a stopping point rather than finishing the activity. At first you will have to help your child find that stopping place. Perhaps you could say, "After these three Legos it is time to stop," or "after that wall we need to go." Assure him that he can finish later.

Many times your persistent Ephraim's Child will not want to stop when you need her to, but being able to find stopping points can be a valuable skill. There will be times when circumstances will not allow a project to be finished right then and there. In the classroom your child may be unable to finish the assignment before it is time to move on. It is likely that there will be times when your child's ride shows up and she must leave, even if she is in the middle of something. The telephone never fails to ring in the middle of large projects as well. The ability to find a good stopping point and then return to a task later will make life much easier.

## Limit the Number of Transitions

Ephraim's Children can only take so many transitions a day. If you overload your slow-to-adapt child with transitions, you can kiss a smooth day goodbye. When planning your day, carefully consider the number of transitions. How many times will you be in a different place? How often will you be in and out of the car? How much will you vary from your regular routine? If you want your child to have a successful day, you must limit the number of transitions required of her.

This can be challenging if you are someone who likes to accomplish a whole list of things in a day. If you prefer to do all your errands at once in a marathon day, it may be hard to leave your list unfinished to cater to your child. Realize that your child is not necessarily being difficult when she refuses to get in the car to make one more quick trip to a store. Sometimes she may have just reached her transition limit and is letting you know that she simply cannot handle any more.

One mother we know realized that she was missing an ingredient for dinner. There was enough time for a quick trip to get it at the grocery store so she informed her Ephraim's Child that they would be leaving in a few minutes. He vehemently resisted the idea. In similar situations in the past the mom got upset and forced her child into the car, but this time she paused to review their day. She realized that her child had already had a busy day and had adapted to a lot of transitions. So she asked her son why he did not want to go to the store. He replied, "I don't want to go anywhere else. I want to stay home . . . please!" He was telling her that he had reached his limit. She changed dinner plans and they stayed home the rest of the evening and had an enjoyable time. Fixing a different meal was a small price to pay to end the day on a successful note.

There will be times when a lot of transitions are unavoidable. Vacations, family gatherings, or holidays will require extra planning on your part. Do whatever you can to help your slow-to-adapt Ephraim's Child. Perhaps you can avoid car pooling and drive your own car so that you can leave when your child has had enough. Sometimes you may need to say no to an activity or find a way to alternate hectic and quiet days so your child can have a break. A chain of different activities may not be a big deal to relatives, but it may be disaster for your slow-to-adapt child.

Understanding your child's transition limit and staying within it will avoid a lot of problems. Remember that if your child is tired or hungry, he will have less tolerance for change than when he is well rested and fed. As your child grows, he will handle transitions better. A four-year-old Ephraim's Child will be able to adapt better than when he was two. When you know your child's transition limit and respect it, your days will be more successful. This will require flexibility on your part, but you can reach a balance between your child's limits and your own needs.

## Changing Plans

Changing plans is also a transition, especially if it is at the last minute. A change of plans is often a more difficult transition when it is accompanied with disappointment. Disappointment is difficult for anyone, but especially so for these children because their intense emotions may overwhelm them.

You can help your child learn to handle disappointment without flipping out, but the emotion is still real and needs to be expressed somehow. Deciding what to do about it before you have a disappointed, intense Ephraim's Child can save you trouble. What you choose as an appropriate outlet for disappointment may vary. Maybe you need to allow your child a brief outburst, then explain that you understand she is disappointed and that you will try to do such-and-such another day. Then you can firmly tell her that she has been able to express herself and it is time to be calm now. Handling disappointment this way acknowledges your child's feelings, but shows her that she can still be in control of them.

One simple way to minimize problems from a change in plans is to wait to inform your child of what is happening until you are sure that it will actually happen. There is a difference between forewarning and speculating. Many times parents will try to distract their child or give them something to look forward to by mentioning an idea like, "maybe tonight we can go over to Brad's house and visit." Do not do voice plans like this unless you have called Brad's parents and are sure it is even feasible. If you say it, your Ephraim's Child will consider the plans set in stone. Then, if it doesn't happen, they consider plans changed. Telling your child possible plans before they are conclusive may set you up for dealing with a distraught Ephraim's Child more than you need to.

You can help your Ephraim's Child brainstorm ways how to cope with disappointment and changing plans. This involves imagining and talking through things that could possibly happen. "What if we go to Primary and your name does not get called for a turn?" "What if the movie is sold out?" "What if the other kids don't want to play the same things you do?" Ask your child how she would feel in that situation and then help her think of what she could do about it. This will help your child see that she is in control of her actions; she isn't a slave to knee-jerk reactions.

Thinking about possible outcomes together before your child is surprised by a change of plans can help her adapt easier because she is already somewhat prepared. You have already talked about how she would feel, and she already has a plan of what to do in the new situations. It will not be such a surprise if the movie is actually sold out. You might wonder if doing this will focus your child on the terrible things that could happen. This will not be the case if you emphasize the solutions rather than the problem. You are helping your child anticipate and prepare for situations that may be difficult for her.

## The Importance of Adaptability

The majority of this chapter has been survival tactics for raising a child who is slow to adapt. It is necessary to be patient with this temperamental trait, but your child needs to develop some adaptability. Schedules are important, but learning how to cope when things happen to mess up our schedule is just as important. Having a somewhat flexible attitude is necessary in life. The unexpected is always thrown at us, and we have to learn how to deal with it.

Adaptability is also important for simple spiritual survival in these last days. Elder Marvin J. Ashton said: "Proper attitude in this crisis-dominated world is a priceless possession. . . . [An] important ingredient of proper attitude is resilience, the ability to cope with change. Adaptability cushions the impact of change or disappointment. Love can be a great shock absorber as we adjust in trials and tragedy."[1]

Not only did Elder Ashton extol the virtue of resilience, but he gave us an important clue on how to be more adaptable—love. With love we can help our children adjust to the smaller trials of childhood, then we can continue to love them as their trials grow in magnitude. We need to teach our children of the love their Heavenly Father and Jesus Christ have for them. A testimony of a loving Father in Heaven is probably the greatest shock absorber and security when our lives take a drastic turn from our plans.

Your Ephraim's Child will need your help to be more flexible. We do not want him to grow into a rigid and inflexible adult who runs the risk of becoming hard-hearted or stiff-necked. Hugh Nibley once talked about how the words *hardness* and *stiffness* mean having a lack of flexibility. A simple lack of flexibility can lead to the more serious problem of unwillingness to repent. Inflexibility can become the inability or refusal to change, yield, or to adapt. This attitude can prevent repentance, and when you have lost all flexibility and won't change, you have reached a certain stage and are "ripening for destruction."[2]

Following the counsel of a living prophet also requires adaptability. Most of his teachings will not be new because they are based on eternal principles and standards, but our prophet also receives ongoing inspiration for the Church in the here and now. Sometimes what we are told now will be different from the counsel given in the past. Flexibility allows us to be more teachable, and less likely to be immovably set in possible incorrect traditions of our fathers.

Many times in the Book of Mormon we are told that the Lamanites had big problems coming to Christ because they refused to deviate from what they knew. In fact, they would not even believe the gospel when it was taught to them because of the incorrect traditions of their fathers.[3] The early Christians also had difficulty in giving up the traditions of their fathers, most especially the law of Moses. Paul and the other apostles had to work hard to get some of the church members to be more flexible to the changes that came through the fulfillment of the law of Moses. Through Joseph Smith the Lord gave further explanation to a passage in 1 Corinthians about this. In D&C 74:4 it states, "And it came to pass that the children, being brought up in subjection to the law of Moses, gave heed to the traditions of their fathers and believed not the gospel of Christ, wherein they became unholy."

The need for adaptability in the Church today was addressed in 1942 General Conference by Marvin O. Ashton. He said:

> This is an age of readjustment. Only those capable of making quick changes fit the times. Those with closed eyes and closed minds are in for trouble. A blind man wants the furniture in a room left unchanged. Only then can he move about with any degree of comfort and safety. Change the setting, and he finds himself bumping into things. No longer can he move freely. In our Church there are many men who act as if they were blind. They too want no changes made. They worship familiar patterns, and new ideas, new methods, new personalities cause them discomfort. Now is the time to remember the law of the survival of the fittest. We survive or we perish according to our adaptability or inadaptability to our environment. Each of us must ask, "What changes must I make in my thinking to fit me to this new environment?"4

How much more needful is this quality in our day, when everything changes even more quickly?

We are here to become more like God. The only way that this can happen is when we allow ourselves to be subject to His will. Only through God's plan for our lives can we be molded into the person that He knows we can become. One instance of a person being molded by the Lord into something great is found in the story of the prophet Jeremiah.

Jeremiah prophesied to the Jews from 626-586 B.C., a period of over 40 years. Jeremiah was fearless in his service to the Lord. He had to face continuous opposition and insults from the priests, the mob, the king, the army, and even from the people of his home town Anathoth. After the fall of Jerusalem, the Jews who escaped into Egypt took Jeremiah with them and eventually stoned him to death.[5]

At the beginning of Jeremiah's ministry the Lord told Jeremiah to visit a potter's house.[6] There the Lord taught Jeremiah that "as clay is in the potter's hand so are ye in my hand."[7] Elder Jean A. Tefan (Area Authority Seventy) comments in his article "Jeremiah: As Potter's Clay," that Jeremiah's willingness to put his life in the Lord's hands, like clay in a potter's hands, was a large part of his greatness in serving the Lord. He says: "A major factor in the molding of Jeremiah's life was his pliability, meaning his readiness to yield to the commands of God, to be flexible in freely and repeatedly bending to the will of God. . . . Jeremiah was pliable enough to do whatever the Lord commanded, no matter how peculiar, unpopular, or foolish it may have made him appear to others."[8]

The Lord's sculpting of Jeremiah's life reminds us of how He can shape our lives, if we let Him. President Heber C. Kimball said:

> There are many vessels that are destroyed after they have been moulded [sic] and shaped. Why? Because they are not contented with the shape the potter has given them, but straightaway put themselves into a shape to please themselves; therefore they are beyond understanding what God designs, and they destroy themselves by the power of their own agency. [These people] have to go through a great many modellings and shapes, then . . . have to be glazed and burned; and even in the burning, some vessels crack.[9]

Humility, obedience, faith, and freedom from pride are qualities of character that can enhance pliability.

Even though letting the Lord shape us can be challenging and even painful, there are great rewards. Heber C. Kimball gives us hope with these words: "All [who] are pliable in the hands of God and are obedient to His commands, are vessels of honor, and God will receive them."[10] Jeremiah will one day reap even greater rewards for his pliability. "His life was a vessel of honor, a guiding light of service, pliability, and long-suffering for Saints today. Our lives may also be vessels of honor, a work of beauty in the hands of the Master potter, if we will respond to His call . . . [and] be pliable in His hands."[11]

As parents, we can help our child understand about putting his life in God's hands through our example and experience. Tell your child about times from your own life when the Lord has had a different plan for you than what you intended. Explain that sometimes the Lord requires you to be pliable. Share scripture stories of others who were adaptable in the Lord's hands. Then express trust in the Lord's plan, and how following His direction has blessed you or others. This may require more flexibility on your part so that you have experiences to share with your child. Together you can help your child build a foundation of trust in the Lord so that she can be more adaptable in obeying Him.

## Learning When to Adapt

Having a child who is slow-to-adapt is not necessarily detrimental, although it may seem like it. When your child refuses to join the fun or even go in the door until the birthday party is almost over, you may feel like just pushing him in and making him deal with it. However, there are strengths to this characteristic. Don't automatically discount your child's slow adaptability. When he is a teenager, your child may hang back to assess situations and become more comfortable instead of jumping into them headfirst like his peers. How many bad situations could have been avoided by a little caution?

When your child's friends try to talk him into doing unwise things, it will be good for him to be extremely cautious and immovable. However, there will be times when it will be important for your child to adapt, like when he is grown and is given new callings in church. Strange as it may seem, both flexibility and inflexibility are important; the key is figuring out when to be which. As parents, it is important that you teach your Ephraim's Child how to know when to rely on his naturally slow adaptability, and when to loosen up a little.

We have examples in the scriptures of those who could not discern when to be flexible, and to their detriment chose poorly. Nephi admonished his older brothers Laman and Lemuel because they were "swift to do iniquity but slow to remember the Lord [their] God."[12] Mormon also lamented on "how quick to do iniquity, and how slow to do good, are the children of men; yea, how quick to hearken unto the words of the evil one . . . and how slow are they to remember the Lord their God."[13]

The Nephites often had difficulty knowing when to accept new ideas and be flexible and when to resist and be inflexible. Think back on the examples of Sherem, Korihor, and Nehor. They were able to lead away many people with their new ideas. In these cases, some Nephites were quick to accept the wrong thing, when it would have been wiser to hold back. Help your Ephraim's Child learn while he is young when it is wise to adapt.

### Recognize the Successes

Transitions are hard for your slow-to-adapt child, so when he handles one well, make sure to recognize it. When he tries and is successful, acknowledge his work. Bring your child's attention to the fact that he was able to cope with the change; that he *can* do it. In recognizing the little successes, you will reinforce that behavior and make cooperation a pleasant experience. Each success creates a stronger foundation for future successes.

Don't forget to recognize your own success as well. It takes thought to recognize and plan for transitions ahead of time. It takes work to constantly forewarn your child. And it takes a lot of patience to give your child time to adjust, but it is worth it. Your Ephraim's Child will feel more confident and flexible, and you will feel better because the days go more smoothly. As your child's adaptability improves, you can both enjoy the rewards.

# 7

# Awareness

*One mother had to plan an extra five to ten minutes for every outing with her two-year-old. This wasn't time to get ready or use the bathroom, but simply how long it always took to get from the apartment to the car. Her son stopped every other step. First he would pick up a rock, closely inspect it, show her the rock, and then throw it. Two more steps and a leaf or another rock would grab his attention. He would then pick it up and inspect it as well. Fallen leaves had to be meticulously crunched underfoot, any bug required intent observation, and if there were toys or other children along the way, she could expect another few minutes to stop and play before making it to the car. Trying to hurry this toddler was an exercise in exasperation because intense and explosive tantrums occurred any time mom attempted to drag him along at a quicker pace.*

It can amaze parents of Ephraim's Children that their child can be so immovably persistent and yet constantly forget instructions. Why does it seem everything in sight distracts their child? How come simple, everyday tasks take the Ephraim's Child six times longer than normal and require nagging and constant attention? Why do these children simply ignore you? These questions are not only puzzling for parents, but frustrating as well.

Imagine that you have traveled to some faraway, fascinating foreign country. The colors are more brilliant than at home; the smells are overwhelming. You see new and interesting textures everywhere that beg for your touch. Myriad sounds bombard your ears. There is so much to see and do and explore that it takes all your effort just to take it in. You speak the language, but the environment around you is so enthralling that it is physically difficult to tear yourself away from it to listen to what people are actually saying. Welcome to the world of the intensely aware Ephraim's Child!

For Ephraim's Children, life is a much more vibrant and intense experience than for most other people. Not only that, but they are much more aware of their surroundings. Ephraim's Children are usually extraordinarily alert and observant.

Many times this trait is apparent in infancy. When other newborns sleep all the time, these children are more often awake. This discrepancy continues as they grow. In contrast with other infants who may stare off into space when they are awake, Ephraim's Children alertly look around with their eyes focused on the world around them. These babies often fret until they are in the middle of the action, or are at least held so that they can see all around. When these kids do sleep, they often fight it with all they possess, afraid that they will miss something. It may seem that your child does not need as much sleep as other children, but sometimes her awareness is making it difficult to get the amount of sleep she does need.

This intense awareness of surroundings will provide even more challenges as the Ephraim's Child grows. When these babies become mobile, baby proofing takes on a whole new meaning. We used to joke that there is baby proofing, and then there is proofing for our child, a process that goes above and beyond normal. Parents soon learn that the Ephraim's Child has an insatiable desire to explore every nook and cranny of his surroundings. He wants to see everything, touch everything, know where everything is, and discover all there is to know about his environment.

Ephraim's Children do not restrict their intense curiosity to your home. Doctor's offices, dad's work, and a neighbor's house are all fair game. It does not occur to these super-aware children that they are invading someone else's property or space. Usually, parents become adept at spotting the trouble spots within the first ten seconds of entering any room. They survey the area and try to beat their child to any boxes of Kleenex, breakable or sharp objects, cupboards, computers, interesting gadgets, or open doorways.

Not only are these children intensely interested in the world around them, but they notice everything. They catch background conversations and see what you are watching on TV as they chase friends through the room. They hear the news on the car radio despite energetically annoying siblings. Even when your child is seemingly engrossed in something else, he notices what is happening around him. Hiding presents from an aware Ephraim's Child can be extremely difficult. One mother tried hiding a gift, wrapped in a plastic bag, on the top shelf in the corner of the garage. Later that day her young son asked her what was in the bag.

This story shows how little actually slips by these kids. The first time one Ephraim's Child came to Primary as a new Sunbeam his mother was in charge of sharing time. He not only wailed loudly the entire time, but he tried his best to climb on her or on the podium. He refused to sit with his class, proclaiming loudly that he did not like his teacher, he did not want to sing the songs, he did not want to stay at church, and he *did not* want to be in Primary! The frazzled mother said that it was the most trying experience at church she had ever had.

Her son was on a rampage the rest of the day. Then at bedtime her son commented, "When I'm twelve I get to go to the temple, right?" She just looked at him in disbelief. She was even more astounded when he started singing the song they had learned that day. He had climbed all over the podium and all over her, had refused to stay in his seat, and had wailed at the top of his lungs the whole time. How in the world could he have heard, much less understood, what she taught during sharing time?

These kids will hear and remember what is often background noise to us. Many parents are surprised at how much news their child will pick up from the radio or television. It is even more important with these children to monitor what is being watched and listened to, because the aware Ephraim's Child will notice. Don't expect that your child will not pay attention to questionable lyrics in a song—most likely he will repeat them. And just because your child is intently involved in an activity and not watching television doesn't mean that she won't see the adult scene in the show you are watching— you may have to explain it. You will need to be careful about what you discuss in your child's presence—he will repeat it to someone else later. If you don't want to have to explain something to your Ephraim's Child, don't expose him to it at all.

## Awareness or Distractibility?

Raising children who are intensely aware of their surroundings can be frustrating. On the way to pick up a toy or get shoes from her room, the aware Ephraim's Child will notice a dozen other things to investigate. With so many interesting distractions, it can be hard to remember why she was going to her room in the first place. Five minutes later, the parent will come stomping up the stairs to see what is taking so long, only to find that his daughter has not even reached her room yet. She is in the hall fascinated by the light coming in through a window and truly can't understand why Dad is so irritated. It can be maddening.

This awareness can often be confused with more serious problems like Attention Deficit Hyperactivity Disorder (ADHD). ADHD is a behavior disorder that means that an individual has difficulty attending, concentrating, and controlling impulses. Distractibility and hyperactivity may also be present. The list of symptoms for ADHD can include: doesn't pay close attention to details, has difficulty sustaining attention in work or play, doesn't follow through on instructions, has difficulty playing quietly, often interrupts, or often does not seem to listen. By themselves, these symptoms seem like a definition of normal childhood. But for ADHD to be diagnosed these behaviors must negatively affect the child's life and be significantly beyond the normal range for the child's age group. It is important to realize an ADHD diagnosis is reserved only for the most extreme behaviors.

The fourth edition of *The Diagnostic and Statistical Manual of Mental Disorders* (the DSM-IV) is the authoritative source in the U.S. for legal and medical definitions of mental disorders and serves as the official handbook for professional diagnosticians. The DSM-IV states that there must be "clear evidence of clinically significant impairment in social, academic, or occupational functioning"[1] before ADHD can be considered as a diagnosis. This significant impairment must persist at a frequency and intensity that is "maladaptive and inappropriate" for the child's age.[2] "If your child shows symptoms of inattention, impulsivity, or hyperactivity that are in the most extreme five percent for children her age, *and* they interfere with her functioning, *and* there are no other causes that explain them better, she *may* qualify for the diagnosis of Attention Deficit Hyperactivity Disorder."[3] We will discuss ADHD further in later chapters.

Ephraim's Children are not immune to AHDH. However, a typical Ephraim's Child will notice everything going on around her, so it may seem she is as distracted as a child with ADHD. The difference lies in what the child is ultimately able to do with these distractions. A child with ADHD would be *unable* to focus and finish many tasks, no matter how motivated she is. An aware Ephraim's Child will be able to process what she notices and then select the most important information if she has received training and assistance from parents. As a result, she will be able to focus on and complete a task. She may be slower than other children because she is processing so much information, but she will be able to finish. Ephraim's Children *can* focus when they want to. The important issue for parents is how to help their child process everything she notices and then choose the most important message. How do you get her to tune out other stimuli so that she can listen to your instructions? How do you get your child to do what you want her to?

## Getting Your Child's Attention

Often just getting the attention of your Ephraim's Child is a challenge. It is very easy to just yell louder and louder to get your oblivious child to notice that you are talking to him. We have found that getting your child's attention through a gentle touch first and then talking works best. Touching your Ephraim's Child lets him know that it is time for him to pay attention to you. Getting eye-level with your child is also another good way of getting his attention, and it will help him understand your words better. It is also harder for him to ignore you when you are right in front of him.

A large part of getting your child's attention is in the presentation of your message. Many times parents fall into the habit of barking commands at their children. Why would your child want to listen to what you are saying if it is always boring or negative? If your child doesn't want to do it anyway, then it is really little effort to just ignore your shrill voice yelling from across the house. Messages that are positive, fun, or interesting will automatically get more attention—just ask the advertising industry.

We are not suggesting that you install flashing billboards or find some gimmick for every instruction. That is not practical or even possible. However, if you try to find words that make your message more interesting, like a slogan, you will greatly increase the attention your aware child will give to your words. Which presentation is more likely to get a response? "Suzy, it is time to go to bed right now and I don't want any more stalling!" or "Let's see how fast we can get into your pajamas. Get ready, get set, go!" Who would even want to acknowledge the first method? Certainly not your child. The second approach uses words that are more fun, and yet both methods move toward the same goal.

Besides choosing more positive words, your tone of voice can make or break your presentation to your child. "Let's clean up" can be much more effective if said in a happy and excited voice than in an irritated or angry voice. Sometimes just varying your voice, a whisper or funny voice perhaps, will work just as well. You can make any task seem more fun just by making it sound like it is. This works wonders with toddlers who sometimes respond to tone of voice more than to the actual words. Again, you do not have to make every word out of your mouth enthusiastic and fun, but it will make your life much easier if you do it more often.

Sometimes, actually making a task into a game or song will work too. We had a terrible time getting our three-year-old to take a bath at the end of the day. One time we just made up a silly song about it being bath time. To our delight, our child stopped what he was doing and marched upstairs to the tub, singing the song the entire way. It was much more fun to take a bath with our new tune. We sometimes set a timer and try to clean up all the toys before it goes off, turning clean up into a game. Children's television shows use music or little games all the time to increase the appeal of their presentation.

When you present your messages positively, your Ephraim's Child is more likely to want to listen to you in the first place. If your child listens to you more, then you both are happier, and the atmosphere in your home will be happier as well. Experiment to see how your child responds best to you. For example, she might do better with verbal instructions, or writing things down may be more effective.

The Ephraim's Child is constantly barraged by stimulation, and when she has all this "noise" clamoring around her it can be difficult to keep her attention for very long. It is important that once you get her attention, you use the time you have the most effectively. Unfortunately, many times adults sabotage their own efforts by giving ineffective directions.

## Giving Effective Directions

In the book *Parenting the Strong-Willed Child*, authors Rex Foreman, Ph.D., and Nicholas Long, Ph.D. address the problem of giving poor directions. They say, "We have observed that parents often give instructions their child cannot easily comply with. . . . They then become frustrated and angry with their child, even though he really did not have a chance to comply."4 Parents need to give clear and simple directions. But how do you know what is a clear and simple direction? Foreman and Long suggest that one way to recognize a clear and simple direction is to contrast it with types of directions that you do not want to use. These ineffective directions are: chain directions, vague directions, question directions, and directions followed by a reason.5

### Chain Directions

A chain direction involves giving several directions at one time. For example, if you tell your child to pick up his toys, go to the bathroom, brush his teeth, and put on his pajamas, you are actually telling your child to do four different things. The problem with chain directions is that your young child may not have the ability to process and remember all four parts of the direction. Therefore he may be unable to comply even if he wants to.

Instead of giving a chain direction, it is more effective if you break your instructions into smaller parts and give each direction individually. Then you can give the next direction after your child has finished the previous instruction. Don't forget to reward your child for following your direction through praise, a hug, a smile, etc. By giving directions individually you increase the chances of your child's obedience.

### Vague Directions

Children also have difficulty with vague directions. "Be good," or "Act nice," are both too vague; they are not clear or specific. When a child receives a vague direction, he may not know what it is you actually want him to do, and his idea of what you mean may be vastly different from yours. It is much more effective to say exactly what you want him to do. "Do not yell at your brother," is much clearer than, "Act nice."

It is also important that your child understands the

words that you are using. If you tell your young child to put something away in the bookcase and he doesn't know what a bookcase is, then you have a problem. Sometimes disobedience may just be confusion. The more specific and clear you are, the more likely your child will be to follow your directions.

### Question Directions

Question directions ask your child whether she will do something rather than directing her to do it. "Do you want to be quiet now?" is not a clear direction. Your Ephraim's Child now has the option of saying no, and he probably will. "If your intent is to give a direction to your child and have him follow it, you should not phrase it in the form of a question and allow him the option of refusing. When a child says "no" to a question direction, many parents become upset with their child for being defiant. However, the parents are responsible for giving their child the option of refusing."6

Before using a question direction, decide first whether you really want to give your child the option to obey or not. If your intent is to let your child choose between being quiet now or being quiet later, then the direction, "Do you want to be quiet now?" is acceptable. However, this is not usually what parents mean when they use directions in the form of a question. Be careful not to confuse questions and directions.

Many adults add the words "okay" and "please" after directions to act as a buffer. If you are dealing with an intense Ephraim's Child who is not going to like you telling her what to do anyway, then it is very easy to slip into this habit. By adding these words, we try to make our directives a little less harsh, and hopefully that will make our child's reaction less intense. These words automatically turn your direction into a question. Unfortunately, if the Ephraim's Child hears your instructions as a question, she will almost certainly respond with a definite "no." Then you are stuck between giving in or going into battle. If you are using the word "okay" to make sure that your child understands, then it would be wiser to ask, "Do you understand?" Saying please is good to be polite, but make sure that you use a no-non-sense tone of voice to let your child know that you are still giving an instruction and that obedience is still expected.

### Directions Followed By a Reason

The last type of ineffective direction is one followed by a reason. "Finish your lunch because we are late and still need to get dressed before going to church," is an example of this type of direction. By the time you have reached the end of the reason your child may have forgotten your instruction. You have effectively distracted your child from your directive. Giving a short reason or explanation is appropriate, but the best way to do so is to give the reason first. That way your direction is the last thing the child hears and he is more like-ly to comply. "We are running late for church, so finish your lunch," is a much more effective direction. People usually remember best what they hear last.

## Components of Effective Directions

You will have more success in getting your aware Ephraim's Child to tune in to you and then obey when you give effective directions. Forehand and Long also give some general components of effective directions.7 These are:

1. Get your child's attention and make eye contact before giving a direction.
2. Use a firm, but not loud or gruff, voice.
3. Give a direction that is specific and simple.
4. Use physical gestures when appropriate, such as pointing to where to put the toys.
5. Use "do" directions rather than "don't" directions.
6. Reward compliance.
7. Think before giving a direction, and make sure you are willing to gain compliance regardless of the amount of time, energy, or effort required—and with the young Ephraim's Child it may often require a lot!

An important tip that we have found through trial and error is to eliminate the amount of stimulation bombarding your child before issuing instructions. Trying to get your child's attention to clean up while the television or radio is on is nearly impossible. Turn the TV or radio off, or even physically move your child to another room if that is the only way to reduce the surrounding commotion. Then your child will have fewer distractions to filter through to listen to what you are saying.

Your child will also be able to tune in to you easier if you give directions slower. A feverish listing of instructions may simply be noise to the Ephraim's Child who is trying not to notice everything else and transition to you. Slower instructions will allow him time to adjust and listen. Like any aspect of parenting an Ephraim's Child, giving effective directions will take concentrated effort on your part, but it will be worth it.

## Applying Awareness

It is great to be observant and aware of surroundings, but what do you do with the awareness? Neal A. Maxwell has said:

> "Some of the critics of contemporary society have spoken about the divorce between knowing and feeling, that in the midst of abundance in which we know so much, in which we are so fact-filled, we are feeling fewer and fewer of the facts in terms of their implications for us and for our times. Our ability to feel facts and to respond to them in appropriate ways as leaders and followers is one measure of our sensitivity and our awareness of the world around us."[8]

In other words—just knowing isn't enough. Wise application is the key, or else we fall into the trap of "ever learning and never able to come to the knowledge of the truth."[9]

A classic example of this principle can be found in *The Book of Mormon* with the brothers Laman, Lemuel, and Nephi. All three had equal access to incredible founts of information: a great father to teach them, a knowledge of

Israelite heritage, the brass plates as scripture, and even angelic ministrations. Yet only Nephi had the sensitivity to move beyond awareness to application. The Ephraim's Child *can* learn how to apply his awareness.

## Other-awareness

Part of being aware of your surroundings is being aware of the people around you. This is not just noticing that there are people around you, but paying enough attention to know what they are doing. One Sunday a husband was assisting his wife to a vacant chair in a classroom. The woman had just recently recovered from a life-threatening illness and the couple was moving rather slowly. Another sister scooted around the slow couple and sat in the very chair that was their destination. This woman was not very aware of others in this situation.

Neal A. Maxwell wrote that "usually helping depends on knowing. . . . While abstract affection can rise to the level of a generalized feeling, customized concern, real charity, and real help are facilitated by knowing what another person needs. Awareness makes it more likely that the helper can provide the kind of help in which real growth occurs in the person being helped. Potential helpers are often . . . unaware that help is needed."[10] We are a service-oriented church, but without an awareness of others and their needs, how will we know who, when, and where to serve?

The Lord often uses human hands to do His work. We are His instruments in helping others and building the kingdom. In order to be His instruments, we not only need to be sensitive to the Spirit, but we also need to be aware of others. J. Richard Clarke said: "How many times have we observed a benevolent act performed by someone and asked ourselves, 'Why didn't I think of that?' Those who do the deeds we would have liked to do seem to have mastered the art of awareness. They have formed the habit of being sensitive to the needs of others before they think of themselves."[11]

During his earthly ministry, Jesus Christ was so aware of the people around Him that He even knew when a woman merely touched the hem of his robe to find healing.[12] When we are in the midst of a multitude, which usually involves jostling and bumping, are we aware enough of others to see someone in need? Do we have other-awareness when we fail to see someone trying to get by us in a crowded hall? We need to notice where we can serve.

The Ephraim's Child already has a marvelous gift in her aware nature. She already notices everything. We need to show her how to use her awareness to do good. When she notices that her sister is sad, even if you didn't, help her think of ways to help. Instead of telling your child to mind her business when she remarks that a stranger looks unhappy, help her brainstorm ways that she could help, like simply smiling at that person. Let your child see that her awareness can help the Lord reach others through her. An aware personality is a good foundation for a life full of service.

## It's Great to Be Aware

Intense awareness can make your life as a parent of an Ephraim's Child more challenging, but it can also enrich and expand both your child's life and the lives of those around him. Your Ephraim's Child probably notices the many quiet miracles that abound in nature that are often overlooked by those of us who are less observant. Sometimes your child can point out blessings or ways that the Lord has influenced your life that you did not see. Enjoy and appreciate your observant child. Channel his powers of observation to also include spiritual awareness.

With our guidance, the Ephraim's Child can apply his awareness. It can help him have a more full life. In his book *The Abundant Life,* Hugh B. Brown said: "The degree of your awareness will determine the measure of your aliveness. Some have eyes but see not, ears but hear not, and hearts that do not understand. No day will dawn for him who is asleep, and no dream will come true for him who only dreams."[13] Several chapters later he continues: "As we become more aware of our surroundings, more aware of the things we see about us, our worship of God is more meaningful and devout."[14] Let's help our child to have eyes and ears that not only notice everything, but that actually see and hear.

# 8

# Sensitivity

*Some young parents had extreme difficulty getting their baby to sleep. He would be obviously tired, but would fuss and fuss until he began to scream for long periods of time. However, the screaming did not wear the baby out; he only became more hysterical as the night wore on. The frazzled parents began to notice a correlation between the type of day they had and how well their baby slept. He would be frantic and fussy after a busy day and calmer at night after low-key days. They concluded that their baby became over-stimulated from their activity, especially in the evenings. The parents limited their activity after seven o'clock, either sending family and friends home at that time or making sure they were home from other places. They made a schedule for their child and insisted that others adhered to it. These measures improved their nighttime success with their child. Their son is two years old now, and still has trouble sleeping through the night. The more hectic the day or the longer he is kept up after his bedtime, the harder it is for him to get to sleep and stay asleep.*

Many people believe that all of us experience basic sensations similarly; however, people actually vary considerably in how they perceive sights, sounds, touch, smells, and movement. Ephraim's Children are often very sensitive. Because they are more aware, Ephraim's Children not only have more stimuli than many of us, but they smell, see, hear, taste, and feel to a greater intensity as well. Therefore, awareness affects the quantity of stimulation that these kids receive, and sensitivity refers to the quality or intensity of the stimulation. When we talk about sensitivity we are referring to two main domains: physical sensitivity and emotional sensitivity.

In his book *The Challenging Child*, author Stanley I. Greenspan, M.D. classifies "The Highly Sensitive Child" as one of his five difficult types of children. He writes about some of the ways that our senses can give us pleasure, like soothing touches or the clean scent of freshly washed clothes. "These sensations, however, are entirely different for the highly sensitive child. A friendly touch might feel harsh to her. Certain sounds may seem to come out of a bullhorn. Certain smells seem oppressive. Even bright colors can overwhelm."[1]

Try to imagine life as an ultra-sensitive individual. Greenspan uses the example of how you would feel if you attended a rock concert after being forced to stay awake the whole previous night. The sound would probably grate through you and the flashing lights and crowded conditions would be overwhelming.[2] Many sensitive children feel this way every day. Take the bad smell you notice in your child's school classroom and multiply it. Maybe then it will not be quite so mystifying why your child always fights going to class. Does your shirt feel a little tight around your neck? Imagine that sensation much greater and you will better understand why your child screams whenever wearing any collared shirt. Does a lot of noise bother you? Chances are the effect on your sensitive child is much greater in intensity. If you could experience the world through the body of a sensitive Ephraim's Child, you could begin to understand why seemingly inconsequential things can set your child off.

These children feel like they have little barrier between themselves and the world, like they are wearing their skin inside out with every nerve exposed. Things that are little irritants to most people can often be unbearable to the sensitive child. Your child truly can taste the difference between yogurt brands, even when you try to sneak the cheaper brand into the more expensive container. An Ephraim's Child can actually have a problem being with someone because they smell funny. The seams in her socks really do hurt her toes. Certain sounds can drive her to tears and the texture of milk can honestly make her gag. Your child has a low sensory threshold.

Not only is the Ephraim's Child sensitive in regard to his physical senses, but he is also emotionally sensitive. Many parents feel that their child is mercurial or moody. You have a child that cares deeply and intensely about *everything*. Losing a game can seem like the end of the world. Your child can cry for hours over a broken toy, or out of the blue burst into sobs about the favorite pet that died a year ago. Perhaps your child turns almost hysterical over a part in his favorite movie—you know, the movie he has seen twenty times and *knows* that the villain does not kill the hero. Sometimes it seems that your Ephraim's Child has too much feeling.

Yet, possessing sensitivity can be a valuable personality trait. "A highly sensitive child is often bright, articulate, creative, and insightful, easily able to tune in to other people and their feelings. She may display a deep sense of empathy and compassion for other people."[3] Your child can develop deep and meaningful relationships. She can also teach us how to more fully enjoy our physical senses. Your Ephraim's Child will point out the beautiful scenery on the way to the grocery store that you never notice. She can call your attention to the feel of grass on your bare feet or the wind blowing through your hair. She smells the first flowers of spring and is first to notice the changing leaves of autumn.

Day-to-day living with a sensitive child, however, can be trying. Sensitivity combined with intensity can drive parents nuts . . . fast. Not only does your child feel more, but he reacts intensely to it. Sensitivity can also be puzzling, especially if you are not a sensitive person yourself. It can also be challenging and puzzling for your child. How would you feel if you were constantly told that you care too much or that things that drive you crazy are really not a big deal? Your child cannot change the depth of his feelings, and being told that he shouldn't feel what he does can negatively impact his feelings of self-worth. Constant belittling of your child's emotions can cause him to resort to hiding his feelings because they are usually treated as unimportant. This can cause emotions to remain unresolved, unexpressed, and to fester into larger problems.

You need to help your child understand his sensitivity and learn to manage it. In order to function, your child will have to know how to put his quick and intense sensations and emotions into perspective. Yes, he can be deeply hurt by something, but it is not the end of the world. Ephraim's Children need your help to be comfortable with their physical sensitivity and deep emotions. That means that you need to be comfortable with them too. Make sure that you use positive everyday names when discussing this personality trait. It is better to be *tenderhearted* or *sympathetic* than *touchy* or *emotional*. As you help your child come to grips with his sensitivity, he will understand that he is not abnormal. Together you can find solutions to free up all that time you spent forcing him to wear the cute outfit from Grandma that just drives him up the wall because it "swishes."

## Monitor and Adjust

We all are constantly bombarded with stimulation. We are even exposed to noise, touch, and light when asleep. If we were unable to screen out some of that stimulation we would never be able to accomplish anything and would always be on edge. Every one of us chooses what stimulation to attend to; it is a necessary skill for survival. This is called screening. Some people are very good at screening. They can focus so well that it takes major effort to even get their attention. Others simply have a harder time avoiding distractions.

Sensitive Ephraim's children take in everything. Unfortunately, they are born with little skill in screening out unnecessary stimuli. As a result, your child can become over-stimulated easier than most people. Being sensitive becomes a problem when your child becomes overwhelmed, either by stimulation or emotional stress surrounding him. "The goal for the parent of a sensitive child is to work around the child's sensitivities in order to provide the basic psychological experiences that she needs for emotional development. But it takes a special kind of parenting to cope successfully with a child who is drowning in a sea of sensations."4 As the parent, you need to be aware of your child's stimulation level and know when she is reaching the breaking point—something that we call a "meltdown." You must become your child's screener while he is young, and then teach him this skill so that he can focus and function when he is older. You will need to monitor stimulation and adjust accordingly.

If your child is tired and low on energy, the amount of stimulation that he can endure will be less than when he is well rested. You may need to be flexible to accommodate your sensitive child. Running errands for hours in a row, while dragging your child in and out of the car, then in and out of different stores is probably not a good idea unless you are prepared to deal with the repercussions. Is it more trouble to fight your child who has completely lost it, or to do some of your errands the next day? Sometimes these children try to block stimuli by using their parent as a physical buffer. They become clingy and whiny. Many times the parent will push the child away. Who wants a loud and irritating leech attached to your leg when you are trying to concentrate on something else? Instead of merely being an irritant, this kind of behavior can be a clue that your child is becoming over-stimulated.

Certain environments just invite trouble. Expect your child to have a challenging time in these environments and limit his exposure. Crowded stores with bright lights, background music, glaring displays, and crowds of people are a prime example. The next time you go to a department store, stop for a minute and note how much stimulation you are exposed to. Sensitive children are catapulted with high levels of noise, sights, sounds, and movement, not to mention numerous people that bump into them and constantly invade their space. This much stimulation, combined with a natural difficulty screening, makes it obvious why Wal-Mart often sends your child over the edge. Some children's activities can also be over-stimulating. Parties, school carnivals, fairs, amusement parks, or beaches are a few of these sensation nightmares.

There are also certain kinds of days that will be harder for your sensitive child. The days when your family is constant-ly on the go are the days when you would think your Ephraim's Child will be so tired he crashes, right? Wrong. Often these children do the exact opposite. They become even more hyper and wound up. Not only are they tired at the end of the busy day, but they are also over-stimulated. Many times an over-stimulated child will seem to be out of control. You know that your child just needs to shut off and rest, but your hysterical child has reached the point where he can no longer handle the information being sent to his brain. He is unable to calm himself down; he has a stimulation "meltdown."

When you have days like this (and every family will, once in a while), try to find ways to give your child some peace before he reaches a critical point. Perhaps turning off the radio in the car as you run from activity to activity will give your child enough of a break from sensation to circumvent a meltdown. Maybe you need to have a minute of silence where everyone simply sits and breathes with their eyes closed before dashing to the soccer game. Preventing the meltdown before it occurs will make you and your child much happier.

It is not surprising that hectic days can cause problems for your sensitive child, but even normal days can some-times produce meltdowns. It is a good idea to institute a daily time of peace and quiet. If your Ephraim's Child does not nap, you could make her stay in her room looking at books or something else quiet for fifteen minutes. Or maybe your child can go in a different room by herself.

Whatever you choose, it is important that she is alone, she is required to be quiet, and that you consistently do the same thing every day. These break times are essential for survival. Your child may fight you on instituting daily quiet times, but hang tough. Some day you may be floored when your child asks for her rest time or tells you that she needs it. A daily rest time has been a lifesaver for our family, both for the Ephraim's Child and for Mom.

Though we can limit sensory input, we can't (nor do we want to) totally avoid it, so every once in a while your child will go over the edge. When that occurs, you will need a plan of action. The first step is to remove her from the situation. Take her to a calm, quiet place where there is less stimulation and she can calm down. Be aware that at this point even your touch may be too much for her to handle. When she calms down some, talk with her about what has happened. Identify for her what may have been too stimulating. For example, you could say something like, "there were a lot of people in that store with a lot of noise and not much room." If your child is old enough, ask her what was bothering her. "Were there too many people? Was it too noisy? Did the lights bother you?"

This will help your sensitive child understand what sets her off and how to verbalize that to you. You need to help her build the tools necessary to communicate with you. Descriptive words are important to have in the sensitive child's vocabulary. Scratchy, stinky, hot, cold, noisy, scared, lonely, sad, irritated, bothered, tight, bright, angry, and sticky are some words that can help your child tell you what is bothering her. Eventually your child will be the one telling you when the stimulation is too much.

It is much wiser to step in before your child becomes over-stimulated, though. As a parent, you need to monitor the stimulation level for your child and adjust. Perhaps the adjustment is reducing the stimulation. Find a quiet spot or room for a few minutes, take a walk outside, remove the sweatshirt so your child is no longer dying of heat, or anything else you can do to reduce the stimulation will help. Perhaps the best adjustment is to just quit. When you monitor your child and how he is handling the stimulation, it is often a good idea to just quit before your child loses it. Leave the carnival, or end the play date before your child starts throwing fits. You will both feel much better ending an outing successfully rather than in screaming and tears.

Learn your child's cues, or observe what situations become too much for him, and try to arrange things beforehand to keep your child from reaching his breaking point. Perhaps Christmas shopping is a situation requiring a babysitter, when you know fighting the crowds will be too much for your child. Visits from friends may need to be limited to an hour, or you may need to discreetly leave family gatherings early. It is much better to take preventative measures and end on a high note before your child is reduced to a whiny, loud, irritating brat.

Do not feel guilty about always being the party pooper at family gatherings and get-togethers with friends. After all, you are the one who has to live with your hysterical child— they don't. You also don't want your child to dread going over to Grandma's house. Plus, your first priority is to take care of your child. Letting a sensitive child reach the point of a meltdown (when it can possibly be avoided) is not being kind to your child. Yes, you will probably have less fun sometimes, but as your child grows and learns how to monitor and manage his sensitivity, he will be able to handle more, and you will have more flexibility.

## Monitor Emotional Stimulation

An overabundance of stress can also over-stimulate your sensitive child. Sensitive children are very good emotional gauges. They sense and react to the emotional undercurrents around them. You may not realize that your child is sensing your feelings, but she is. You may be surprised to find out that your child's emotional outbursts often correspond to your own moods. The times when you are tired, stressed, harried, or frazzled are when your child is the most difficult. Unfortunately, these are the worst times to be testing your patience as a parent.

Many times the best way to reduce the emotional stress of your sensitive child is to reduce your own stress. Your little four-foot-tall emotional gauge can let you know when you need to review your priorities, take a day off, or just chill out. It will help if you talk with your sensitive Ephraim's Child about your feelings. If you are uncomfortable doing so, just remember that your child senses these feelings anyway. If you don't talk with your child, then she is left alone to try and cope with the emotions bombarding her, which can be frightening. If you have an introverted child you may need to give her space and time when dealing with feelings. She will open up when she is ready, but she still needs you to communicate with her.

You also need to monitor your child's own emotions. As a sensitive and intense individual, life will have many emotional tempests for the Ephraim's Child. Help your child understand that although he cannot control the emotions he feels, he is in control of his actions. It is okay to be sad and cry. It is not acceptable to throw a screaming fit. It is perfectly acceptable to go take a break in his room if he is angry with a sibling, but it is not appropriate to lose control and pummel his little sister. Parents can help their child come to grips with difficult feelings and move on. Your child needs you to acknowledge his feelings. In fact, many times your verbal acknowledgment of your child's emotions will help to diffuse them. Then, you need to show your child how to appropriately express his feelings. We will address this issue in greater depth in another chapter.

Above all, you need to be sympathetic to your child's feelings. Greenspan emphasizes that "no matter how extreme or unrealistic your child's feelings may seem to you, try to empathize with them."5 A sensitive Ephraim's Child sometimes needs more empathy and compassion than other kids. He feels emotions more intensely and is more disturbed by them. Many times your child feels over-loaded by the sensations and emotions constantly assaulting him and needs parents to react compassionately. Try to treat your child as you would an adult friend who is having a rough time. Would you tell your friend that he is being ridiculous, or listen to him and then try and help him? Do our children deserve less?

## Control Media

Public places and gatherings are not the only environments that can over-stimulate your child. Far too often, our homes are full of stimulation that can also send a sensitive child over the edge. Sensitive children need a place where they can retreat and regroup from the outside world, and if they cannot do that at home, be ready for fireworks. Remember that what may be merely background noise to you is just one more thing thrown at your child's senses. For example, a radio or television being on for long periods of time can further agitate your child.

The biggest offender in our homes is probably the television. Like many kids, Ephraim's Children love to watch TV. It can be tempting for frazzled parents to use the TV as a babysitter or "sedative," letting their child watch television just to have some peace. In *Living With the Active Alert Child*, Dr. Linda S. Budd remarks that "parents who live day-in and day-out with . . . [these children] . . . may administer the TV drug without realizing the price they pay. Even those who realize the consequences of television may feel the temptation to gain half an hour or so of relief. Used this way, television is, indeed, an addiction—for the parents."6 How many of us have not decided to just leave on the cartoons for another 30, 40, or 60 minutes so that we have some free time? What harm can it do? Unfortunately, you usually have to pay a price for that extra 30 minutes.

Dr. Budd continues that for some reason, "after the television set goes off, there is a universal release of energy in these children."[7] Whatever the cause, Ephraim's Children will often be wilder after television viewing. Many times they reenact the shows they just viewed. In other words, your child doesn't just watch Tarzan, he *becomes* Tarzan. The child who was calmly watching TV just seconds before is now tearing around the room, leaping over things, and swinging on the curtains.

In truth, television is very stimulating. The sound, the colors, the flashing lights, and the quickly changing picture can overwhelm your child, and an overwhelmed Ephraim's Child is an out-of-control Ephraim's Child. Limit the amount of television your Ephraim's Child watches. Suggest other activities like drawing, painting, cooking, building, playing outside, playing games, etc. This way you also teach your child how to use her internal resources (like imagination) to entertain herself instead of relying on television.

## Blessed Sleep

One of the main factors in determining the quality of interaction between you and your child on any given day is sleep. If either of you have not gotten enough sleep, then it is going to be a rough day. Unfortunately, many Ephraim's Children have difficulty with sleep, which means that parents of Ephraim's Children have sleeping difficulty as well. And taking on a high-maintenance, demanding, and intense child on inadequate sleep is not a formula for success.

High sensitivity is one of the reasons that these children may have problems sleeping. They not only have problems screening when awake, but also when they are trying to sleep. Too much light, talking in the other room, sound coming in from outside, the cold, the heat, the wet diaper, uncomfortable pajamas, or bunched-up blankets may be culprits. At this point, your child is already tired and less able to cope with over-stimulation. He may even get so wound up that he becomes hysterical and unable to calm down, like the boy in the story at the beginning of this chapter.

If your Ephraim's Child has problems sleeping, try calming the surroundings. Decorating experts advise people to make their bedrooms calm, restful places where their brains as well as their bodies can take a break. Why do we often do the opposite with our kids? Toss out the neon-colored bedding. Try dimming or removing the night light in your child's room. It may be waking him up, and then there is too much to see and do. Stuffed animals on your child's bed may be too tempting to play with, at just the wrong time for your child to be more stimulated.

Although the sleeping environment of your sensitive child may contribute to your difficult nights, the most likely culprit is the activity level before bed. Sensitive Ephraim's Children *require* time to wind down before they can sleep. Let's repeat that so you don't miss it. These children *must* have time to wind down before bed. How much time is needed varies. Some may require thirty minutes to an hour to unwind. Others require less. Experiment to find the right formula for your child. Be careful of too much stimulation during wind-down time; you don't want to wind your child up again. This is not the best time to wrestle with dad. However, no matter the amount of time required, if your child does not get his down time, he will often have a rough night. A regular bedtime routine can also cue your child that it is time to wind down.

This will require sacrifice on your part at times. We are always the first to leave family gatherings, which is not always easy. But we have found that if our children are too wound up immediately before bed, they wake in the night and many times even wake earlier the following morning. We feel that the sacrifice required by us to get our children to bed on time is worth it.

We discussed the importance of regular schedules in the adaptability chapter. Routine is also very important in sleeping schedules. Dr Marc Weissbluth, M.D., author of *Healthy Sleep Habits, Happy Child*, strongly recommends continuity in sleeping schedules. He says that parents need to help their children develop healthy sleep habits, otherwise they will then grow into adults who do not have healthy sleep habits. "It comes as a surprise to many parents that healthy sleep habits do not develop automatically. In fact, parents can and do help or hinder the development of healthy sleep habits."[8] For those parents who still hesitate, he continues to say: "When thinking about sleep schedules . . . consider sleep to be 'food' for the brain. . . . You don't withhold feeding because it is socially inconvenient; you anticipate when your child might become hungry. Same for naps . . . a parent coming home late from work would not starve his baby by withholding food until he arrived and could feed the child. Same for the bedtime hour; let's not 'sleep-starve' our baby's brain by keeping her up too late."[9]

Like most children, the sensitive Ephraim's Child will appear "wound up" when tired. Fatigue actually causes increased arousal, so the more tired your child is, the more difficult it is for him to sleep. He enters a hyper-alert state when he is too tired to sleep.[10] Dr. Weissbluth talks about studies confirming this. "These studies support the notion that when an overtired child appears wired, wild, edgy, excitable, or unable to fall asleep easily or stay asleep, he is this way precisely because of his body's response to being overtired."[11] In a sensitive child, who is already bombarded by stimulation, this hyper-alert state may be more pronounced. It is better to get your child to sleep before he is too tired to sleep. A consistent and possibly earlier bedtime can be a large help in getting your family the sleep it needs.

### Getting Dressed

Getting dressed is another common battleground with the sensitive Ephraim's Child. It is amazing how many wars are fought over clothing! When our Ephraim's Child was born, we were given a list of tips for new parents to help them prepare for parenthood. It suggested that we dress a live, slimy octopus to practice getting our new baby dressed.

For parents of Ephraim's Children, it should suggest we practice dressing a rabid wolverine that screams, fights, whines, complains, runs away, cries, and then proceeds to undress the minute your back is turned. Nothing can ruin your day like finally getting your Ephraim's Child into his clothes, only to follow a trail of discarded clothes strewn all over the house to find him smug and naked when it is time to get in the car.

Clashes over clothing are often rooted in your child's temperament. He is not intentionally driving you nuts. Nor is he merely being stubborn or rebellious or doing this to you "on purpose." Your Ephraim's Child is sensitive to textures, "pokey" things, little nubs of fuzz, seams, etc. The tags in clothing really *do* drive him nuts. The sound of nylon pants *can* hurt his ears when he moves. Collars make him feel he is choking. Sweaters are too scratchy. The shoes actually do feel funny. He can smell the difference between detergents. His socks are too tight or too rough, and the little microscopic rock it took you ten minutes to find in his shoe, like the famous Princess and the Pea, really can make his entire foot ache.

Your child is so sensitive that these kinds of things really do physically affect him. He is not just being exasperating. Once you accept this simple fact, you will have taken the first step to a smoother time getting dressed. You should also take into consideration the other temperamental traits of your Ephraim's Child that make this such a difficult time. Persistence will make dressing take longer for a child who wants to do it himself. Intensity makes any setback such as problems with buttons, a favorite shirt being dirty, or uncomfortable clothing a major calamity. Getting from pajamas to clothes is a transition that can set off a slow-to-adapt child. The television or radio can be so distracting that your child cannot focus on getting dressed. Is it any wonder that getting an Ephraim's Child dressed is a terrain full of land mines?

The first step to successful dressing is planning. Here are some examples of ways to plan for getting dressed. Plan enough time, either for you to help your child or for her to dress herself. Forewarn her when it will be time to change clothes. A consistent morning routine can help your child know what is coming. Dress in a place with fewer distractions: turn off the TV or radio, remove toys, or leave the blinds drawn. Give your child choices of appropriate clothing. Either you pick a number of outfits from which your child can then choose, or organize your child's drawers or closet so that she can pick out appropriate things. You can have a play drawer and a school drawer, for example. If you don't want your child wearing shorts in December, do not leave them in her room. A mirror to check progress may help your child remain focused (unless it is too distracting). If you have an active child, you may have to find a way for her to dress on the move. Maybe you can time her to see how fast she can put her pants on, or challenge her to put her socks on while upside down. Games and humor can always motivate a child more than ultimatums. If you find ways to work *with* your child instead of against her, your mornings will be less battle-scarred.

Probably the best way to prepare for getting dressed is to listen to your child. If he cannot stand a certain style of clothing—collared shirts, for example—then don't force him to wear them. He will always complain, and it will always be a fight. Is wearing a shirt with a collar worth it? If your child says he is hot, then he is probably hot. Let him take off the sweatshirt, even if you are huddled under a blanket. Sensitive people often have a narrow temperature range of comfort. Realize that your child isn't pretending to be uncomfortable just to irritate you.

Purchase clothing that your child will actually wear. If your Ephraim's Child will not wear overalls, don't buy them. It is probably a good idea to go shopping with your child. Have him try on the clothing in the store, and together you can discover what he is comfortable wearing. This may be an arduous undertaking, but you will be showing your child that you believe him and respect his sensitivity. Be warned, this may require several shopping trips. When you finally find something, buy it! You could even buy more than one. If your child can stand wearing this piece of clothing, buy it in different colors. Once you have finally found clothes your child can handle, don't rip off the tags as soon as you get home in celebration. Never take off tags until your child has tried the item on again at home and has pronounced it wearable.

Working with your Ephraim's Child is important, but there will still be occasions when your child must wear clothing that drives him nuts. Family pictures, special occasions, parties, or church are some of those times when your child's preferred clothes may not be acceptable. If you have to force your child to wear something tight, hot, bumpy, or scratchy, don't push your luck by making him endure his discomfort longer than necessary. It will be a more successful undertaking for both of you if you get your child in the clothes, get the job done, and then get him out of them. When that time comes, explain to your child your expectations. Tell him you understand that he does not like wearing a tie, but that he must. Before he launches into a screaming fit, work out some sort of reward or concession on your part. You could say something like: "We will take the clothes to the studio where you can change into them just before we take the pictures. As soon as we are finished you can change out of them immediately. I know you can handle wearing that shirt for fifteen minutes."

A little planning can go a long way. Even though it may not seem like it now, eventually you will have more success with your sensitive Ephraim's Child when it is time to dress. As you have more days when your child gets dressed with minimum fuss, the less difficult it will be. Success builds upon success. You do not need to start every morning with a wrestling match or battle of wills over clothing.

You may be thinking at this time that we are suggesting that you allow your sensitive child to run the household and tell you how and when he will do things. However, often when your child is having fits over things like getting dressed and not eating certain foods, he is not doing it to manipulate you. Usually the shoes *do* hurt his feet. He is not saying it just to drive you crazy. How would you feel if you had a shirt that was uncomfortable almost to the point of pain, yet no one would believe you, and you were forced to wear it? Yet we often treat our children this way, simply because they are children.

There will be times when you are suspicious that your child is taking advantage of his sensitivity and trying to gain the upper hand. Then you must decide when to let him have his way and when to lay down the law. Sometimes your child will just have to wear the uncomfortable pants or eat a bite of the food. Just remember that with these kids, you must pick your battles. When your child is squaring off with you over an issue, you must decide if this is worth the fight. Is it really imperative that your child wear this particular pair of socks? Is that shirt worth the power struggle? Will clothes come between you and your child?

## Refining Sensitivity to Charity

The sensitive Ephraim's Child is naturally in tune with others. She can sense others' pain, happiness, or stress. This is an amazing gift. When you are having a bad week and your child is acting out, this trait may not seem so wonderful, but with time and refinement your sensitive Ephraim's Child can expand her sensitivity into true charity.

After a wonderful discourse by Mormon on the subject of charity, the seventh chapter of Moroni tells us that this highest of Christian virtues is more accurately labeled "the pure love of Christ."[12] As the love of Christ, charity is characterized as selfless and self-sacrificing,[13] emanating from a pure heart, a good conscience, and faith unfeigned.[14] Thus, more than an act, charity is an attitude, a state of heart and mind[15] that accompanies one's works and is proffered unconditionally.[16] Charity as the pure love of Christ is an attribute.

An attribute is an inherent quality or characteristic. It is part of what we are; part of our personality makeup. Elder

Dallin H. Oaks has said:

> The Apostle Paul taught that the Lord's teachings and teachers were given that we may all attain "the measure of the stature of the fulness of Christ" (Eph. 4:13). This process requires far more than acquiring knowledge. It is not even enough for us to be *convinced* of the gospel; we must act and think so that we are *converted* by it. In contrast to the institutions of the world, which teach us to *know* something, the gospel of Jesus Christ challenges us to *become* something. Many Bible and modern scriptures speak of a final judgment at which all persons will be rewarded according to their deeds or works or the desires of their hearts. But other scriptures enlarge upon this be referring to our being judged by the *condition* we have achieved. . . . The gospel of Jesus Christ is the plan by which we can become what children of God are supposed to become.[17]

Jesus said, "Therefore what manner of men ought ye to be? Verily I say unto you, even as I am."[18] We are here to become more like God. In other words, we are striving to develop His divine attributes. Joseph Smith also talked about the pure love of Christ. He said: "Love is one of the chief characteristics of Deity, and ought to be manifested by those who aspire to be the sons of God."[19]

Your sensitive child is already headed in the right direction. To some degree, he can feel what others are feeling. In order to refine this innate sensitivity towards others, your child needs to know what to do with his empathy. Someone who has developed true charity does not say, "Oh dear. She is feeling very bad and overwhelmed today. That's rough," and then go about his/her day. Action of some sort is required. Teach your child how to go a step beyond sensing others' emotions. Help your Ephraim's Child expand her empathy into charity.

Service to others is a good way to develop charity. "The term 'compassionate service' is used in the Church to refer to love-inspired assistance willingly given to meet physical, spiritual, and emotional needs. It requires a sensitivity that perceives human distress beyond spoken words (Luke 10:30-37; cf. 8:43-48), an eye that recognizes the good in people (Mosiah 4:16-18), and an understanding heart attuned to the Holy Spirit to discern what is appropriate to say and do (3 Ne. 17:5-8; John 19:25-27)."[20] This will be especially helpful if you discuss how the person you have served may be affected by your service. Help your child sympathize with the widow who is lonely, and then is cheered by a visit. Point out the good that you can do. Your child may be moved to alleviate someone else's loneliness in the future without your prompting because she has already experienced the gladness of that first widow. You cannot pay lip service only, however. You must practice what you preach. You may be surprised at how quickly your sensitive child will find others in need of service, perhaps some who you never noticed yourself.

Another area of your child's natural sensitivity which should not be neglected is her sensitivity to the Spirit. When you feel the promptings or presence of the Spirit, point it out to your child. Chances are good that she is feeling it as well and just doesn't know it. With your help, she can learn to recognize the feelings associated with the testifying of the Spirit and spiritual promptings. Your child may be more sensitive to the still, small voice than you think, simply because she is highly sensitive anyway. Recognizing the Holy Ghost is an invaluable tool for anyone, and one of the most important skills that you can teach your child.

Sensitivity is a valuable trait in leadership. The best leaders are those who are sensitive to the ones following them. In the Church, our leaders are often given the gift of discernment, which is a type of sensitivity. *The Encyclopedia of Mormonism* quotes Stephen L. Richards as saying: "The gift of discernment [embodies] the power to discriminate . . . between right and wrong . . . [and] arises largely out of an acute sensitivity to . . . spiritual impressions . . . to detect hidden evil, and more importantly to find the good that may be concealed. The highest type of discernment . . . uncovers [in others] . . . their better natures, the good inherent within them."[21]

Having sensitivity is a positive characteristic, especially when put into perspective and not allowed to overwhelm your Ephraim's Child. Try and remember this when he is throwing a tantrum over the seam in his socks or is inconsolable because his friend couldn't play today. When your child is sobbing in the middle of a sad part of a cartoon, or loses control when others are upset, remind yourself that he is already a step closer to true charity than many others.

# 9

# Activity

The popular children's book *If You Give a Mouse a Cookie,* by Laura Joffe Numeroff, begins with a boy offering a mouse a cookie. This kind gesture results in a request for a glass of milk, which gives the mouse an idea for a project. In the middle of that project he has another idea for a different project, and then another, and another until the mouse eventually sweeps the whole house, washes all the floors, and draws a family picture to hang on the fridge. Being near the refrigerator reminds the mouse that he is thirsty. He asks for milk again and then wants a cookie to go with it, starting the whole chain of events over again. The boy spends the story fetching things for each of the mouse's projects and then cleaning up after him when the mouse leaps to the next activity. The final page shows the mouse happily eating a cookie next to the exhausted boy asleep on the kitchen floor, surrounded by a mound of debris from the mouse's many projects.[1] This book captures the essence of life with an active Ephraim's Child.

Ephraim's Children who are active are intensely active; they can leave all others in the dust. This is probably the most noticeable attribute to others. These kids are constantly moving, going from thing to thing to thing in a state of perpetual motion, leaving you to chase after them. But they can accomplish a lot. The mouse in the story managed to do a great many projects, and, like the boy in the story, many of us are often left exhausted in the wake of this high energy.

Perhaps you first became aware of your child's high activity level in the womb, when you felt black and blue from the inside out from your baby's energetic movement. In infancy, this high activity level may exhibit itself as sleeplessness. The advice for new mothers to sleep when their infant does only works if their baby sleeps enough to do it. Most newborns are expected to sleep a majority of the time, unlike our wide-awake Ephraim's Child who would take three or four twenty-minute naps the whole day. Needing less sleep than average as a young child is a common trait of Ephraim's Children. Try not to feel cheated that your friend's five-year-old will still take three-hour naps while your two-year-old has abandoned them altogether. You have an active Ephraim's Child.

The extroverted, active Ephraim's Child is enveloped in sound as he bounces from one thing to another. These children are easy to spot because not only do you notice their constant motion with your eyes, but they talk, sing, screech, hum, and yell while they do it. The introverted Ephraim's Child can also move from activity to activity, but does so without the accompanying noise. Therefore, he may not seem to be as active, but when you really watch, he is just as full of energy as the loud Ephraim's Child.

Many times parents wonder if there is some way to calm down their active kids. In responding to this we will use an example from Mary Sheedy Kurcinka's book, *Raising your Spirited Child*. She writes to imagine that you are confined to a room for the next five hours with no available rest room. A quick mental check on your bladder should let you know how uncomfortable the next five hours may be. Inside you may note a growing pressure. Your bladder may be announcing a grave need for release. Your brain might tell you to tough it out and ignore the mounting tension, but if you were born with a small-capacity bladder, no matter how tough your brain might tell you to be, this may not be a case of mind over matter. You might feel more and more strained as your body practically screams for release. How would you feel in this situation? Would you realistically be able to ignore your bodily needs?

Just as your bladder signals a need for you and creates a pressure when that need goes unanswered, a child who is temperamentally active has a body that not only likes to move, but *needs* to move.[2]

This characteristic recalls some of Brigham Young's words about the tribe of Ephraim: "They are so full of life that they cannot contain themselves . . . their bones fairly ache with strength. They have such . . . life, strength and activity, that they must dispose of them."[3] It is important to understand that your active Ephraim's Child is not diving off furniture to scare you. She isn't constantly falling out of chairs to irritate you. She is not simply being a pest when she uses every person sitting down as a jungle gym. She isn't trying to wear you out or distract you with her constant motion. The active Ephraim's Child was born with high energy; she *needs* to move her body, and she needs to move often.

## Activity vs. Hyperactivity

The active Ephraim's Child's average state of being is in motion. He is constantly moving, bouncing from one activity to another, to another, to another. Many can mistake this tireless motion for hyperactivity. However, constant activity is different from hyperactivity. The term "hyperactive" is often used as a synonym for ADHD. When used as a diagnosis, hyperactivity is activity that cannot be stopped and is often a problem in multiple contexts. Many times your child will seem hyper in certain contexts, like when thrown into new situations, but not appear hyper in other contexts. As we have discussed before, most Ephraim's Children can focus when they want, and if you watch, even the most active Ephraim's Children are usually able to stop their movement for periods of time. It is important to notice this and not wrongly pigeonhole your Ephraim's Child into the category of hyperactive.

Stanley Turecki, M.D., author of *The Difficult Child*, cautions people against using just one temperamental trait—activity level—to define your child. He discusses the ramifications if another aspect of temperament, like normal mood for instance, were used in this manner. If your child is normally serious, analytical, prone to sulk, and slow to enter new situations, how many of us would automatically jump to the conclusion that she is depressed or "hyperwithdrawn?" Yet this is often done based solely on activity level. "If no other characteristic [by itself] defines a child's condition, why should activity level?"4

Many times these children go quickly from activity to activity because once they have figured out a task they are ready to move on to the next thing. Then they no longer even have any interest in the things they have just done. They are ready for something new. If your active Ephraim's Child is like this, boredom is a big challenge. It is difficult to continually think of different, mentally stimulating, interesting activities when your child runs through each activity quickly.

## How Your Child Learns

Not surprisingly, active Ephraim's Children usually learn by doing. They are kinesthetic—or movement—learners. Linda S. Budd, Ph. D., devotes a chapter of her book, *Living with the Active Alert Child,* to understanding how your child learns. This information becomes even more important once your child is in school settings. The following section is a summary of Budd's discussion of the three basic learning modalities—kinesthetic, auditory, and visual—as defined by psychologists Walter B. Barbe, Ph.D., and Raymond H. Swassing, Ed.D.5

### The Kinesthetic Learner

All children begin life as kinesthetic learners; they learn by doing, touching, tasting, etc. To master physical tasks like crawling, standing, and walking, children need to be in tune with their bodies. As they approach school age, some children begin to prefer another modality or style of learning.

However, highly-active children usually remain kinesthetic learners for a longer time. As they age, perhaps by seven or eight, they may mix kinesthetic and auditory or visual styles, but they still keep a very strong kinesthetic response. "There is no way around it: the kinesthetic approach is basic to their learning."[6]

Dr. Budd states that according to Barbe and Swassing, approximately 15 percent of school-age children are kinesthetic learners.[7] Children who learn kinesthetically emphasize action and doing. They prefer action stories. Even when they talk they use action words. They "jump for joy" or "bounce off the wall." They spell words by "feel." Their first response is to move into action and, therefore, they appear impulsive. They gesture with their hands when they speak and "fidget" when required to sit still; they take a lot of breaks and frequently change body positions. Because kinesthetic learners move around so much, people tend to think of them as "distractable" children or, later, as "nervous adults."

*Once my young grandson asked me to read some books to him. Reading to this Ephraim's Child, however, is not a quiet, calm experience. He does not simply sit, listen, and look at the pictures while you read. He continuously asks questions, so reading a book not only involves reading the original story, but explaining the story and incorporating all of his input into the narrative as well. Reading books to him is a significant mental effort, and by the end of a few books my body has taken a toll as well. My grandson fidgets constantly, and I also serve as a Jungle Gym. He leans on me to see better, then he climbs in my lap, scrambles off my lap, stands next to me on the couch, sits down next to me, climbs up behind me on the back of the couch to peer over my head, lays down, and frequently falls off the couch as he changes positions. After a couple books, I feel a little battered. By the end of the reading session, I am ready for a nap.*

### The Auditory Learner

Auditory learners learn best through listening. They enjoy conversations, but may have a difficult time waiting for their turn to talk. They love to read dialogue and usually dislike lengthy written descriptions of scenery. Young auditory learners often hum, sing, and talk to themselves. They probably talk through their problems in order to reach a solution. Sounds may distract them. Because they are sensitive to noise, they express emotion by changing the volume and pitch of their voice.

According to Barbe and Swassing, approximately 25 percent of school-age children are auditory learners.[8] They take in information and instructions through listening. A phonics approach to reading is the most successful with auditory learners. These learners usually do well in the typical school setting, which often involves a lot of verbal instruction.

### The Visual Learner

Visual learners learn by seeing. They think in pictures. They learn to read by recognizing words by sight or through the whole-word recognition approach, which relies on the way a word looks. Appearance and order are important to them. Disorder or movement distracts them. They are often deliberate and make plans in advance, jotting notes or making lists.

According to Barbe and Swassing, 30 percent of school-age children are visual learners.[9] They feel more comfortable with teachers who are organized and write directions on the board. They like examples and visual application of concepts.

You may have noticed that 30 percent of children are unaccounted for. That is because approximately 30 percent of all children learn through a mixed-modal style. Most people eventually develop a mixed-modal learning style that combines elements of two or three of the basic modalities. Successful adults develop ways to transfer from one mode to another, but often retain a preference for one style, especially with new or difficult material. Knowledge of all three basic modalities will give you tools to help your kinesthetic Ephraim's Child strengthen his auditory and visual skills. It will also help you work with your child to understand why certain things come easily to her and other things are difficult.[10]

Very energetic children are usually kinesthetic learners. They use their bodies to solve problems, which is why they take things apart or automatically climb over the table or a sibling to get something rather than asking for it. Their thinking is inseparably connected with their body. As a result, it is extremely difficult to direct your child with words alone. You need to involve his body. One way to do that is to gently touch your child while giving instructions. Make sure that your touch is gentle; grabbing him will often merely provoke your child's determined streak and result in a struggle. You already know that you cannot arm-chair parent these kids. This is even more true with the active Ephraim's Child.

## Expect and Plan for Energy

It is not your imagination that your active Ephraim's Child moves more than other children. For instance, all toddlers are on the move, but the high-energy toddler is *more* active, and maintains high energy into adulthood. A high activity level is a prized and valued characteristic as an adult. These are the people who excel at "multitasking"; they are able to do three things at the same time. This is not something that we want to discourage. Our active kids need to hear from us that we appreciate and value their abundant energy. Get comfortable with it and use your new everyday names. For example, replace the word *wild* with *energetic*. Instead of telling your child he is out of control, comment that his body is full of energy. Tell him that he could make a good athlete or energetic worker.

Part of becoming more comfortable with your child's normal activity level is learning to expect and plan for it. Expect that your child is full of wiggles, don't fight it. Plan active play times in your day. Go to a park regularly. Play soccer in the backyard. Exercise together. Sing songs that use your whole body. Create places where your child can release energy. If the weather is bad, put a mattress on the floor and let your child jump, tumble, and roll around. We open up an old hide-a-bed and let the kids use it as a trampoline. If your child can release some of the pressure to move his body, he will be better able to manage his energy at other times.

Part of planning for energy is choosing activities and environments carefully, especially in public. When you eat out, go somewhere that has a play area. When traveling, plan stops to stretch little active legs. Extended shopping trips are often best done with a babysitter at home with the kids, unless you don't mind them darting in and out of clothes racks and grabbing everything in sight. Waiting in long lines for anything, even at an amusement park, is likely to be torture. Don't neglect planning at home either. Let your child sit on a swivel chair so that he can move as he stays in his seat. Have your child be the errand runner at dinner: getting more napkins, another carton of milk, etc.

In situations that are more rare, like church or family gatherings, try to plan a way for your child to wiggle and move. If you do not find ways for your child to move appropriately, then he will move inappropriately. At church, commandeer an entire pew so that your child has room to maneuver without disturbing others. Understand that a leisurely family dinner at a restaurant is going to be a problem, and a movie directly after dinner is most likely to be a disaster. Try to plan movement time in between sitting spells. After some time at Grandma's fragile knick-knack filled house, take your child outside for a little walk to explore.

Extremely active kids demand a lot of attention from their parents. You are always concerned about safety and must be on guard, monitoring your child's whereabouts and activities. If you are a high-energy person yourself, you may be doing okay keeping up with your active child. However, if you have a lower energy level, you may feel haggard at the end of each whirlwind day. Even if you have a lot of energy yourself, these kids can still wear you down. Part of planning for energy is planning a break for yourself.

The obvious solution is to get a babysitter so you can have a break. Unfortunately, this often is not as easy as it sounds. Who do you get to watch your children? You worry that your active Ephraim's Child will wear out an older person, yet a younger babysitter may not be able to keep him safe. Do not lose hope. You can find a babysitter with enough energy and maturity to keep your little whirlwind safe. It may just take some effort on your part to find him/her. Teenagers are a viable option. Get recommendations from adults who work with teens, like at the high school or with the youth in church. Then, arrange a time to try out new babysitters. Invite the sitter to your home while you are there and observe their interaction with your child. This gives your child important time to adjust to another person and also gives the babysitter a preview of what they are in for if they tend your child. You could also arrange for a night out after your child is in bed, but forewarn him so that he doesn't flip out if he wakes and finds you gone.

Once you stop resisting your child's high activity level, you can start enjoying it. Expect that your child is going to be all over the place, and if he isn't then you will have a pleasant surprise. If you plan for your child to be active, then you can spend less time worrying about it. Planning for energy also shows your child that you understand his need to move.

**Winding Up**

Just like an over-stimulated child may become frantic and out of control, a tired, active child will often become more active rather than less; he winds up rather than winds down. It seems paradoxical that your child speeds up when he gets tired. After all, he has been going non-stop since the crack of dawn. You may notice, however, as the day wears on, that the quality of your child's perpetual motion changes. It moves from focused energy to frenzied activity with no focus. That is when your child is on his way to spiraling out of control. You could even say he is heading for a "crash and burn" episode. When that happens, you will be faced with an intensely tired, irrational, unstoppable bundle of emotion and nothing you do seems to help.

As parents, it is vitally important that you intervene before your child "crashes and burns." Sensitive children need relief from stimulation, and active children need help slowing down and unwinding. Your child is not able to calm her activity by herself until she is taught how. Everyday rest time is also a good idea for the active Ephraim's Child. However, don't be surprised if your child spends her "down" time differently than you expect. It is not unusual to discover that your child has stripped the bed and is lying in the middle of the bedding on the floor, or has emptied the clothes from all the drawers or the closet. To you this might not seem like resting, but to the kinesthetic Ephraim's Child, this activity may be calming. The goal is to give her time every day to unwind, however she does it.

Because your child winds up instead of winding down when she is tired, it may be hard to find that window of "actually tired" that lies between "not tired enough to sleep yet" and "out of control." Your active Ephraim's Child will rarely admit that she is tired, so don't wait for her to tell you that it is time to retire. Try to find your bedtime window of opportunity and then stick to it.

## When High Activity Is the By-product of Another Temperamental Trait

Unexpected company arrives and your child begins flinging himself off every piece of furniture while yelling, "To infinity and beyond!" He runs around in circles, dodging through the guests' legs and acting like a wild thing. Or you are in the middle of a week of Christmas activities and your Ephraim's

Child is falling apart at the seams. One of your child's friends comes over to play, and as soon as he walks in the door your son leaps on top of him and wrestles his friend to the ground. In these cases, is your Ephraim's Child's high energy really the issue, or is it another underlying emotion being expressed?

Sometimes when your child's activity level explodes out of control, the real problem is not his natural energy, but emotion tied up with some other temperamental trait. Just as frantic activity at the end of the day is how your child signals to you that he is tired, wild behavior may be another signal that he is overwhelmed by something else. If this is the case, focusing only on the frenzied energy is equivalent to treating the symptoms rather than the disease. Try to objectively view the situation and see what trait really needs attention.

In the above examples, other temperamental traits are most likely the origin for the unacceptable behavior. Guests who show up at the doorstep with no warning present a sudden transition for your slow-to-adapt child. An extended holiday season will often drown your sensitive Ephraim's Child in stimulation. And Ephraim's Children are so intense that when they are excited and happy to see a playmate they may have trouble controlling themselves. In their exuberance, they can literally knock the other child over in joy.

If you have a very active child, watch carefully for when his activity gets out of control. When that happens, try to determine if your child is simply being his normal, extremely active self, or if he is having trouble with another temperamental trait. If it is another trait, then you need to address the underlying need. Find the real reason for the behavior. Don't let his movement conceal the true issue.

### Active From the Beginning

The unceasing activity of an Ephraim's Child probably did not begin with the advent of a body. These spirits were most likely "doers of the word"[11] before ever coming to

Earth. Writing in *The Mortal Messiah*, Elder Bruce R. McConkie stated:

> When we pass from pre-existence to mortality, we bring with us the traits and talents there developed. True, we forget what went before because we are here being tested, but the capacities and abilities that then were ours are yet resident within us. Mozart is still a musician; Einstein retains his mathematical abilities; Michelangelo his artistic talent; Abraham, Moses and the prophets their spiritual talents and abilities. Cain still lies and schemes. And all men with their infinitely varied talents and personalities pick up the course where they left it off when they left the heavenly realms.[12]

Ephraim's Children have the energy and drive to accomplish much. Their high activity level is an integral part of who they are. It is not out of the realm of possibility to suppose that their active spirits helped determine their role in mortality at this time. We don't want to calm our kids down. What we need to do is help these children harness and direct their abundant energy into productive channels. Great amounts of energy and activity are needed to accomplish the Lord's works.

## Channeling High Activity

The amount of things that these children can do in one day is astounding. How many times do you watch your child from the couch where you have finally collapsed, unable to chase after him one more minute, and wish that you could have just a small amount of his energy? Energy that is not channeled and under control is destructive, but once it is harnessed it can accomplish miracles. Electricity, for example, is vital to our society. We use it to power almost everything in our homes. If it is not channeled properly, however, it is extremely dangerous and destructive. It is important to teach our Ephraim's Child how to channel his energy so that he can use it productively. We need to help our child be anxiously engaged, rather than merely rushing about expending energy.

We have been told that "men should be anxiously engaged in a good cause, and do many things of their own free will."[13] Elder Mark E. Petersen talked about how being anxiously engaged is a way of showing love for the Lord. He said: "You remember the Lord also said that we are to be 'anxiously engaged' in a good work. He has told us that we are to bring forth much fruit. He has told us that we are to thrust in our sickle with our might. In many other ways he has indicated that not only must we be whole hearted in our love for him but that our love must be translated in terms of doing things for him."[14] As you direct your child's activity in a positive way, you can help him channel energy into diligent work.

Our Heavenly Father and Jesus Christ have shown us by their examples and teachings that work is an important activity in heaven and on earth. God worked to create the heavens and earth. Jesus Christ said: "My father worketh hitherto, and I work."[15] J. Richard Clarke has also said:

> Work is a blessing from God. It is a fundamental principle of salvation, both spiritual and temporal. When Adam was driven from his garden home, he was told that his bread must be produced by his physical toil, by the sweat of his brow. Note carefully the words: "Cursed shall be the ground for thy sake" (Moses 4:23), this is, for his good or benefit. It would not be easy to master the earth; but that was his challenge and his blessing, as it is ours. . . . Most important, the Lord knew that from the crucible of work emerges the hard core of character.[16]

Direct your child's energy to good use. Your active child can expend his energy in idle pastimes, or he can learn the value and satisfaction of work well done. Weeding the garden, mowing the lawn, cleaning house, sweeping the driveway, or washing dishes will provide outlets for your child's abundant energy. Not only will you lessen the load of work for parents, but, more importantly, you will be teaching your child how to work.

The loss of a good work ethic is a growing concern in our society. Generations of children are growing up never learning how to work, and then they enter the workforce and are expected to know how. If people don't know how to work, then they are missing a critical skill needed to return to their Heavenly Father. Neal A. Maxwell once said that "those who do too much for their children will soon find they can do nothing with their children. So many children have been so much done for they are almost done in."[17] The only way to learn how to work is to do work, and the best place to learn this is in the home.

President David O. McKay said: "Let us realize that the privilege to work is a gift, that the power to work is a blessing, that the love of work is success."[18] The greatest success is eternal life, and work is a requirement. "Work is a key to full joy in the plan of God. If we are righteous, we will return to live with our Heavenly Father, and we will have work to do. As we become like him, our work will become like his work. His work is 'to bring to pass the immortality and eternal life of man' (Moses 1:39)."[19] The Lord expends large amounts of energy in his work. Let's help our active Ephraim's Child learn how to channel his energy as well.

## Enjoy Activity

You are not going to change your child's need to move, so why not accept it and enjoy it? Understand that your child will not be the one who sits totally still and reverent through an entire sacrament meeting, but he will most likely not become a couch potato either. As your child ages, the demands on you to keep him physically safe and occupied will lessen. If you have taught your child how to direct and focus his active nature, you can experience the joy of seeing a child who knows how to work and has the energy to accomplish a lot. When your child grows up, his high activity level will be an asset. He will be able to juggle many things in his life and still have steam left over to devote to righteous pursuits.

# 10

# Intelligence

Be prepared! The Ephraim's Child is usually very intelligent. She may walk early, talk early, or learn the alphabet, colors, and numbers early. Then again, she may not accomplish these things earlier than average. At some point, however, you will realize that this child is definitely bright. Maybe it happens when you get into a deep discussion with your three-year-old about why ice floats on water, and suddenly you are involved to a depth that rivals fifth grade science. Perhaps it occurs when you listen to the accomplishments of your friend's children and have to bite your tongue, smile, and not share the fact that your child has been able to do those things for quite a while. Or maybe it is when a young child contributes an insightful thought on a spiritual discussion, showing that not only was she paying attention, but was internalizing the concept as well. These flashes of brilliance can make you forget the difficulties and swell with pride. Your child can make you laugh, think, and reason, as well as scream in frustration.

Ephraim's Children can be wonderfully alternative thinkers. They may not use their toys in "normal" ways or give the predictable answers to questions. Their answers are intelligent and correct, but often are the result of different ways of viewing the question. Linda S. Budd relates a story of a preschooler who is asked what windows are made of. He replies that they are made of squares and rectangles.[1] The answer is correct, but not the "normal" answer.

Part of being an alternative thinker is the ability to creatively solve problems. These children may surprise you with the different approaches they use to get what they want. One baby could not reach a toy on the other end of a blanket so she pulled on the blanket until the toy was within reach. Another child wanted to join his dad who was running an errand. The problem was, his father was already gone with the family's one car. He thought of the solution to ask a neighbor who has a car for a ride to the store. His mother pointed out that they might miss daddy because they wouldn't know where he is. Her son said that they could call him on the phone. But Dad doesn't have a phone. The bright little boy had the solution to that dilemma as well. The store has a phone. We could call the store and have them look for Dad, then we could tell him to wait for us while we get a ride with our neighbor. This intelligent Ephraim's Child found multiple ways of getting around the obstacles in his path.

Viewing things differently can be a valuable asset. We all need alternative thinkers—someone who can see new solutions to the same problems. You can help cultivate this gift by encouraging your child as he explores new ways of looking at the world. Don't immediately tell your child that he is wrong when he does not see things the normal way. Applaud his alternative thinking.

Many times these children can astound you with their memory. One dad laughingly remarked that his Ephraim's Child has a better memory than he does. One time a member of the Stake Presidency visited a Primary and referred to his visit a year earlier when he had told them his favorite church song. To his amazement, a young girl raised her hand and told him the name of the song. She had remembered that small bit of information from a year before.

Don't forget that an Ephraim's Child usually learns by doing (see the chapter on Activity). He prefers to move, touch, and manually manipulate things. He likes to explore. This child will often physically attack a problem rather than talk about it or ask for your help. This can become a big headache when the problem he is physically addressing is an irritating sibling. Many parents have watched their Ephraim's Child launch himself at a hapless child. Teaching him to express himself verbally in these kinds of situations can be difficult, but are possible because the Ephraim's Child is often verbally gifted. He is very comfortable debating, questioning, or just chattering nonstop.

Sometimes Ephraim's Children run into difficulties because their intellect may outweigh their years. They have the ability to grasp knowledge, but still have the emotions and maturity of their physical years. You can imagine how frustrating it would be, for instance, to understand that if you put these Legos together just so, you can create a wonderful robot or bridge, and then not have the manual dexterity to accomplish the mental vision. This frustration can easily lead to tears, anger, and tantrums.

A high intellect combined with high awareness creates special challenges for parents. The Ephraim's Child will pick up information all the time and from anything. Many times these bright children will delve deeply into topics. What causes an earthquake? Why does the sun travel across the sky? How do germs get in our bodies? Why must we wear shoes outside? A vague answer that would satisfy most kids usually will not satisfy your Ephraim's Child. Instead of brushing him off, help your child find ways to get his answers and learn new things. Work with your child's intelligence. Instead of trying to stop the flow of curiosity and creative behavior, focus it. Find ways to structure your child's desire for knowledge and find appropriate environments for learning.

## School

The intensity of their various temperamental traits can make school problematic for Ephraim's Children. But many do well and even prosper in school. They love to learn, and if they are able to do so at their own pace, they can be happy and satisfied. However, if your child is having problems, there are some things that you can do to help.

The first step is work with the principal of your child's school to select teachers before the year begins. This alone could prevent numerous problems from occurring. Try going to the school and observing different teachers. Make sure that the teachers know that you are not judging whether or not they are good teachers, but are merely observing their teaching style and how it might fit with your child. When in the classroom, pick a child that reminds you of your own and watch him. Does his teacher allow movement, or is she most comfortable with children who sit quietly and listen? Does she present material in various ways, or prefer one method? How does this teacher handle exuberant, intense children? Do you think the teacher's personality will clash with your child's? Is the child you are observing happy in the classroom atmosphere?

When you find the teacher that you would like your child to have, approach the principal with your preferred choice. You can do this in person or in writing. Pick one or two important qualities and explain that your child would do best in a classroom where, for example, movement is integrated into the learning. If it is possible, could your child please be assigned to Mrs. Smith's classroom, or put with another teacher with a similar teaching style? Most principals will try to work with you. If you give your input in the spring, when there is much more time and flexibility, many schools will do their best to cooperate.

If you are already in the middle of the school year or unable to choose teachers, work with your child's teacher. Discuss your child's characteristics that might be problematic. Remember to use your positive everyday names. If the teacher knows that your child needs to move, his frequent trips to the pencil sharpener may not irritate her so much. Perhaps your child is very verbal and loves to ask questions. If the teacher knows this she can be prepared. Don't tell the teacher what to do, but let her know that you want to work together as a team to make the school year a success for your child. Listen to her concerns and ideas as well. Throughout the year meet with the teacher to see how things are going. She may have suggestions for things for you to work on at home, like raising his hand and not blurting out answers.

A little preparation beforehand can also help your slow-to-adapt child. Before the school year begins, arrange to take your child to the school. Walk with her to find the restrooms, the drinking fountains, and her new classroom. If you can meet the new teacher, that would be even better. This way your child is already familiar with the layout before the first day of school, when she will be dealing with noise, activity, and twenty other children as well. You can also talk with your child about school before it starts. Find out what she may be nervous about. Do what you can to make her as comfortable as possible and less stressed. Then your child will have more energy to cope and adapt. Some forethought from parents can make a big difference in school success.

## Multiple Intelligences

Often, the Ephraim's Child is bright according to the standard ideas of intelligence. Yet there are other ways that your Ephraim's Child may be smart. This goes beyond book learning and rote memory to multiple intelligences and, what may be most important, emotional intelligence.

When we think of intelligence we usually think only in terms of IQ. Thomas Armstrong challenges this concept in his book, *Seven Kinds of Smart*. He says that "by definition intelligence is the ability to respond successfully to new situations and the capacity to learn from one's past experiences."[2] A broader view of intelligence has gained respect in recent years. Psychologist Howard Gardner developed the theory of multiple intelligences and suggests that there are at least seven intelligences worthy of being considered important modes of thought.[3]

*1. Linguistic intelligence*—the intelligence of words.

People who are smart in this area can argue, persuade, entertain, or instruct effectively through the spoken word. They often love to play around with the sounds of language through puns, word games, and tongue twisters. They tend to read voraciously and can write clearly. Journalists, story-tellers, poets, and lawyers often rank high in linguistic intelligence.

2. *Logical-mathematical intelligence*—the intelligence of numbers and logic.

A logical-mathematically-inclined individual has the ability to reason and think sequentially. They think in terms of cause-and-effect, create hypotheses, look for conceptual regularities or numerical patterns, and enjoy a generally rational outlook on life. These are often the computer programmers, scientists, and accountants.

3. *Spatial intelligence*—the intelligence of pictures and images.

Architects, photographers, artists, pilots, and mechanical engineers usually possess great spatial intelligence. This is the ability to perceive, transform, and re-create different aspects of the visual-spatial world. Highly spatial individuals often have sensitivity to visual details and can visualize vividly, draw or sketch their ideas graphically, and orient themselves in three-dimensional space with ease.

4. *Musical intelligence*—the intelligence of sound.

This is the intelligence of composers and musicians. Yet any individual who has a good ear, can sing in tune, keep time to music, and listen to different musical selections with some degree of discernment also possesses musical intelligence. Key features of this intelligence are the capacity to perceive, appreciate, and produce rhythms and melodies.

5. *Bodily-kinesthetic intelligence*—the intelligence of the physical self.

Athletes, surgeons, mechanics, and craftspeople have this kind of intelligence. Talent in controlling one's body movements and also in handling objects skillfully are measures of bodily-kinesthetic intelligence. Body-smart individuals can be skilled at sewing, carpentry, or model-building, or they may just enjoy physical pursuits like hiking, dancing, jogging, camping, swimming, or boating. They're hands-on people who have good tactile sensitivity and need to move their bodies frequently.

### 6. *Interpersonal intelligence*—the intelligence of others.

Interpersonal intelligence is the ability to understand and work with other people. It requires a capacity to perceive and be responsive to the moods, temperaments, intentions, and desires of others. People with high amounts of this intelligence have the ability to get inside the skin of another person and view the world from that individual's perspective. They often make good networkers, negotiators, and teachers.

### 7. *Intrapersonal intelligence*—the intelligence of the inner self.

Someone who is strong in this kind of intelligence can easily access her own feelings, discriminate between many different kinds of inner emotional states, and use her self-understanding to enrich and guide her life. These people can be very introspective and enjoy meditation, contemplation, or other forms of deep soul-searching. On the other hand, they might be fiercely independent, highly goal-directed, and intensely self-disciplined. Either way, they prefer to work on their own rather than with others.

Every one of us possesses all seven intelligences to some degree, but vary in how strong we are in each of them. Unlike the traditional view of IQ, the theory of multiple intelligences states that any normal person can develop and grow in every one of the seven kinds of intelligences to a reasonable level of mastery. So even if your Ephraim's Child may not seem to fit the traditional idea of high intelligence, chances are she is highly smart in other areas that may not be measured by an IQ test.

## Emotional Intelligence

Daniel Goleman, Ph.D. and author of *Emotional Intelligence,* noticed that Gardner's theory of multiple intelligences failed to address a vital aspect of human life: that of emotions. Why do some people with a high IQ flounder and others with a modest IQ do surprisingly well? Gardner argues that the difference quite often lies in the abilities that he calls emotional intelligence. These include self-control, zeal and persistence, and the ability to motivate oneself. Unlike genetically based IQ, these skills can be taught to children, "giving them a better chance to use whatever intellectual potential the genetic lottery may have given them."[4]

Goleman breaks down emotional intelligence into five main domains:[5]

### 1. Knowing one's emotions

The keystone of emotional intelligence is in self-awareness. This is the ability to recognize a feeling as it happens. Being able to monitor feelings from moment to moment is crucial to psychological insight and self-understanding. Goleman contends that the inability to notice our true feelings leaves us at their mercy. People who know their emotions are better pilots of their lives because they have a surer sense of how they really feel about personal decisions.

### 2. Managing emotions

Once an individual is aware of his feelings, the next step is knowing what to do with them. This emotional skill includes the capacity to soothe oneself, to shake off rampant anxiety, gloom, or irritability. People who are poor in this ability constantly battle feelings of distress, while those who excel in it can bounce back far more quickly from life's setbacks and upsets.

### 3. Motivating oneself

People who have this skill tend to be more productive and effective in whatever they undertake. Marshaling emotions in the service of a goal is essential for paying attention, for self-motivation and mastery, and for creativity. Emotional self-control, the delaying of gratification, and stifling impulsiveness underlies accomplishment of every sort. Being able to get into an emotional "flow" state enables outstanding performance of all kinds.

### 4. Recognizing emotions in others

Empathy is the fundamental "people skill." People who are empathic are more attuned to the subtle social signals that indicate what others need or want. This is another ability that builds on emotional self-awareness. One needs to recognize his or her own feelings in order to decipher other's emotions.

### 5. Handling relationships

In large part, the art of relationships is skill in managing emotions in others. These are the abilities that undergird popularity, leadership, and interpersonal effectiveness. People who excel in these skills do well at anything that involves smooth interaction with others; they are "social stars."

If you are not naturally proficient in these emotional skills, where can you learn them? Schools do not concern themselves with emotional issues unless children are out of control or obviously have something wrong. Most of society focuses on the traditional view of IQ, which is usually equated with academic intelligence.

Academic intelligence offers virtually no preparation for the turmoil—or opportunity—life's vicissitudes bring. Yet even though a high IQ is no guarantee of prosperity, prestige, or happiness in life, our schools and our culture fixate on academic abilities, ignoring emotional intelligence, a set of traits—some might call it character—that also matters immensely for our personal destiny. Emotional life is a domain that, as surely as math or reading, can be handled with greater or lesser skill, and requires its unique set of competencies.[6]

Not surprisingly, emotional skills are best learned at home.

## Being an Emotional Coach

Numerous prophets have said that our most important work is done in the home, and helping our children appropriately deal with their emotions is a large part of our work. We are examples to our children in every way. This is true in the realm of emotions. Goleman says:

> Family life is our first school for emotional learning; in this intimate cauldron we learn how to feel about ourselves and how others will react to our feelings; how to think about these feelings and what choices we have in reacting; how to read and express hopes and fears. This emotional schooling operates not just through the things that parents say and do directly to children, but also in the models they offer for handling their own feelings and those that pass between husband and wife. Some parents are gifted emotional teachers, others atrocious.[7]

That parents are the primary teachers of emotional intelligence has also been supported by science and research. Daniel Stern, a psychiatrist at Cornell University School of Medicine, conducted research on the small, repeated exchanges that take place between parent and child on a daily basis. He believes that the most basic lessons of emotional life are laid down in these intimate moments, the most important of which are those that let the child know her emotions are met with empathy, accepted, and reciprocated, in a process Stern calls *attunement*. He contends that the countlessly repeated moments of attunement or misattunement between parent and child shape emotional expectations as the child grows into adulthood, perhaps far more than the more dramatic events of childhood.[8]

From repeated attunements a child develops a sense that other people can and will share in her feelings. A prolonged absence of attunement between parent and child takes a tremendous emotional toll on the child. When a parent consistently fails to show any empathy with a particular range of emotion in the child (joy, sadness, or the need for reassurance, for example) the child begins to avoid expressing, and perhaps even feeling, those same emotions. By the same token, children can come to favor a certain range of emotion, depending on which moods are reciprocated.9

As parents, we play a vital role in shaping our child's emotional intelligence, whether or not we make a concerted effort to do so. How do we deal with our child's emotions? Are we good or bad emotional teachers? In his book, Goleman also discusses the three most common emotionally inept parenting styles.10 These proved to be:

1. *Ignoring feelings altogether.*
Such parents treat a child's emotional upset as trivial or a bother, something they should just wait to blow over.

2. *Being too laissez-faire.*
These parents notice how a child feels, but hold that however a child handles the emotional storm is fine. Like those who ignore a child's feelings, these parents rarely step in to try to show their child alternative and appropriate emotional responses.

3. *Being contemptuous or showing no respect for how the child feels.*
Such parents are typically disapproving and harsh in both their criticisms and their punishments.

Rather than these three styles, the goal is to become what Goleman calls an emotional coach or mentor. This is when you see your child's upset as an opportunity for emotional growth. In order to do this, you must first take your child's feelings seriously. It requires that you spend time and effort to try to understand exactly what is upsetting your child and then help him find positive ways to soothe his feelings. Emotional coaches help a child discover his own feelings and put a name to them. So, for example, instead of just feeling "awful," a child can know that he is feeling frustration.

In her article "How Children Learn to Behave," author Barbara Vance writes that children who can recognize, label, and talk about their feelings in an atmosphere of acceptance are more likely to keep the commandments and resist temptation. In general, children are more at the mercy of their external environment than are adults. They respond impulsively, quickly, and often highly emotionally to stimuli in their environment.[11]

Sometimes figuring out what your child is feeling can be challenging. Children throw a lot of "noise" at us when in the grip of emotion. We can get caught up in the noise instead of addressing the root of the problem. When a child comes home from school, throws his stuff on the floor, and immediately starts picking on his little sister, yells at the dog, and is rude to mom, do we calmly try to talk to him about what may have happened to make him so upset? Do we try to get at the reason for his behavior, or do we focus on the mess on the floor and the rude words? He is probably not being impossible just to make your day awful. Something has happened to make him feel a certain way, and he does not know how to deal with it.

After we help our child label his emotion, our job is not finished. We must then teach our child what to do with his emotions. Being an emotional coach does not mean that you let your child get away with inappropriate behavior just because he is in the grip of emotion. You can tell him that even though he feels frustrated, angry, sad, rejected, etc. that he cannot be rude to others. Let's say that your child is angry with his brother. Most parents have no problem instructing an angry child on what not to do. For example, he cannot hit or punch his brother. It is important to teach your child that certain behavior is inappropriate, but your child still feels angry. What does he do with his feelings? Ignore them? Wait for them to just go away?

Many parents fail to take the next step and teach their children how to manage their feelings in an appropriate way. As a result, we have children who are growing up without a clue on what to do with their emotions. This lack of emotional savvy can result in tragic circumstances. Chances are that someone who kills another in a fit of road rage never learned how to deal with frustration and annoyance when he was young. A youth who shoots a classmate for teasing him probably did not learn how to deal with embarrassment and anger at home.

In order to teach our children what they are feeling and how to manage their strongest emotions, parents need to be able to do it themselves, which is not always easy. Children will follow our example of how we deal with our own emotions like anger, frustration, and fear. Mary Sheedy Kurcinka writes in her book *Kids, Parents and Power Struggles*:

> Learning to express strong emotions, like anger and frustration, respectfully and selectively is learned behavior. You don't have to be a victim of your emotions. You can choose your response. You don't have to react. And as you make those choices, your children are watching and listening. You are their role model, teaching them with your words and actions what adults do when faced with a rush of powerful emotions.[12]

Through everyday interactions and opportunities, you can teach your child how to manage his emotions. Just understand that learning to manage one's emotions does not happen overnight. It takes effort, time, and repetition to learn. You can support and encourage your child as she practices. As you work with your child to increase her emotional intelligence, you become your child's emotional coach, her guide to self-discipline.

Due to their intense natures, Ephraim's Children often have very strong emotions. Dealing with the intensity of your child's emotions can be draining, and yes, sometimes even scary. How is your child supposed to deal with them unless you help him? Some people naturally manage their emotions well, but most of us require help and practice. Guiding the Ephraim's Child to grow to her potential requires emotional management. Greater understanding and control of our emotions can also help us in spiritual matters.

## Using the Heart to Understand

When we discuss emotion, we often talk about the heart. Love comes from the heart, we can have a broken heart, or we feel heartsick. Many times it is the heart, not the head, which guides our actions. Often the Spirit of the Lord speaks to our hearts—our feelings. "Yea, behold, I will tell you in your mind and in your heart, by the Holy Ghost, which shall come upon you and which shall dwell in your heart."[13] For true understanding of spiritual matters, we must use our hearts as well as our minds. King Benjamin told his people to "open your ears that ye may hear, and your hearts that ye may understand, and your minds that the mysteries of God may be unfolded to your view."[14] Abinadi told the priests of King Noah: "Ye have not applied your hearts to understanding."[15] One of Laman's and Lemuel's biggest obstacles to spiritual understanding was that they "were past feeling, that [they] could not feel his words."[16] If we are more in tune with our hearts, then we may better understand and feel the still, small voice of the Holy Ghost.

Our hearts also play a key role in truly dedicating ourselves to righteousness. Paul said: "For with the heart man believeth unto righteousness."[17] It is our hearts that the Lord requires,[18] "for the Lord seeth not as man seeth; for man looketh on the outward appearance, but the Lord looketh on the heart."[19]

Marvin J. Ashton talked about how at the end of our lives the Lord will not look at our intellect, or our possessions, or any other worldly measure of a person, but He will use our hearts as the measuring stick.

> When the Lord measures an individual, He does not take a tape measure around the person's head to determine his mental capacity, nor his chest to determine his manliness, but He measures the heart as an indicator of the person's capacity and potential to bless others. Why the heart? Because the heart is a synonym for one's entire makeup. We often use phrases about the heart to describe the total person. Thus, we describe people as being "big-hearted" or "goodhearted" or having a "heart of gold." Or we speak of people with faint hearts, wise hearts, pure hearts, willing hearts, deceitful hearts, conniving hearts, courageous hearts, cold hearts, hearts of stone, or selfish hearts. The measure of our hearts is the measure of our total performance.[20]

Only through both the heart and the mind can we be truly converted. It is not enough to just intellectually understand the doctrines of the gospel. It has to do more than just make sense or seem reasonable. We need to understand the gospel in both mind and heart for a sustaining testimony that moves us to a "mighty change of heart."[21] Only then can our Ephraim's Child, and us as well, be moved to righteous action through our thoughts and emotions.

### "Saving Intelligence"

*Random House Webster's College Dictionary* defines intelligence as: "1. capacity for learning, reasoning, and understanding; aptitude in grasping truths, relationships, facts, meanings, etc. 2. mental alertness or quickness of understanding. 3. manifestation of a high mental capacity. 4. the faculty or act of understanding."[22]

As we've already mentioned, and as this definition confirms, most equate intelligence with knowledge, or the ability to acquire knowledge. In our society a great deal of time, effort, and money is spent acquiring it. Many times worldly success is a reflection of one's education and knowledge. The Lord tells us, however, that there is more to intelligence than just knowledge.

Bruce R. McConkie quotes Joseph F. Smith in explaining the difference between intelligence and knowledge:

> Knowledge can be obtained and used in unrighteousness; Satan gains his power on this principle. But intelligence presupposes the wise and proper use of knowledge, a use that leads to righteousness and the ultimate attainment of exaltation. The devil has tremendous power and influence because of his knowledge, but he is entirely devoid of the least glimmering of intelligence. An intelligent person is one who applies his knowledge so as to progress in the things of the Spirit; he glories in righteousness.[23]

Remember that "to be learned is good if [we] hearken unto the counsels of God."[24]

In his book *The Abundant Life*, Hugh B. Brown asserts that cultivating our intelligence is part of the gospel of Jesus Christ as we understand and proclaim it. He writes: "We believe that a man is saved in the kingdom of God no faster than he gets knowledge, that he cannot be saved in ignorance. We believe that the glory of God is intelligence [see D&C 93:36] and that every man's glory will be determined by the quality and degree of his intelligence."[25] Intelligence, knowledge, and education are therefore worthy pursuits and can help us get far in this world. But only when our intelligence is applied to eternal things can it helps us get closer to the glory of God. Only then do we have the knowledge necessary to save, or as Joseph F. Smith calls it, "saving knowledge."[26] And if intelligence is the application of knowledge, then when we apply our "saving knowledge," we have "saving intelligence."

The Ephraim's Child can repeatedly amaze us with her intelligence and understanding. It is natural to cultivate her intellect when it comes to academic pursuits, but we cannot neglect the weightier matters. As parents, we are "commanded to teach our children to understand the principles of the gospel. . . . If parents neglect this important duty then the sin will rest on the parents."27 We need to help direct our Ephraim's Child's intelligence on eternal, saving paths so that she can develop her own "saving intelligence."

When can our children begin to cultivate this "saving intelligence?" When the Savior visited the people in the Americas, he loosed the tongues of the children so that "they did speak unto their fathers great and marvelous things—even greater than he [Jesus] had revealed unto the people . . . . yea, even babes did open their mouths and utter marvelous things. And the things which they did utter were forbidden, that there should not any man write them."28 Joseph E. Taylor talks about the power in these children to speak such great and marvelous things. He says that rather than being like machines merely set in motion, these children uttered "marvelous things" by virtue of the understanding that they already possessed. Through His power, Jesus gave their bodies the ability to exhibit the full strength of their intellect.29

Many times Ephraim's Children can understand things at a much younger age than we think. Many leaders have counseled us to teach our children while they are young. We are to read to them from the scriptures and teach pure doctrine, because they can understand much. We don't need to water down gospel truths. In fact, we may do our children a disservice when we are too vague in what we teach them. They are growing up in a very dangerous world, and they must be properly armed. We may be surprised at how much our Ephraim's Child does understand. These kids will recognize and understand truth when they are taught it.

Hugh Nibley tells us that the highest state of spirituality is to be filled with the spirit of God, "which has no other effect than that of releasing our intelligence. . . . Intelligence was not created (D&C 93:29), . . . like other latent forces, intelligence is there and just waiting to be released."30 As parents, we can help release the powerful intelligence of our Ephraim's Child. We must do our best to help him become what he has been sent here to become, and to accomplish what he has been sent here to do. We need to set him on the path where he can use his intellect for the Lord's purposes. This requires more powerful teaching on our part. That way he does not merely have intelligence, but "saving intelligence."

# 11

# Control

*"The thing that impresses me the most about America
is the way parents obey their children."*[1]
—King Edward VIII

Everyone likes to have their own way, especially children. But some children like to have their way so much that you may feel like you are living in a budding dictatorship. A number of Ephraim's Children are almost fanatical about being in control. They want to choose which chair they sit on at meals; which plate, cup, or silverware they use; what the family will eat and how it is prepared; not to mention where each food item is placed on their plate and to what level you fill their cup with milk. They also tell you which road to take when driving, which store to go to, and how to discipline your other children. Many times they take over with peers, telling the other children what they will play, how they will play it, and sometimes giving the others the lines they are supposed to say.

Ephraim's Children often have a high need to be in control. This may be related to these children's high sensitivity. Their environment greatly affects them, and they often feel a loss of control over their own bodies and emotions, so they seek control whenever they can. Take an Ephraim's Child who wants to be in control and add a large dose of natural intensity, and parents often feel they have a tyrant in their midst.

What may feel like tyrannical behavior now can be shaped and refined into leadership. These children have natural tendencies towards leading others. They seem to be born with a talent for directing others and achieving goals. As James E. Talmage reminds us, "The natures, dispositions, and tendencies of men are known to the Father of their spirits, even before they are born into mortality."[2] The propensity of Ephraim's Children to take charge is likely a personality trait that has carried over from premortality. They probably led others and had many responsibilities there, so they are used to being in control. And if these spirits are used to being in charge, is it any surprise that they try to be in charge still? This chapter is to help us work with these children who want to take charge because that is what they are accustomed to.

Your child's desire to be in control may make you feel that your authority is constantly questioned or undermined. It is important to remember who is in charge. You are the adult and know more about the world and what your child and your family needs. This does not mean, however, that you get to become the dictator. It does mean that on certain issues, you have the final word. For the issues not set in stone, which usually crop up on a daily basis, there are things that you can do to help your controlling Ephraim's Child without relinquishing your authority.

If you are worried about giving your child too much control, remember that control is not the same as authority. You can and should maintain parental authority, but you can often do that best when allowing your Ephraim's Child some control. In *Parenting with Love and Logic: Teaching Children Responsibility*, Foster Cline and Jim Fay address the issue of parental control:

> Control is a curious thing. The more we give away, the more we gain. Parents who attempt to take all the control from their children end up losing the control they sought to begin with. These parents invite their children to fight to get control back. In the battle for control, we should never take any more than we absolutely must have; we must always cut our kids in on the action. When we do that, we put them in control on our terms. We must give our children the control we don't need to keep the control we do.[3]

## Routine

Establishing a consistent routine can reduce some of your child's tyrannical behavior. If he knows what to expect, then he will feel more in control. When he tests the routine, which he will do over and over again, many times he is just making sure that the boundaries are unchanged. When those boundaries do not shift according to parental mood or nebulous factors, your child will feel that he is still in control. Remember that the Ephraim's Child hates surprises, and a life that is rarely consistent is always surprising.

## Give Choices

One way to help your Ephraim's Child feel more in control is to give her some choice in what is happening in her life. As the adult, you pick what choices your child is offered. That way your child has power to decide between acceptable options. At dinnertime, for example, you can allow your child to decide which of two vegetables she wants to eat. You are not giving her the choice of whether or not to eat dinner—that is non-negotiable—but letting her choose between pre-approved options. Your child has some control over dinner, but has not taken over your authority.

However, be wary of giving too many options or vague choices. This can backfire with young children. If you open the closet and say, "What do you want to wear?" there may be too many choices. Your child may get lost in the huge number of options and be unable to make up her mind, which will make her feel even less in control. It is often a better idea to give two or three choices for your child to choose from. For example, you could ask your child if she wants to wear the blue sweatshirt or the red sweater, or pick out three outfits for her to consider.

You can also help your child see that her actions are choices too. "You can choose to stay here and be respectful of your brother, or you can choose to go somewhere else." Although she may not understand it, actions are choices. She can choose to be mad, or choose a different way of reacting to a situation. With your help, your control-hungry Ephraim's Child can realize that she actually has more control than she thinks, because she is always in control of her actions.

Often parents are too rushed or preoccupied to allow their young children the power of choice. It would be much easier if your child just did things your way because you say so. Many times parents use their authority to try and enforce their way of doing things, even if it is on insignificant matters. Chances are your Ephraim's Child has already questioned "your" way of doing things. Looking for ways to give your child choices may be a change of thinking for you, but if you make a consistent effort, it will become much easier. And imagine how much more pleasant life will be with less struggles between you and your Ephraim's Child over control! That alone should inspire many of us to make the effort.

There are occasions when a power struggle with your Ephraim's Child seems inevitable, despite all your best efforts. It is probably a good guess that this is one of the reasons that you turned to this book in the first place. How do you work through these struggles without feeling like either a tyrant or a pushover? Now we will address the situations when your child vies for control with you.

## Power Struggles

*"It's time to go home," Nathan's mother calls cheerfully to her toddler. She has already given her son warnings to allow him time to get used to the transition. He looks directly at his mother, shouts, "No!" and takes off in the other direction. His mom calmly follows him and gently, but firmly, grasps his hand to lead him to the door. The toddler immediately tries to break free with all his strength. His mother tries every possible method to gain her child's cooperation. Finally she has to pick him up and take him, kicking and screaming, to the door. There she has to dodge flying fists and kicking legs to put on*

*his coat and shoes. The entire time her son is screaming at the top of his lungs and doing everything possible to escape. The mother finally has had enough and loses her cool. She yells, drags her son to the car, and physically wrestles him into the car seat. She slams the car door and stands for a while trying to gather her strength to enter the car with the screaming monster in the backseat. She swears to herself, "I am **never** going to do this again!"*

This scenario probably sounds familiar to any parent that has ever had a two-year-old, but what about when it happens constantly with children who are supposedly not in their terrible two's? Often power struggles are the norm rather than the exception with a controlling Ephraim's Child. In her book *Kids, Parents, and Power Struggles,* Mary Sheedy Kurcinka contests that power struggles with children are rooted in emotional needs. Power struggles are often the symptoms of emotional needs, and until the need is taken care of, more symptoms will keep popping up. "Emotions are the real fuel source behind power struggles. When you identify those emotions you can select strategies that teach your kids what they are feeling and how to express those emotions more respectfully and suitably."4 This is when emotional intelligence and emotional skills can come in handy. Instead of focusing on the struggles, Kurcinka suggests that we address the emotions behind them and work with children to understand and control their emotions. Then the number of power struggles will decrease as your child develops her emotional intelligence.

In order to work with your child, you need to have a common vocabulary. It is imperative that you identify emotions as they happen. Give them a name, describe them, point out examples from movies or memorable experiences. Your child will begin to understand that he isn't just the victim of some nebulous feeling that is upsetting him. He can identify the feeling, even in its beginning stages. When kids recognize their emotions, they are less likely to be surprised by strong feelings and can catch emotions in the early stages when they are more manageable. It is much easier to deal with frustration than a full-blown tantrum.

With this self-understanding, your Ephraim's Child can then learn how to manage her own intensity. She can recognize rising emotional intensity and take steps to soothe and calm herself. The next step, and ultimate goal, is to identify triggers so that she can predict, prepare, and choose the appropriate emotional response. With these skills, children are better able to cope with life's ups and downs. They learn to recognize their stress cues and better identify their fears and anxieties. Then they can make adjustments for them. These children can learn that there are things that they can actually do about stressors, and feel empowered to take charge of their reactions knowing that they do have some control.

Increased emotional awareness of themselves also helps children recognize the emotions of others. They learn how to work with others' emotions like they do with their own, and so are able to avoid power struggles with others. Emotionally intelligent children are better able to maintain healthy relationships.

As discussed in the previous chapter, we can help our Ephraim's Child learn these emotional skills through emotional coaching. You don't ignore the emotion or get mad at it, but address it and help your child understand and appropriately deal with it. Approaching power struggles from the standpoint of an emotional coach will help diffuse intense emotional situations. You have to listen carefully. It helps to get down on your child's level and look into her eyes. Let your child know she is worthy of your attention. Your child will know that you can see things from her point of view and, instead of pitting you against each other on opposite sides, you are on the same side, working together. It is this emotional connection that keeps your child working with you. This does not mean, however, that you always say yes, constantly negotiate, or allow your child free reign with his emotions.

Becoming your child's emotion coach begins with a decision on your part to interact with your child differently. You must approach impending power struggles with a different goal in mind. You need to decide this before you are in the middle of a power struggle. It can be hard to step back in the heat of the moment. Rather than being blinded by all the noise, you need to search for the reason your child is acting this way. It is vital that you realize that your child is not "out to get you." Your child is refusing to get dressed for a reason other than to make you frustrated. Put yourself in your child's shoes and try to address the emotional need behind the screaming and stubborn behavior. Perhaps you have been rushing your child, maybe the clothes you picked are uncomfortable, or maybe your child is scared to go to school for some reason. Unless we take the time to find out the "why" of behavior, we cannot emotionally coach our kids.

Once you can figure out what your child is feeling, help her vocalize the feelings. Your Ephraim's Child needs your input to build her emotional vocabulary. Then you can help her find solutions to the real problem. Make sure to guide her and not take over. Give her some time and space when developing these skills so that she can use them when you are not around.

Coaching your Ephraim's Child through discovering and managing his emotions will help him build some of the most valuable skills he will possess in life. Not only that, but in addressing the underlying emotions that fuel the power struggles, you can connect with your child rather than being backed into opposing corners. You can be on the same side. It is harder to fight with someone who is on the same team.

Although many times emotions will fuel power struggles, there will be times when your Ephraim's Child is struggling with you over more trivial reasons. Like you, sometimes your child just doesn't feel like doing something, whether out of laziness or sheer contrariness. Sometimes he just wants to see what we will do when he defies us. Parents losing control can be great entertainment. Maybe your child just wants your attention. Use your own instincts to determine whether this power struggle is one when emotional coaching is needed or just a firm hand.

## Expanding Bossiness Into Leadership

Do you ever think to yourself, "Boy, my kid is bossy?" Ephraim's Children like to be in charge of everyone and everything. Bossiness, though often irritating, can be an asset if channeled properly. If you teach your child to develop emotional control and communicate well, his bossiness can be transformed into assertiveness and leadership skills.

"People everywhere are looking for someone to follow— for someone to lead them."[5] Nearly every person at some time, somewhere, in some way, leads another person or a group. Our lives touch the lives of others, and we influence them whether or not we intend to. Since in one way or another nearly all of us are leaders, it is important that we learn to be good leaders and teach these skills to our Ephraim's Child, who will lead anyway.

Elder Sterling W. Sill stressed the value of good leaders when he said, "A soldier can fight harder, a salesman can sell more goods, a child can do better school work, and a missionary can make more converts if he works under the direction of someone who knows how to teach and inspire and train and supervise and love and motivate and do those other important things that [good leaders do]."[6] Good leadership skills help us improve ourselves, help others, and strengthen our relationships with our friends and family members. As the Church is organized in all parts of the world and the Lord's work continues to expand, many of us will be called to lead others.

Leadership is first learned at home. This is where we learn how to work with others, how to accomplish tasks, how to delegate assignments, and how to ask for help. "Because the need for leadership increases with the importance of the institution that it serves, leadership in the home assumes the greatest possible importance. 'No other success can compensate for failure in the home.'"7 As parents, we are the leaders of our families, so we should strive to be the best leaders possible. As we do so, we can encourage and help our children become good leaders.

Children develop the sense of confidence necessary to be an effective leader by small, consistent successes. Provide leadership opportunities for your child, but make sure they are things he can usually succeed at. We say usually because it is important that your child have some experience with failure and the accompanying emotions so that he knows how to deal with it. Perhaps your child can teach a lesson in family home evening, lead a family discussion, plan a family activity, or help a younger brother or sister.

Teaching your controlling Ephraim's Child better communication skills can also help. Show her better ways to express her ideas and opinions. Encourage your child to express herself, but show her how to offer suggestions rather than give orders. When she starts barking out commands, point out that she needs to say things more gently. You can explain that you are more willing to listen when you do not feel that you are being run over by a bulldozer. Help your child brainstorm more appropriate ways of verbalizing her desires, and then practice with her.

The Lord has revealed in the scriptures the qualities that make a good leader. As the Lord indicates in D&C 121:41-45, leaders should have the following qualities: persuasiveness, long-suffering, gentleness, meekness, love unfeigned, kindness, and charity. It is our job to guide our Ephraim's Children as they refine bossiness into persuasiveness and impatience into long-suffering. Our children need us to show them how to be meek and follow as well as lead. Only when they learn how to cooperate and incorporate other's ideas will our children be the type of leaders the Lord wants them to be. We help these Ephraim's Children be better leaders as we lovingly show them how to turn their sensitivity into gentleness, love unfeigned, kindness and charity.

## Leading As Jesus Led

The best way to expand bossiness into leadership is to find a good leader and copy him/her. We can choose no better model of leadership than our Lord and Savior. Not only can we follow His pattern in raising our little ones to be good leaders, but we need His example ourselves as we lead our own children.

"Behold," Jesus told the Nephites, "I am the light; I have set an example for you."[8] The Savior is the perfect role model. Through studying his example we can learn skills and qualities that "are important for us all if we wish to succeed as leaders in any lasting way."[9] Here are some ways that the Savior led (adapted from Neal A. Maxwell and Spencer W. Kimball).[10]

### Lead by Example

Jesus said several times, "Come, follow me."[11] He inspired others to "do what I do," rather than just "do what I say." Leaders not only tell others what to do and how to do it, they also show them by example. A true shepherd leads his sheep. Like a true shepherd, a leader inspires others to follow him and to fulfill their own duties. He shows the way by living the principles he teaches and by understanding and responding to others' needs. Children are often great at finding the discrepancies between what we do and what we say. Parents must practice what they preach.

### Be Consistent

"Jesus operated from a base of fixed principles or truths rather than making up the rules as he went along. Thus, his leadership style was not only correct, but also constant."[12] Jesus was consistent in obeying the commandments. He did not change His standards or behavior to please others. As we willingly follow His example and control our actions in righteousness, we will become good examples for our followers. We must live the standards of the gospel in every way if we want our children to do the same.

## Love

"Love one another; as I have loved you."[13] Jesus loved the people He led. Love is perhaps the most important quality leaders can have, because it means they genuinely care for those they lead. If they love those they lead, they want to help them improve their lives. Loving leaders are concerned for their followers' needs and want to help them reach their goals. It is only through our love that we can help others accomplish the common goal of us all to return to live with our Heavenly Father. Love is a powerful motivator. Elder Neal A. Maxwell said that "leadership is love in action."[14] Most parents love their children, but we need to make sure that they know we do.

## Serve

True leadership can only lift others through service. Instead of thinking of leading others as being in charge of them, we need to see it as the opportunity to serve them. Spend the majority of your time serving your children, not telling them what to do. "The Savior's leadership was selfless. He put himself and his own needs second and ministered to others beyond the call of duty, tirelessly, lovingly, effectively."[15] Children will be able to tell if you are serving them grudgingly, out of a sense of duty, or to get them out of the way so that you can move on to more important things. Be careful that you don't fall into the trap of seeing your children as obstacles to your life.

## Be Prepared

Jesus prepared Himself. He fasted, prayed, and studied, always seeking to learn the will of the Father. We have been encouraged to study and prepare ourselves.[16] As we fast, pray, and study, we also can know the will of our Heavenly Father and increase our ability to serve our children as He would have us do.

## Teach

Jesus taught His disciples the purpose of His work. He helped them to understand their part in His work and to gain a vision of their important responsibilities. The best leaders are those who are able to share their vision with their followers, thus inspiring them to fulfill that vision. Through our new everyday names we can help our Ephraim's Children catch the vision of what they can become. We want to first see our children through Heavenly Father's eyes, then pass along that vision to our children.

## Allow Agency

Jesus based His leadership on the principle of agency. He did not force His disciples to follow Him. He invited them. He cared about the freedom of his followers to choose and did not try to control them. When we attempt to force anyone to follow, we are using Satan's method. If we are to lead in a Christlike manner, we must allow our children the freedom to choose.

## Delegate

Jesus gave His disciples tasks that were meaningful and challenging. Meaningful and worthwhile tasks help us feel needed. Good leaders help their followers feel that what they do is worthwhile. However, everyone must recognize that at times there are necessary but tedious tasks to be performed. As leaders we must learn to delegate authority to others. This means giving others the responsibility to do tasks under our direction and then allowing them to do the work.

President Harold B. Lee said: "Let them do everything within their power, and you stand in the background and teach them how to do it. I think therein is the secret of growth, to fix responsibility and then teach our people how to carry that responsibility."[17] Delegating tasks to your Ephraim's Child can be hard to do, especially if it would be quicker, easier, or more effective for you to just do something yourself. Your child needs to learn to do things himself, and he can also have the added enjoyment of working side by side with you.

### Be Responsible

Jesus showed He was responsible both to His purposes and to His people. He felt a responsibility to help His people grow. He not only wanted to build His Father's kingdom, but also to exalt His people. This should be our purpose—to help our followers grow and gain exaltation.

Being responsible also means requiring that same quality from others. In describing what He expected of His followers, Jesus was honest. As we lead, we also must let others know what we expect from them, and what they can expect from us. Let your children understand what is expected of them. Giving children specific instructions can help them better perform their tasks in the home. Your children also need to see you fulfill your responsibilities.

### Listen

Jesus was a good listener. He created an atmosphere of love and acceptance that made His followers comfortable, because He listened with a loving ear. He took time to listen to them and to understand their needs.[18] We too must exercise this kind of concern. This can be challenging with a child when we have a million other things to do, but your Ephraim's Child will learn how to listen to others because she first saw how you listened to her.

### Allow Others to Learn

Jesus often helped His followers think through their own ideas by asking them questions.[19] This helped them understand what He was trying to teach. To be good leaders, we must help people solve their own problems and meet their own challenges.

Instead of jumping in to solve every dispute, we need to help our children learn how to solve problems themselves.

We can ask them questions to help them consider possible solutions. We must express confidence in them and motivate them to find solutions and make decisions. This way our child is not only learning that he must share, but is learning how to work with another person to find a solution that will work for both parties.

### Be a Good Follower

A good leader is also a good follower of those in authority over him. Good followers earn the trust and confidence of both their leaders and those they lead. "Jesus Christ was the model leader because He learned to follow perfectly the will of His Father. In order to become truly effective leaders, we must learn to obey the Savior's admonition, 'Come, . . . follow me' (Mark 10:21). This requires that we learn to do what the Savior did and follow His example."[20] Do we honor our parents? Do we sustain our local church leaders in word and in deed? Do we follow the counsel of the prophet in all things?

As in everything, Jesus Christ has given us a model to follow, both as leaders ourselves and trainers of future leaders. Elder Wendell J. Ashton reminds us, "The lasting lessons in leadership do not change. They are eternal. They helped make Noah and Abraham and Moses giants in the land, giants in character, in leadership, in bringing men and women closer to God. . . . These eternal principles can help you lead in a world that cries out for real . . . leadership."[21]

Elder Ashton then gave his sons this advice, which is even more applicable today. He said:

> The most powerful lessons . . . come from that leader among leaders, Jesus the Christ. And so . . . from the prophets and from the Prince of Peace, learn how to lead, beginning with yourselves. Stand on your own feet. Stand tall. Hold your heads high as though you are truly [children] of God, which you are. . . . Move on the good earth as though you are partners of the Lord in helping to bring immortality and eternal life to mankind, which you are.

Walk quietly . . . but walk fearlessly, in faith. Don't let the ill winds sway you. Walk as . . . leaders in the government of God. Walk with hands ready to help, with hearts full of love for your fellowmen. But walk with a toughness in righteousness.[22]

Many Ephraim's Children are born leaders. They just need our help to hone their skills. Find new everyday names and use them. Your Ephraim's Child is not bossy; she knows how to accomplish goals. She is not a control freak, but likes to know what is going on. And she is not a tyrant or dictator, but a leader. Our homes do not need to be a battleground for control. When you wish your child didn't want so much control, remember that you are raising one of tomorrow's leaders.

# 12

# Independence

*A young girl was going to Primary for the first time. Her mother wanted to go with her to make certain that she arrived at the right room. The child kept saying, "No. You stay. I go. You stay here." Eventually the child made her way down the hall to Primary—by herself—with another member of the ward secretly following behind so that the concerned mother could be sure that her daughter arrived in the right place.*

*One small boy refused to let his mother help him on the apparatus at his Little Gym class. The other mothers looked at this woman like she was neglecting her child and letting him hurt himself, but the child would push away his mother's hand, and say loudly, "Move!" Then he would leap off unassisted.*

*A new Primary Chorister asked each small child who volunteered to lead a song if he/she wanted help. The Chorister would hold the child's hand and move his/her arm in time with the music. The answer was yes for every-one, except one little girl. She refused any assistance, shak-ing her head and hiding her hand behind her back. "I know how," she insisted. She directed the song all by herself, com-plete with holds to draw out the count, her little hand going all over the place without any pattern in the air at all.*

*A young mother was trying to feed lunch to her upset seven-month-old who was sitting in his high chair. Her son usually enthusiastically ate his food, yet this whole day he refused to eat any food she offered. A visiting grandmother suggested to the frustrated mother that she let the child feed himself, so she dropped the food on the highchair tray. The boy immediately calmed down and started to laboriously feed himself. Even though it was more work, this independent child wanted to do it himself.*

If you have an independent Ephraim's Child, then you have a persistent and intense child who wants to do everything himself. He wants to buckle himself in the car seat, he wants to operate the microwave by himself, he wants to walk without your hand, and he wants to dress himself. It doesn't matter to him if he is unable to do it, he wants to anyway. When this child is confronted with a task that he cannot do, he often gets frustrated and angry. He is fiercely, intensely independent.

We live in a society that often sends a dual message about independence. In some instances doing things on your own without help from anyone is applauded. Being strong and not asking for help, even if it is needed, is often admired. On the other hand, in some aspects of our lives we are sometimes advised to completely rely on others. For example, there are some who want to rely on the government for retirement, health care, or even their own livelihood without any of their own effort. This second attitude can foster a sense of entitlement—that we deserve some things as our right—which is problematic when people are unwilling to expend their own effort to reap rewards.

It is important to teach our Ephraim's Children that there are appropriate times for both dependence and independence. However, the goal in many situations is a mixture of the two, which is called interdependence. We need to teach these children how to combine elements of dependence and independence to make interdependence. We will discuss dependence, independence, and interdependence in more detail.

## Dependence

The fiercely independent Ephraim's Child may be so set on doing his own thing that he automatically refuses assistance—even when it is needed. He needs to learn that it is okay to ask for help sometimes. The very thought of dependence is repugnant to a highly independent spirit. However, there are times when dependency is reasonable and useful. There will be times in life when every person needs help and must depend on others like doctors, repairmen, friends, parents, teachers, etc. When situations arise that are beyond what we can handle effectively alone, then we must depend in some degree on others. This kind of dependence is not crippling or undesirable, but necessary in life.

The most important dependence that we need to realize is our dependence on God. Ultimately we all must reach an understanding of our dependence on Him and on the Atonement so that we can progress spiritually. We *cannot* gain eternal life by ourselves, no matter how much we accomplish on our own. It is absolutely impossible to have salvation independent of our Savior. He is the only means and way. We need to help the fiercely independent Ephraim's Children learn to lean on the Lord. One who is so independent and self-willed will have a hard time turning to the Lord in times of necessity, and more especially during easier times.

Being dependent on the Lord is not a weakness. He has said that He "will make weak things become strong,"[1] not make strong things become weak. But relying solely on ourselves *can* be a weakness. Nephi said that "cursed is he that putteth his trust in the arm of flesh. Yea, cursed is he that putteth his trust in man or maketh flesh his arm."[2] In *The Book of Mormon*, the Nephites were able to keep the Lamanites at bay when they depended on the strength of the Lord. When they relied on themselves, they began losing battles. Our children are in a very real battle with the forces of evil. We will be able to keep evil and wickedness at bay when we do as the Nephites and depend on the Lord. When we fail to rely on Him we will lose battles, just like the Nephites.

In some things we want to be independent. After all, the Lord says, "It is not meet that I should command in all things."3 However, we must eventually learn to turn our independence over to the Lord. It is a test to take that agency that we fought so hard to keep in premortality and place it in the Lord's hands. Neal A. Maxwell reminds us that "only by aligning our wills with God's is full happiness to be found. Anything less results in a lesser portion (see Alma 12:10-11)."4 But only by aligning our will with the Lord's can we become the person that He knows we can be, especially when our vision of who we are is not the same as the Lord's.

We all have a hard time voluntarily giving up independence, but the independent Ephraim's Children may have even more difficulty doing this. Neal A. Maxwell also tells us that "the submission of one's will is really the only uniquely personal thing we have to place on God's altar. The many other things we 'give' . . . are actually the things He has already given or loaned to us. However, when you and I finally submit ourselves, by letting our individual wills be swallowed up in God's will, then we are really giving something to Him! It is the only possession which is truly ours to give."5

### Independence

The prophet Lehi talked about two types of things in this world: the "things to act" and the "things to be acted upon."6 "God gave unto man that he should act for himself"7 and "not to be acted upon."8 We have been granted the freedom to act for ourselves. Our loving Heavenly Father has insured that we have the opportunity to exercise our independence while on this earth.

Independent Ephraim's Children need opportunities to exercise their independence. William G. Dyer comments in his *Ensign* article "Interdependence: A Family and Church

Goal" that many parents see independence in their children and often try to stifle, reduce, or change it. "Children don't want to share their toys with others, but parents want them to share. Children want to run around the church during Sunday School, but adults want them to sit still; children don't want to eat certain foods, but mother wants them to clean their plates. There seems to be a subtle (and sometimes not so subtle) struggle going on between the adults, who want to channel or control, and the youngsters, who want to be independent and free to do as they please."9 Unfortunately, struggles over control and independence can develop into rebellion, and continual struggling can make rebellion a habit. Some people are so used to resisting authority that they spend extraordinary amounts of time and energy just automatically resisting. Sometimes we must stop ourselves and let our independent Ephraim's Child be independent.

It can be challenging to stand back and let your child do things for herself, especially when she has a hard time or sometimes even fails. Parents want the best for their children and do not like watching them struggle, but this is an important part of growing up. Donald K. Jarvis talks in his *Ensign* article "Leaving Eden: A Lesson for Parents" about how the most important task for children for the first part of childhood is obedience. However, as children grow older, they gradually must learn to act independently. He says that shifting from obedience to independence is difficult. "Ideally, parents should help their children make a gradual transition by carefully guiding the children as they exercise increasingly more independence. But in practice, it is very difficult for parents to know when and where to step back and allow their children freedom. Parents understandably make mistakes—by either giving too much or too little leeway. But even if parents' timing is perfect, they simply cannot smooth out all the bumps: at some point, all children will make mistakes and have the opportunity to learn from them."10

Instead of automatically assuming that your child is

unable to do something that he wants to do, let your child try it. You may be surprised at how much your Ephraim's Child can do without you in the way. You can stay nearby to offer help if it is needed. And then perhaps the best help is verbal help so that your child can still do the task herself. It will often take extra patience to not jump in and do it yourself so that it can be done more quickly, but the growth your child can experience is ultimately worth the inconvenience.

Independent Ephraim's Children can be very motivated to do things on their own. They can get very frustrated when their bodies are unable to do what they want them to. Perhaps a two-year-old's hand coordination is just not developed enough to operate a car seat buckle. You will need to help your child find appropriate ways to express her frustration. Then show her how to break down the task into small steps that can be accomplished easier.

The young independent Ephraim's Child often requires more supervision. He truly believes himself capable of doing anything by himself, so why shouldn't he cross the street by himself? Why does he need to hold your hand in a public place if he is able to walk unassisted? The independent Ephraim's Children are often daredevils, with little concept of possible danger. Safety is often a major issue during the early years.

While you are grinding your teeth in frustration because your Ephraim's Child refuses to let you help him put his socks on despite five minutes of his failed attempts, just imagine what he must have been like before coming to Earth. These spirits were probably just as independent. Most likely they did not wait around for anyone to do things for them or help; they did it themselves. They were probably dependable and capable. It is not surprising then that they are so adamant to do things for themselves. They know that they can.

The Lord needs strong people like this who are willing to go against the tide of worldly pursuits and values. If the independent Ephraim's Child is set on a righteous path, then her fervent independence can be a protection for her and a tool in the hand of the Lord. Joseph F. Smith has said:

> It requires no especial bravery on the part of men to swim with the currents of the world. When a man makes up his mind to forsake the world and its follies and sins, and identify himself with God's people, who are everywhere spoken evil of, it takes courage, manhood, independence of character, superior intelligence and a determination that is not common among men; for men shrink from that which is unpopular, from that which will not bring them praise and adulation, from that which will in any degree tarnish that which they call honor or a good name.[11]

## Interdependence

There is a time and place for both dependence and independence. However, there is another type of relationship that is both possible and desirable: interdependence. Being interdependent means being mutually dependent, or dependent on each other. William G. Dyer, Ph.D., author of the article "Interdependence: A Family and Church Goal," defines interdependence as the cooperative or collaborative using of each other's resources.[12]

Interdependence is neither complete independence, nor complete dependence. A person is not free from all authority; he is not independent of others. But neither is a person dependent on others with no responsibility of his own. Interdependence is a mixture of both independence and dependence. We are an interdependent people. In order for society to work smoothly all the parts work independently yet are mutually dependent on the other parts. Unfortunately, many people do not learn interdependence with others. We can teach this important skill at home.

On the consequences of and remedies for rebellion, William Dyer has said:

> In our society we see all around us the consequences of young people in rebellion. They are either in revolt against

authority or have never learned how to work with authority persons. Training in collaborative problem-solving and team effort must be taught in the home. This does not mean parents allowing their children license to do whatever they please, nor does it mean children slavishly carrying out the whims of parents; rather, it is a solid condition of mutual effort based on love, concern, and trust.[13]

William Dyer also gave five guidelines to help us develop greater interdependence.[14]

## 1. Love and Concern
The Ephraim's Child must know that his parents really care about him as a person, and not only if he does what he is told. Parents need to talk about their feelings of love and concern, no matter how awkward or difficult it may be.

## 2. Trust
Persons in authority need to display greater confidence and trust in those under them. Parents need to trust their children to make correct decisions and need to give them the opportunity to do so. Joseph Smith said that he governed the Latter-day Saints by "[teaching] the people correct principles and they govern themselves."[15] Our job as parents in authority is to teach correct principles, and then trust our children to govern themselves within age-appropriate situations.

## 3. Open Communication
To have interdependence there needs to be open communication. This means opportunities for both parties to speak and to listen. If we want true understanding we must do both. "Most parents share little of their own feelings or ideas with their children. Giving directions, orders, and commands is not sharing. Sharing comes first, before the decisions are finally made, and is a process of getting thoughts and feelings out in the open so a good decision can be made."[16]

## 4. Shared Decisions

Interdependence requires that decisions be made in a collaborative way. Shared decisions are not necessarily fifty-fifty decisions, when each person always demands an equal part in everything. Most times both parties will listen to each other and work out a solution both can support and implement.

## 5. Joint Action

Interdependence means working together. In too many instances, parents tell the children what to do. The parents pressure, control, or punish until the child complies. Often, too little is planned and carried out together.

We want to teach our Ephraim's Children the skill of inter-dependence so that they can be more productive as adults. The ability to work interdependently with others will be a prized asset for your child in the job market, and an essential skill for a successful marriage. Interdependence is not only valuable in the temporal sphere, but eternally as well.

In his book *An Introduction to the Gospel*, Lowell L. Bennion talks about the strength of the gospel of Jesus Christ that lies in the interdependence of Deity and man. Man is not saved by grace alone, but neither can he save himself without it. Salvation from the grave comes to us through the grace of Christ; we are wholly dependent upon Him for this thing. But the ultimate goal—eternal life—requires individual work as well as the resurrection. In order for man to develop the intelligent, moral, and spiritual state required for eternal life, he must do some work. It cannot be done for him. Thus, salvation is a goal that requires interdependence between Deity and man.[17]

"This is our earnest belief. It robs God of nothing precious. He and the Son are eagerly striving to lead, teach, persuade, and inspire man to help him gain eternal life. But we, too, must play our part, assume our responsibility. It is a law of life, which we see operative everywhere, in nature, in education, in human relations, even as in religion."[18]

Independent Ephraim's Children possess a valuable trait. A better understanding of dependence, independence, and interdependence can help these children be better tools of the Lord in building His kingdom.

# 13

# Disciplining the Ephraim's Child

Ephraim's Children need parents who are willing to be just as persistent and adamant as their strong-willed children when it comes to teaching basic rules and values. As parents, we have the primary responsibility to teach our children; to train them to become righteous adults and parents themselves. It is our job to direct them to "walk uprightly before the Lord."[1] This requires discipline. "If parents do not discipline their children, then the public will discipline them in a way the parents do not like. Without discipline, children will not respect either the rules of the home or of society."[2]

The Ephraim's Child not only requires more discipline, but takes more effort and knowledge on your part as well. This chapter was born out of our desperation and feelings of failure in attempting to discipline our own Ephraim's Child. Parents who are truly trying to find joy in parenthood feel despondent after the day ends and they review the number of times they lost their temper, yelled, became frustrated, and fought with their Ephraim's Child. They understand the importance of disciplining children to become righteous, responsible adults, but are at their wits' end on how to do it with this child. This chapter is what we found in answer to prayers and honest searching.

## Obedience

A principle purpose for discipline is to teach obedience. To many people, the very word "obedience" is a term signifying oppression. They feel it is tyrannical to expect obedience from another human being. In one book the authors stated, "We define obedience as following rules without question, regardless of philosophical beliefs, ideas of right and wrong, instincts and experiences, or values."3 Often, the word *obedience* is linked with the word *blind*, implying that to obey is to not see.

In contrast with blind obedience is faith obedience, which is obedience that comes from understanding. Boyd K. Packer sheds some important insight on obedience. He said:

> Latter-day Saints are not obedient because they are compelled to be obedient. They are obedient because they know certain spiritual truths and have decided, as an expression of their own individual agency, to obey the commandments of God. . . . Those who talk of blind obedience may appear to know many things, but they do not understand the doctrines of the gospel. There is an obedience that comes from a knowledge of the truth that transcends any external form of control. We are not obedient because we are blind, we are obedient because we can see.4

Rather than oppressing us, obedience can give us freedom. Marion G. Romney talked about the freedom that is obtained through faith obedience, rather than blind obedience. In his article, "The Perfect Law of Liberty," he stated: "Freedom thus obtained—that is, by obedience to the law of Christ—is freedom of the soul, the highest form of liberty. And the most glorious thing about it is that it is within the reach of every one of us. . . . All we have to do is learn the law of Christ and obey it. To learn it and obey it is the primary purpose of every soul's mortal life."5

Obedience is not harmful or oppressive. It is an eternal concept and is required to obtain blessings. "There is a law, irrevocably decreed in heaven before the foundations of this world, upon which all blessings are predicated. And when we obtain any blessing from God, it is by obedience to that law upon which it is predicated."6 Obedience is also essential to obtain salvation.

It is important to realize that you cannot force your Ephraim's Child to obey just because you demand it, and Ephraim's Children will almost assuredly not obey just because they are supposed to. Remember, your child does have a choice whether or not to obey, and sometimes he will choose not to just to prove that he does have a choice. We all know people that immediately get their hackles up when they are told they have to do something. It doesn't matter what, they will refuse to do it simply because they were told they had to.

Often parents use words that sound like ultimatums, which can escalate conflict rather than diffuse it. Phrases like "you must," "you have to," or "there's no way you're going to" can make your child automatically want to disobey. Sometimes getting your child to obey is simply a matter of presentation and communication. When you tell your child, "Don't talk to me in that tone of voice!" you are using words that may come across as ultimatums. An alternative could be, "I will listen when you can talk in a calm voice." Sometimes we just have to search for the right phrase and keep from ordering our kids around all the time. As you choose your wording, you may find that your Ephraim's Child cooperates more.

Requiring obedience is important and necessary, but taken to extremes it can become unrighteous dominion. As we are told in D&C 121:39, "it is the nature and disposition of almost all men, as soon as they get a little authority . . . they will immediately begin to exercise unrighteous dominion." As we guide our children in learning obedience, we need to rely on the Spirit because when we try "to exercise control or dominion or compulsion upon the souls of the children of men, in any degree of unrighteousness, behold, the heavens withdraw themselves."[7]

William Arthur Ward, author, once said, "Every great person has first learned how to obey, whom to obey, and when to obey."[8] As children of our Eternal Heavenly Father we are all destined for greatness. "Obedience," James E.

Faust has said, "helps us develop the full potential our Heavenly Father desires for us in becoming celestial beings worthy someday to live in His presence."9 It is vital that we teach our children how to obey, and that is a tall order with an Ephraim's Child.

## The Challenge of Disciplining the Ephraim's Child

Some parents are fortunate to have a child who is anxious to please and whose mild temperament makes discipline easy. In *Setting Limits with Your Strong-Willed Child*, author Robert J. MacKenzie remarks that parents of these kinds of children often do not need to learn effective discipline techniques because their child is so compliant that even ineffective discipline works. Parents of an Ephraim's Child do not have this luxury. These children will often argue about everything and test parents repeatedly. "To them, the word 'stop' is just theory. They want to know what will happen if they don't stop, and they know how to find out. They continue to test and push us to the point of action to see what happens."10

Does this sound familiar? Regularly, the Ephraim's Child will test the limits, demand, pester, argue, and persist until you have one nerve left and are praying for a miracle to find more patience. He knows how to push buttons to reduce you to rage in seconds. He constantly chooses to do things the hard way. Nothing seems to work. You look at other children who just obey and wonder what is wrong with you or your child. Be assured that nothing is wrong with either of you. You have been blessed with the challenge of disciplining an Ephraim's Child.

Why are these children so hard to discipline? It often has to do with your child's temperament. Once you understand your child's temperament, it is easier to understand why your discipline techniques aren't working and why he repeatedly needs to "test" you. This is why we discussed temperamental traits of the Ephraim's Child before we addressed discipline. If you skipped those chapters, then go back! You need the background of why your child is the way he is. Dr. MacKenzie comments that "the problem many parents experience is that they invest too much time and energy trying to change the one thing they can't change—their child's temperament. We can't change temperament, but we can understand it, guide it, and shape it in positive directions."[11]

How come your Ephraim's Child either defies or challenges your rules or just ignores them? These children do much of their learning "the hard way." They often need to experience the consequences of their own choices and behavior before they can learn the lesson we are trying to teach. Dr. Mackenzie explains that your child frequently tests the rules by "doing research" to see what he can get away with. If ignoring the rule lets him get out of doing something that he doesn't want to do, then he is unlikely to listen. Even if he delays doing something for five or ten minutes or if you give in half the time and let him out of doing it, that is usually enough to reinforce his defiance. And as in the case with scientific research, the experiment is duplicated multiple times to double-check the findings. "[These] children need to experience your boundaries repeatedly before they accept them as mandatory, not optional."[12]

Ephraim's Children test frequently, and consequently they require more frequent discipline than children who do not test as much. This is a fact of life. When you can accept this rather than let it drive you nuts, you can change your attitude and perspective. MacKenzie writes about his own experience in learning this lesson. He writes: "[My child's] job was to test, and my job was to guide him in the right direction. . . . My new perspective didn't change his behavior, but it sure made my life a lot easier. I stopped taking it personally."[13] When you stop taking it personally, you no longer spend the energy being upset because your child is the way he is. You can move on to more effective discipline.

## Discipline vs. Punishment

The first thing to understand is that discipline is not punishment. The word "discipline" has the same root as the word "disciple." A disciple is a student; someone to be taught. Therefore discipline is training that corrects, molds, or perfects. In the *Ensign* article "Punishment—or Discipline," the authors point out that punishment, on the other hand, "calls for 'retributive suffering.' Punishment is directed at the child himself. Discipline is directed more at the objectionable behavior of the child; it is something we do for our children, not to them."14 Punishment is more of a release of tension for the person delivering it, and usually will not teach a child better behavior.

We can change our vocabulary and replace the word "punishment" with the word "discipline," but it is still punishment if the motivation is wrong. Discipline is motivated by love. Love is not an action or a technique that you can learn. It is a feeling that guides our actions. "When love fills our hearts, our actions reflect that love, and our desire is to do only that which will benefit our children. When we feel love, our actions toward a child who is arguing with his brother will not be a result of our own frustration. Rather, they will reflect our desire that he not harm himself through a habit of contention."15

Christ was the perfect example of how love can be used to discipline and to teach. He was patient with the imperfections of his disciples, and in spite of their imperfect behavior he maintained a loving relationship with them. But he did not condone or ignore their undesirable behavior. When they needed correction, he taught them. While doing so he always showed them the respect due children of our Heavenly Father.

Our children deserve this same kind of relationship as we teach and train them. Many times, however, we view our children more as objects than as individuals—pushing them around or putting them away when not in use. When we forget that our children deserve our respect, our relationship with them becomes one of correction and commands. We need to remember that the child you found decorating the bathroom with chocolate syrup is still a child of God with infinite worth. President Gordon B. Hinckley reminds us that:

> The Lord, in setting forth the spirit of governance in his church, has also set forth the spirit of governance in the home in these great words of revelation: "No power or influence can or ought to be maintained . . . only by persuasion, by long-suffering, by gentleness and meekness, and by love unfeigned. . . . Reproving betimes with sharpness, when moved upon by the Holy Ghost [and only then I think]; and then *showing forth afterwards an increase of love* toward him whom thou hast reproved, lest he esteem thee to be his enemy; That he may know that thy faithfulness is stronger than the cords of death" (D&C 121;41, 43-44). . . . When little problems occur, as they inevitably will, restrain yourself. . . . There is no discipline in all the world like the discipline of love. It has a magic all its own.[16]

Eugene Mead, Brigham Young University professor of Child Development and Family Relations, has said, "I think there are two main principles involved in effective discipline. The first is one where parents take a positive approach to discipline—looking for things children do right instead of punishing them for their shortcomings. The other principle operates on the idea that families can train their children to be responsible."[17] We will discuss the first principle briefly, and then delve into the second in the rest of the chapter.

### Reward the Good

Behavioral Psychology views human behavior in terms of reinforcement. Very simply, behavior that is reinforced is likely to be repeated, and those behaviors that are not reinforced will likely disappear. In his book *Parenting With Love: Making a Difference in a Day*, Glenn I. Latham states:

Of all the consequences that reinforce the behavior of children, I have found nothing to be more powerful than parental attention. Over the years . . . I have been interested to note that, on average, more than 95 percent of all appropriate child behavior never receives any parental attention whatsoever. . . . On the other hand, parents are five to six times more likely to pay attention to their children when the children are behaving inappropriately. . . . For the most part, ironically, the very behaviors that annoy and concern parents most are the very behaviors parents are encouraging.[18]

Ordinarily parents try to *make* their children behave, and then punish them when they don't. Latham contends that research has shown that the most effective way to reduce problem behavior in children is to strengthen the desirable behavior through positive reinforcement rather than try to weaken undesirable behavior through negative means.[19] Rewarding your children when they are good is more effective because it motivates children to want to behave.

To reward the good, you need to catch your children being good. For many parents this requires a change of outlook. How can you reward good behavior when you focus primarily on what children do wrong? At first you may need to create opportunities to offer praise and give credit. Carol McAdoo Rehme wrote in the *Ensign* about her family's efforts to reward the good. She says:

We became vigilant observers, alert to small acts of obedience and deeds of kindness, and we were lavish with our compliments. We discovered that the younger children needed to see immediate results for their actions, and they soon began thriving on our renewed applause. The older ones sought our approval for their choices, our appreciation for their efforts, our admiration for their accomplishments. . . . To our amazement, we saw our children respond to our new emphasis with a desire to please us.[20]

The question then arises: what do you do when your children behave well? In this Latham also gives some guidance. He suggests acknowledging appropriate behavior verbally, through touch, or through positive eye contact. These positive interactions should be numerous—aim at having twenty or more brief, intermittent positive interactions per hour with children, particularly young children.[21] Vary the positive reinforcers—do not just say "good job" all the time.

When you reward the good you will naturally increase the positive environment in your home. You may be surprised to see less misbehavior as this happens. Family members will be more cheerful and comfortable in the home, making it more of a safe haven from the world. However, you will still have times when discipline is required. How can we more effectively discipline our Ephraim's Children?

## Be Clear

"Behold, mine house is a house of order, saith the Lord God, and not a house of confusion."[22] "Order is an eternal principle—an important characteristic of the kingdom of God. We are instructed to follow the pattern and set our own houses in order. Frederick G. Williams was told: 'And now a commandment I give unto you—if you will be delivered you shall set in order your own house' (D&C 93:43)."[23]

Effective discipline should be done with order, not confusion. The first step is to have a game plan. This includes a plan for discipline as well as family rules. Without a plan, parents are likely to rely simply on instinct and react emotionally to each situation. Rules are the things that you as adults will dig in your heels and go to battle over. These matter so much that you are willing to meet your child head-on.

If you don't want to argue with your Ephraim's Child all day long, it is essential that your basic ground rules are very clear and precise. Ambiguous rules are open for testing because the Ephraim's Child will always look for clarification. In our household, we do not allow the children much sugar, and we were constantly arguing over what was "enough" sugar. It was frustrating to have our persistent Ephraim's Child pestering us for candy, and he was frustrated because his view of "enough" sugar was vastly different than ours. Finally, we decided to make it clear so that the arguments would end. He gets one "sugar" per day, and only during certain times of the day. Clarifying this rule has not stopped our child from asking for more than one sugar on the off chance we will give in, but the Candy War of 2002 has ended at our house. Look at your rules. Some may need to be clarified and made less subjective. Give clear, unquestionable parameters such as "one candy" versus "enough candy." There is no question over the definition of "one," like there is over what exactly "enough" means.

If your children are old enough, take some time to discuss your rules with them. Explain why you have the rule and what is expected. Give children some say in establishing family rules. As the adult, you are the ultimate authority, but each child may have something to contribute that you have not considered. Rules can be merely orders if autocratically imposed, or they can be responsibilities that children agree are essential to an orderly home.

## Be Consistent

Once rules are clear, you will have fewer battles with your Ephraim's Child, but she will still test them. And she will test you numerous times. Ephraim's Children constantly check their boundaries. All children feel more secure knowing their boundaries, but Ephraim's Children are even more this way. They go crazy if the rules keep changing or aren't enforced every time. Just like a night watchman who still checks all the doors even though they were locked the last time he checked, these kids continually rattle the doorknobs of our rules to make sure they are still locked.

We were once told a story about a young boy that always sat down to dinner without washing his hands, even though the rule was that he had to wash his hands first. Exasperated that she had to send him to wash his hands every day, his mother asked him why he always ignored the rule. He replied, "Because one time you forgot." He did not wash his hands on the chance that his mother would forget again.

The Ephraim's Child requires consistency in discipline. When rule violations happen at an inconvenient time or place, we may be tempted to let things slide. If you relax on enforcing rules, chances are your child will not let you forget it. Then, when you are ready to adhere to the rules again, you have made life more difficult for yourself. One mother let her child avoid his naptime one day when a cousin was over. For the next two months her Ephraim's Child reminded her at naptime that the other day he did not have to do it. Do not reward your child's "research" with laxness. You *must* be consistent.

It is important that both parents are on the same page and are disciplining the same way. Discipline cannot be consistent if both parents do not agree. Elder Dallin H. Oaks has said that "the father presides and has the ultimate responsibility in the government of the home, but parenting is obviously a shared responsibility. Both parents occupy a leading role in teaching their children, and both must counsel together and support one another. . . . In the sacred task of teaching the children of God, parents should unite and combine their efforts to dispel the powers of darkness from the lives of their children."[24] Once parents are unified in purpose, they need to be willing to make sacrifices to consistently act in that purpose.

In the article "Punishment—or Discipline," authors Layne E. and Jana Squires Flake write:

> In order for discipline to be effective, it must be both pre-dictable and consistent. Children need to know that Mom and Dad will do what they say they will. If discipline is a "sometimes" proposition, children soon learn that certain situations and environments provide a sanctuary from misbehavior. Church services, restaurants, or grocery

stores are frequently such sanctuaries. Even home can become a sanctuary for misbehavior when guests are present. Some children find they can misbehave in these circumstances without the threat of discipline because their parents don't wish to be embarrassed or inconvenienced. On other occasions parents may feel too tired or too busy to be bothered with enforcing family rules. When children feel their parents cannot be counted on to maintain discipline, they lose respect for parental authority. . . . And they may become insecure if they are never sure what reaction their behavior will evoke from their parents.[25]

Being consistent between spouses is important, but you must also be consistent with yourself. Your words and actions must be consistent with each other. Many times we say something but our actions speak otherwise. When our words do not match our actions, children learn to ignore our words and base their beliefs on what they experience. When your words are consistent with your actions, then your child will begin to take what you say seriously and tune in more. How does your Ephraim's Child know that your spoken rules are really the rules you practice? He tests. Remember the difference between rules and expectations, and when you need to be immovable or more flexible. When your child does break rules, he needs to know that *every time* he does it you will stop him.

## Be Firm

Once your rules are clear and consistent, you need to move ahead confidently. Your child needs clear, consistent, and firm limits to guide him in the right direction. To enforce rules with the persistent Ephraim's Child, you must be firm. The word *firm* means showing resolute determination. This does not mean yelling or using an angry voice, but using a voice that shows you are serious; you mean business. If you do not feel confident enough as a parent, try practicing. New missionaries go through practice and training before going out in the field. Follow their example. Grab a spouse or friend and role-play so that you can practice being firm. When alone, practice in front of the mirror.

Being firm does not mean that you are a bad parent, nor does it indicate that you care less. The Lord is very clear and firm with his children when it comes to rules. Thou shalt not steal. Period, end of discussion. To gain exaltation, certain steps must be taken for everyone. The Lord does not equivocate on His rules. He is very firm, but He still loves us.

When you say "no" to your kids does it really mean no? Or does it actually mean yes, sometimes, or maybe? In *Setting Limits with Your Strong-Willed Child*, author Robert J. MacKenzie discusses the difference between firm limits and soft limits.[26] Firm limits are clear signals. They are words supported with effective action where compliance is both expected and required. Soft limits are mixed messages or unclear signals about our rules and expectations.

Soft limits are rules in theory but not in practice. Words are not supported with action, so compliance is optional. As a result, children learn to tune out and ignore our words and push us to the point of action more often. "[Soft limits] invite testing because they carry a mixed message. The words seem to say stop, but the action message says that stopping is neither expected nor required."[27] Many times children will acknowledge the signal, but continue to do what they want anyway. For Ephraim's Children, soft limits often lead to testing and power struggles.

Chances are that you use soft limits more than you realize. Here are some typical examples of soft limits (adapted from *Setting Limits with Your Strong-Willed Child*):[28]

1. *Wishes, hopes, and shoulds.* "I wish you would stop taking your sister's toys all the time" is an example. This gives the message that stopping would be nice, but you don't really have to.
2. *Repeating and reminding.* When you tell your Ephraim's

Child to turn off the TV and she does not do it, many parents repeat themselves four more times before doing anything to ensure compliance. How is your child supposed to know which time you really mean it?

3. *Warnings and second chances.* In actuality these just let your child misbehave numerous times without a meaningful consequence.

4. *Explanations and reasoning.* Your child just has to listen to you explain something, and she still doesn't have to obey.

5. *Speeches, lectures, and sermons.* If your child can tolerate an annoying lecture, she can do what she wants.

6. *Ignoring the misbehavior.* We have already discussed why this often does not work with the Ephraim's Child. Robert J. MacKenzie also says, "What makes us think that the absence of a green light is equivalent to a red light? At best it's a yellow light, and we know how strong-willed children respond to yellow lights."[29]

7. *Poor role modeling.* When you yell at your kids for yelling at each other, then you are modeling the same behavior you are punishing.

8. *Pleading, begging, and cajoling.* This sends the message to do it when you feel like it.

9. *Bargaining and negotiating.* To the Ephraim's Child, this often makes compliance feel optional.

10. *Arguing or debating.* These send the message that your rules are subject to argument and debate.

11. *Bribes and special rewards.* Cooperation can be seen as optional and contingent upon receiving a reward.

Firm limits, on the other hand, clearly communicate rules and expectations. Parents' words say stop, and by their action they enforce their words. Firm limits are stated in clear, direct, concrete behavioral terms where the words are supported by actions. With firm limits, "children understand that we mean what we say because they experience what they hear. Words are consistent with actions. They learn to regard our words seriously, test less, and cooperate more often for the asking. The result—better communication, less testing, and fewer power struggles."[30]

Firm limits give clear information so that your child can make his own choice. You tell your child what his choices are and then hold him accountable. "Go pick up your toys on the floor or I will put them away for a week" is an example of a firm limit. "Your friends will have to go home if you cannot share your toys" is another example. Both of these examples are firm limits, but only if you follow through if your child chooses not to comply.

Part of being firm is being calm. Anger, drama, and strong emotion reduce the clarity of your message and distract you and your child from the issue. In her book *You Can't Make Me*, Cynthia Tobias talks about how your actions will always be more effective than your emotions. She agrees that parents of these kids often have good reason for becoming angry and upset with their children's behavior. "But anger is usually the least effective way to change [your child's] attitude or behavior. If you allow your anger to control your use of discipline techniques, you are almost certainly doomed to failure."[31]

To be firm you also must take responsibility as the authority figure instead of foisting it off on someone else. This happens when parents say things like, "Grandma would not like you to play with that picture," instead of, "Do not play with that picture or you will have to go in another room." The first statement almost makes Grandma a scapegoat, so that our child gets mad at her rather than us. When you know that you are going to get a strong reaction from your Ephraim's Child, it can be tempting to try and diffuse it or direct it somewhere else. Using firm limits requires that we take responsibility, but also puts us in full authority.

You have clarified your rules, you are committed to being consistent, and you are ready to be firm and stop your Ephraim's Child when she is doing something she shouldn't. However, we need to take discipline one step further and teach children the importance of choice and consequences.

"Whom the Lord loveth he correcteth."[32] Yes, we need to "correct" as the Lord would have us do, but how?

## Using Discipline to Teach—Natural Consequences

"Discipline is not simply a means of maintaining control until children mature into responsible adults. Rather, it should be a means by which we teach and instill that responsibility. . . . Discipline is an excellent means of teaching self-control and responsible behavior."[33] To raise responsible, faithful children, we must teach them to govern themselves. Children who have learned to govern themselves take responsibility for their feelings, thoughts, actions, and decisions. Since our children will not always be under our supervision, we want to equip them as early as possible to use sound judgment and understand how to evaluate the consequences of their own choices.[34] Using discipline to teach requires more work than scolding or ignoring misbehavior. When discipline involves the natural result of misbehavior, it is more effective.

"We lived in the spirit world as intelligent beings and as the spirit children of God had free agency, were endowed with the capacity to choose, but we were and are now warned, as was Adam, that we must take the consequences of our choice."[35] The Lord has made sure that we have the freedom to choose, but each choice is irrevocably linked to a consequence. If you choose to run across the street without looking for cars, you might get hit by one. That is a consequence of your decision.

Unfortunately, many want to avoid the consequences of their actions. We need to allow our children to experience the repercussions of their actions, whether they are good or bad. "Don't protect your child from the consequences of his actions. When you as a parent step in to protect your child against the natural consequences of his . . . actions, his opportunities to learn life skills are impeded."[36]

True discipline teaches children to learn from their

mistakes so that they do not repeat the same ones when parents are not around to protect them. This requires that they accept their role in creating the outcome. When disciplining with consequences, we must make a concerted effort to switch emphasis from guilt and blame to planning future behavior change. Your child is not a bad person because she broke a rule, but she does have to experience the repercussions. By so doing, hopefully she will learn from her mistake and change her behavior in the future.

In the book *Discipline With Dignity*, the authors Richard L. Curwin and Allen N. Mendler advocate disciplining with natural consequences rather than using punishment. They see punishment as less effective because often the punishment has no natural connection to the rule. If your child hits, he goes to time out. If your child disobeys, he goes to time-out. If your child dumps his food on the floor, he goes to time-out. But what does time-out have to do with any of the rules violated? Punishment seems to work because there are fewer violations visible, but there is less learning about responsibility. Through punishment, children usually learn that they do not want to get caught.

In contrast to punishment, consequences are directly related to the rule, are both natural and logical, and help the rule violator learn acceptable behavior from the experience. "Their intent is instructional rather than punitive because they are designed to teach [children] the positive or negative effects of their behavior."37 When we use consequences instead of punishment we allow our children to experience the repercussions of their actions. A child learns that if he chooses to do something, even if his parents are not there to punish him, he has to face the consequences of his actions. He is learning an important fact of life.

## Consequences Work Best When . . .

### 1. They are natural and/or logical.

When you use consequences for discipline, they need to be natural and/or logical (natural outcomes of a rule violation) to be effective. In life, consequences are usually natural; they naturally result from an action. For example, when we are caught breaking the speed limit, we receive a speeding ticket; we are not thrown in jail as we would have been if we committed armed robbery.

Here are some examples of natural consequences. A child makes a mess, then is required to clean it up. If a child constantly fights with friends who come over to play, then the friends are sent home until the child can restrain himself from fighting. If a child refuses to eat her lunch, then she does not get any snacks before dinner. Natural consequences make sense because there is a natural progression from cause to effect.

If, for some reason, a natural consequence is not an option, then consequences need to be logical. For example, you cannot let your child experience the natural consequences of playing in a busy street, so you must find an alternate consequence that is logically linked. In this example, a logical consequence could be that your child is restricted from the front yard for a period of time. Another example of a logical consequence is if your child refuses to stay in bed at night, then she is not allowed a bed and must sleep on the floor for a while. Natural consequences are usually logical as well.

When the consequences are natural and/or logical, then they make sense. It is harder to argue with such a reasonable result, and as parents you will not have to wonder if your discipline is appropriate. This is how life works. Action and consequence are linked, and when consequences are natural and/or logical, you can teach proper behavior through experience, rather than scolding.

### 2. They are related to the rule.

If your child hits his sibling and you make him sleep on the floor, then what good will that consequence do? Sleeping on the floor has nothing to do with hitting. Can your child make a clear connection between his actions and the consequence? This is one of the reasons why time-out sometimes does not work. Parents use time-out for a wide range of rule violations, yet time-out is only related to a very small percentage of the rules being broken. If the consequence is not related to the rule, then the child will have difficulty seeing the link between the two.

### 3. They are consistent.

Predictability is important to help children understand what the results of their behaviors will be. When consequences are random, children begin to doubt they can influence their future. If adults let minor things go as they slowly reach the breaking point, then blow up over some little infraction (like the straw that broke the camel's back), mixed messages are being sent to children. They will have a harder time predicting the results of their actions.

### 4. They are clear and specific.

In order for your Ephraim's Child to govern himself, in the early years you need to be very clear and specific. You will need to tell him why you are setting the consequence that you are. In the early years, a child has a very hazy idea of cause and effect. He needs to be taught the nature of things and why certain decisions garner certain results. This does not mean launching into a lengthy explanation full of "what if's" that will lose your child's attention. Keep your reasoning brief, clear, and specific. "You chose to track mud in the house, so you need to mop the floor to clean it up."

### 5. The severity of the consequences matches the circumstances of the behavior.

The consequence needs to match the behavior. Some

rules are more important than others and usually demand harsher consequences. Hitting or biting are more severe than dumping sand on the floor, for example. Consequences can become punishment if delivered too aggressively, and they are less effective if they are too harsh or incongruous. On the flip side, if you impose consequences that are not severe enough, your child will not gain a realistic idea of the repercussions of his actions. Perhaps the biggest mistake that parents make when disciplining is loss of control.

There are few occasions when spanking is as effective as other methods of correcting misbehavior. The Church's guidelines for parents suggest using physical punishment rarely and with restraint.[38] Physical punishment, in fact, loses its effectiveness when used with any frequency. And it is often not effective at all with an Ephraim's child. Some sleep-deprived parents, frantic to find anything that would keep their young child in bed at night, decided to try spanking. After every spanking the child looked at the parents as if to say, "Is that the best you can do?" And he still got out of bed. What finally worked with this persistent Ephraim's Child was using consequences.

The big problem with spanking is that it is generally used for the wrong reasons. No discipline, particularly physical discipline, should be used to vent our anger. Sadly, many parents go way too far in their use of physical discipline. Recently, much attention has been given to child abuse, both in and out of the LDS Church. It is wise to steer clear from something so fraught with the danger of getting carried away.

### Using Consequences Takes More Effort

Disciplining with consequences requires more control and thought. Parents need to slow down and learn to act instead of react to a situation; they can't fly off the handle and send their children to their room for every infraction. Mothers and fathers should step back from their emotions to review each circumstance and decide what to do. And then they should act, despite how tired they are, despite the inconvenience, and despite who is watching.

"Sometimes when we correct children, we merely react to the circumstance. The child's action upsets our plans or our image of ourselves as good parents, and we become frustrated or angry. Action taken with such an attitude is seldom helpful. It erodes the relationship we have developed with our children and lowers their feelings of self-respect. But as we learn to discipline our own feelings, yielding to the whisperings of the Spirit, we can make discipline a learning experience."39

Disciplining through consequences may take more effort than you are used to, especially at first. Is the extra effort worth it? If you are tired of feeling like the wicked witch (or warlock) of the west, then it is worth it. If you want to punish less and enjoy your Ephraim's Child more, then it is worth it. If you want a child who is responsible and can govern himself, then it is worth it. Remember the ancient proverb: "Train up a child in the way he should go: and when he is old, he will not depart from it."40 After all, it is easier to build children than to repair adults.

# 14

# When You Don't Like
# Your Ephraim's Child

We all begin the journey of parenthood with preconceived ideas about what it will be like. Maybe your vision resembled a commercial: parents wait by the Christmas tree while angelic children rub the sleep from their eyes and look around the room in delight on Christmas morning. Or maybe you envisioned spending one-on-one time with your daughter, getting her dressed up in frilly dresses and doing her hair. Most likely, your vision included you and your child spending time together doing things that you like to do.

Chances are that your vision did not include the holy terror that visits you on Christmas Day in the body of your Ephraim's Child, or the daughter that refuses at the top of her lungs to wear dresses because she can't stand the way they feel. You probably didn't see yourself trying to talk your child into doing something fun while she resists with every fiber of her being. And most of us did not dream about the child who yells things like, "Stop choking me!" in the middle of sacrament meeting when we try to keep her quiet. What about that child of your dreams?

Those times when you stand outside the closed door of your child's room listening to him rip the blankets off his bed in rage and frustration you might think, "I didn't sign up for this!" Life with an Ephraim's Child sometimes feels like a constant roller coaster ride, with each day bringing another battery of ups and downs. Some nights you collapse into bed, wondering if it is possible to get enough sleep to have the energy you know you will need for tomorrow. Sometimes you are afraid to even let other people sit down in your house because they become automatic jungle gyms. And then there is the embarrassment when your child does things like go through your boss's lunch—in his office—at work.

He's difficult. He's loud. He flips out over nothing. He doesn't comfort easily. He's demanding. He rules the house with emotional outbursts. He won't let you sit and rest for even a moment. He wears you out. You don't dare leave him with babysitters very often and the extended family members look stricken if you suggest babysitting to them. People look at you like you are greatly lacking in parental skills, or like you are a tyrant when you have to be so controlling of your child in public. If you could check the option box "return to sender," would you? What about those times when you feel that you don't like your Ephraim's Child?

If your Ephraim's Child does not share the characteristics you envisioned in your dream child, you may have a hard time reconciling reality with your fantasy. Letting go of your dream child can be very difficult. It can even be one of the most difficult tasks you face as a parent, but it is essential. Your child needs you to do it. If you are too busy regretting what your child is not, then you may not be able to see the unique qualities that your child does have. You may be spending energy and effort trying to change your child into the "perfect child." In these cases your dream child can interfere in your relationship with your real child.

## What You May Feel

Ephraim's Children manage to bring out strong emotions in others, especially their parents. Many of these emotions are difficult to deal with and may leave you feeling alone and resentful. But you are not alone. Other parents have similar problems and challenges. Here are some common feelings shared by parents of Ephraim's Children (adapted from *Parenting the Fussy Baby and High-Need Child* by William and Martha Sears):[1]

1. *Doubtful*—Others seem to be able to control their children, why can't you? Many parents question their parenting abilities.

2. *Alone*—Because your child has different needs and is so much *more*, your parenting is naturally different from most others. This leaves you open to judgment or unwanted—and unworkable—advice.

3. *Defensive*—When your child is the one who won't behave you may feel constant embarrassment. You may also get angry when others accuse you of doing something wrong to cause your child to behave this way.

4. *Resentful*—You resent your plight and then resent yourself for having uncharitable feelings.

5. *Thrilled and scared*—There are moments when your child's delightful personality shines and you feel blessed to be the parent, then seconds later you plunge into despair as your volatile child flips out again.

6. *Controlled or manipulated*—Most of us enter parenthood expecting to be in control of our child, or at least in charge. Instead, you may feel that not only are you unable to control your child, but imagine that he's controlling you.

7. *Tied down*—The Ephraim's Child is *more*, and as such demands more of your time and energy.

8. *Inadequate*—There are days when nothing you can do seems to do any good.

9. *Lost*—With the demands from your child, somewhere you have lost yourself.

10. *Worried*—You wonder if she is normal or worry that your kid will turn into one of those annoying kids you have known and swore you would never let your child become.

11. *Disillusioned*—Parenting this child is not what you expected.

12. *Stretched or burned out*—Parenting these children force you to extend yourself, which can make you feel worn out.

## Your Child Is Not "Out to Get You"

It is vitally important that you constantly remind yourself that your Ephraim's Child is not "out to get you." She is not acting this way to drive you nuts or being difficult on purpose. Your frustration level will automatically decrease once you stop taking things personally. Dr. MacKenzie reminds us that these children "are not part of some conspiracy to make life difficult for others. They just do what strong-willed children do. They test harder and more often, resist longer, protest louder, use more drama, and carry things further than most of us would ever imagine. They're movers and shakers, powerful kids who bring out strong reactions in others."[2] That is the Ephraim's Child.

## Work with Temperament

Brigham Young said, "Bring up your children in the love and fear of the Lord; study their dispositions and temperaments, and deal with them accordingly, never allowing yourself to correct them in the heat of passion; teach them to love you rather than to fear you."[3] Likewise, you can love your Ephraim's Child rather than fear her.

We have reasons for devoting the majority of this book to temperament. Once you understand your child's temperament, you can better predict his behavior. Why your child does what he does is no longer such a mystery. Many times problems with our Ephraim's Children stem from misunderstanding. You have absolutely no idea why the new and improved packaging on the favorite cereal box incites an explosive reaction. If it tastes the same, why on earth does your child even care? His behavior is confusing.

If you do not know that your child is slow-to-adapt and finds change very frightening, then you would be clueless to the reasons behind this crisis. However, if you do know your child does not take change well, you can work with him to get through this issue. Your child's behavior makes sense now. You will have more patience that stems from understanding.

You no longer need to spend all your energy wondering why your child does something. You can now focus your energy on what you need to do to guide your child when he does it. You can navigate the minefield of potential triggers and help your child refine his characteristics into strengths. You can enjoy your Ephraim's Child more.

## Use Correct Tools

"Do you sometimes question whether your child's behavior is normal? Perhaps you worry that you've done something to cause your child to behave this way. If so, you'll be relieved to know that the problem, in most cases, is not parents. Most are doing the best they can with the discipline tools they have. The problem is not the child either. Most strong-willed children are just being themselves. The real problem is a bad match between the child's temperament and the parents' discipline methods. The parents' tools are not well suited for the job. The predictable result is conflict and power struggles."4

Find out what methods work with your child and then use them. We have shared many of the tools given through books that we have read and studied. This will probably require that you get out of your comfort zone. Your natural way of dealing with situations may not be the best way to deal with your Ephraim's Child in those situations. If nothing else, Ephraim's Children force their parents to grow and develop as parents.

## Our Children Help Raise Us Too

Part of becoming more like God is having children. We are commanded to multiply and replenish the earth. But this is not merely so that we can be in charge of new spirits entering the world. Having children is required so that we can learn important lessons that cannot be learned other ways. So an important thing to remember is that our children help raise us too. We learn important things from them that are necessary for reaching our full potential. "Nevertheless the Lord seeth fit to chasten his people; yea, he trieth their patience and their faith."5 Often children try patience and faith more than anything. The truth is that we need them as much as they need us.

## Don't Get Too Busy

One thing that will greatly affect how you feel about your demanding child is how busy you are. It is not difficult to be irritated with something that you feel keeps interfering with what you really want to do. "Children should not be seen as interruptions to the main thing of life; they are the main thing."6 If you find yourself feeling that your Ephraim's Child is getting in the way of your life, maybe it is time to review your life.

Elder Richard G. Scott gave us this counsel:

As a mother or father, are you in trouble because the pressures of the world lead you from effectively fulfilling your divine role? Is your life unconsciously fueled with the burning desire for more things that could compromise eternal relationships and the molding of a child's developing character? You must be willing to forgo personal pleasure and self-interest for family-centered activity, and not turn over to church, school, or society the principal role of fostering a child's well-rounded development. It takes time, great effort, and significant personal sacrifice to "train up a child in the way he should go." But where can you find greater rewards for a job well done?7

## Do the Best You Can

When you are lucky enough to have one of "those days," you may have to just do the best that you can. Just be the best parent you can on that day. Then be glad you can start over tomorrow. Sometimes we just have to persist and do what we have to. Neal A. Maxwell wrote, "Sometimes that which we are doing is correct enough but simply needs to be persisted in—patiently—not for a minute or a moment but sometimes for years. Paul speaks of the marathon of life and how we must 'run with patience the race that is set before us' (Heb. 12:1)."8 Some days you may just have to endure to the end of the day.

But the endurance required for parenthood is not merely putting up with a circumstance. Neither is it the out-lasting of a situation, or suffering through one, or just tolerating one. Resigned endurance is not what you need with your Ephraim's Child. You cannot guide him to his potential if you are merely "putting up" with him or "out-lasting" him until he leaves for college. Neal A. Maxwell has said: "Patient endurance is to be distinguished from merely being 'acted upon.' Endurance is more than pacing up and down within the cell of your circumstance; it is not only acceptance of things allotted to us but also the determination to 'act for ourselves' by magnifying what is allotted to us (Alma 19:3, 6)."9

To magnify what is allotted to us is one way of enduring well. Neal A. Maxwell also says, "With enduring comes a willingness to 'press forward' even when we are bone weary and would much rather pull off to the side of the road."10 Enduring with an Ephraim's Child is work. He is usually high-maintenance; emotionally and physically labor-intensive. However, the scriptures are filled with promises for those who endure well. "And then, if thou endure it well, God shall exalt thee on high; thou shalt triumph over all thy foes."11 "But he that shall endure unto the end, that same shall be saved."12 Endure the tough times well, and you can reap the rewards of a good relationship with a delightful Ephraim's Child who is growing to his potential.

### If the Savior Were Babysitting

If Jesus Christ were babysitting your child, how would He act towards her? If you are ever concerned over your feelings or actions towards your child, ask yourself, "What would

Jesus do?" You could expand that question to, "How would Jesus feel?"

If you need to, pray with "all the energy of heart"[13] that you will be filled with the love that Christ feels for each of us. His love, the pure love He has for all mankind, is manifest in the atonement that He made. As Mormon tells us in Moroni 7:48, we can pray that the effects of the atonement, which is the greatest gift of all, will fill us. This is charity, or the pure love of Christ. When we know how Christ loves us and are filled with His love, then it is possible to love as He does. Then we "shall be like him"[14] and we can love these precious Ephraim's Children as surely as the Savior does.

Seek strength and wisdom from the Spirit. Enlist the Lord's help. Sister Gayle M. Clegg, second counselor in the Primary General Presidency, reminds us: "Your child is the child of Heavenly Father, and you can expect His help. In fact, you can't do it alone. You need Heavenly Father's help in raising His child."[15] That help is there for you. After all, "ask, and ye shall receive; knock, and it shall be opened unto you."[16]

## Others Think You Have a Brat

*One Sunday a primary teacher was in charge of the class presentation for Sharing Time. She valiantly tried to do her job with one of her Ephraim's Children glued to her side and another one trying to climb up the front of her dress. Usually the intensity of her two children does not bother this mom, but in this situation she became frustrated. She tried to push her children away, but her attempts to extract herself only exacerbated the problem. The other adults watched her lack of control, some with sympathy and others with disapproval.*

Sometimes you might intercept looks from others that make you worry. Do others think you have a brat? You can begin to doubt yourself when you see people watching your child critically. They disapprove of your active

Ephraim's Child that zings around the cultural hall during ward parties, or shake their heads at your lack of control when your toddler escapes to the microphone to "participate" in the Primary Program. Whether it is true or not, you feel that these other people must have had perfectly behaved children and that the reason that you don't is due to some vital parenting flaws that they can see and you can't. Nothing can undermine your confidence in your parenting more than other people.

The first thing is to realize that other adults who are obviously disapproving probably have not experienced an Ephraim's Child. Either they do not have children (nothing changes your ideas of raising children faster than actually trying to raise children), their kids are grown, or their children were not as temperamentally challenging as Ephraim's Children. They have probably not had the joy of a close relationship with one of these special spirits, and so really they should be getting your pity, not the other way around! Use your positive everyday names when talking with others, and perhaps they will begin to see your child in a new light.

One woman expressed her frustration with the young children in her ward who "are just rude!" She thought that mothers of these young children were not teaching their children proper behavior because they ran around and were noisy all the time. This belief is based in the idea that all children can be easily restrained and compliant. There will probably be people who see your child's "misbehavior" as a shortcoming of your parenting. It is important that you do what you feel is best for your child and don't let these opinions upset you. After all, you know your child. They don't. You need not shun public situations just because you are afraid that others will disapprove of your child's behavior. In time, your child will learn the acceptable behavior for different situations. In time, he will be able to sit still at ward parties, but maybe not right now.

Perhaps the most stressful disapproval can come from

your own family. Hopefully this book will help you foster a more understanding relationship between other family members and your Ephraim's Child. It will be much better for your child if he does not feel censure whenever you spend time with family, so try to educate them. If it is slow going, keep trying. Despite your efforts, Aunt Bertha may still harp on those "out-of-control troublemakers" whenever your child is in her presence. When this happens, it may just be best to limit contact with that person. You can still visit, only less often.

Many times the critical looks you think others are sending your way may just be looks of understanding or sympathy. When you see a lady laughing while your child throws one of his most spectacular overstimulated Ephraim's Child fits, it doesn't mean she thinks you are the worst parent around. It just may be because it looks so familiar to her and she is glad it is not her child this time. You may be a little over-sensitive yourself. When you find yourself sending other parents sympathetic glances when they are in the middle of battles with their kids, they may be relieved to hear something from you like, "It's a relief to see other kids acting just like mine. Tomorrow has to be better."

### Church

Unfortunately, the Ephraim's Child does have an amazing capacity to be disruptive. She is just more intense than others, which makes her more noticeable. Understand that she is not being disruptive just to be disruptive, but there is usually a temperamental and emotional reason behind her behavior. You cannot avoid going places where your child has prime opportunity to be disruptive, but there are things that you can do to help minimize the chances of it while your child learns how to behave.

Church is often a challenge for the Ephraim's Child. Seventy minutes spent trying to keep an Ephraim's Child quiet and still can make sacrament meeting feel like a torture session. Good luck trying to physically hold an active

Ephraim's Child so that she remains still. Usually her struggles to free herself increase exponentially every minute. You can almost give up trying to keep your child quiet if she becomes distraught for some reason.

Sacrament meeting behavior usually requires extra effort and creativity by parents. Some parents resort to treats. Just beware the potential mess of wrappers, chocolate, or sticky residue. You have to decide if the mess is reverent and respectful of our Lord's house. The other downside to using treats during church to reward behavior is the increase in activity that sugar can cause in children. Isn't that the opposite of what you are trying to do? You may be making the remainder of church more challenging and alienating your child's primary teacher at the same time.

You can provide other activities for your child, such as quiet books that you can make or buy. If you have an Ephraim's Child that gets bored once he has mastered an activity, then even a quiet book may only keep him occupied for a short time. We have a church bag, full of books, activities, coloring books, and puzzles that our children only get to use during Sacrament Meeting. Every couple of months we rotate the contents and are always on the lookout for new church activities. From our own experience, be careful with things that need sound effects like action figures or cars. The little cars were removed from our church bag after we had a race on our bench complete with squealing breaks, crashes, and engine sounds.

The next potential hot spot in church is Primary. Your child may have just spent an hour being still and quiet—for him. After sacrament meeting he will probably want to move and be loud for a little while, and if he is told to sit still and be silent again for two more hours, you may have a rebellion on your hands. The adults in charge could be doing things that you just know will not work for your child. What do you do?

The first step is working with your child at home on the acceptable behavior for Primary. That way you can communicate in ways that your child understands the type of behavior that you expect. The next step is to set the tone in sacrament meeting. Sending your child to Primary with a stomach full of candy is probably not setting him up to succeed. If you have already kept your child calm (do your best!), then he won't start primary stressed.

Finally, include the primary workers. Give them information about your child and ideas of things that work for you. For example, you could say something like, "I know that Timmy is a very active child and needs to move his body. We have found that if you get him involved in physically acting out a scripture story he will stay tuned in better than if he is required to sit in his chair. Then after the story he is more able to sit because he has expended some energy." Approaching the situation diplomatically and offering suggestions will usually work better than telling a teacher that she is doing it all wrong. Chances are she will be glad of any ideas to help. Use your positive language to give her a happier picture of your child.

Another situation may be that you spend enough time in the primary that you can recognize other Ephraim's Children. Diplomatically suggesting solutions or alternative methods to adults in charge may give you a chance to help. You could begin by pulling aside the Primary President and saying, "As I have spent time in here with Jenny, I have noticed that there are several other children that remind me of her. Through our own trial and error we have found that _____ works well with Jenny's temperament. You could try it in Primary and see if it will help these other children as well."

## The Medication Concern

Because of the intensity of Ephraim's Children, it is not unlikely that someone will suggest you get your child on medication to help him chill out. The number of children being medicated for behavioral problems is rising. The most well-known example is the prescribing of Ritalin to treat

ADHD. In an article in *Education World* online magazine, author Diane Weaver Dunne states that "the increase in the number of prescriptions doctors write for treating ADHD is staggering. According to the Congressional Testimony of Terrance Woodworth, a deputy director of the Drug Enforcement Administration, the number of prescriptions written for methylphenidate (Ritalin) has increased by a factor of five since 1991."[17]

However, the use of stimulant medication is not seen just in school-aged children. The number of preschool children using stimulant medication for ADHD has increased significantly as well. "A study, 'Trends in the Prescribing of Psychotropic Medications to Preschoolers,' published in the *Journal of the American Medical Association* . . . found that psychotropic medication use tripled in preschool children ages two to four over a five-year span."[18]

It is a legitimate concern that our society is over-prescribing drugs to make children easier and more compliant. Pressure may come from others for you to medicate your Ephraim's Child. This pressure may come from anywhere: neighbors, friends, strangers, or school teachers. Lawrence Diller, M.D., who practices behavioral pediatrics in Walnut Creek, California and is the author of *Running on Ritalin: A Physician Reflects on Children, Society and Performance in a Pill,* comments on the stampede of people in education trying to get parents to medicate their children. Dr. Diller expresses alarm with the widespread reliance on pharmaceuticals by educators. He is afraid that they do not always explore fully the other options available to deal with learning and behavioral problems in their classrooms. In his article "Just Say Yes to Ritalin!" Dr. Diller says:

> Public school administrators, long the enthusiastic adherents of a Just Say No! policy on drug use, appear to have a new motto for the parents of certain tiny soldiers in the war on drugs: Medicate or Else! It is a new and troubling twist in the psychiatric drugs saga, in which

public schools have begun to issue ultimatums to parents of hard-to-handle kids, saying they will not allow students to attend conventional classes unless they are medicated. In the most extreme cases, parents unwilling to give their kids drugs are being reported by their schools to local offices of Child Protective Services (CPS), the implication being that by withholding drugs, the parents are guilty of neglect.[19]

The pressure from local schools on parents has become so intense in some areas that resolutions to have teachers restrain from recommending medical evaluations and Ritalin for students are under consideration in several states. At the same time as the issue of parents' rights is being considered in some areas, the stakes have dramatically increased in others. Some schools are seeking the intervention of CPS to get parents to medicate their kids. "It is no longer simply an issue of which school or which class a child will attend," Diller says. "Instead, some parents are being threatened with the possibility of losing custody of their children if they refuse to comply with suggested treatment for an alleged medical condition . . . . These policies . . . demonstrate a disquieting belief on the part of educated adults that bad behavior and underperformance in school should be interpreted as medical disorders that must be treated with drugs."[20] Dr. Diller and others are concerned about families being forced against their will to put their children on psychiatric medication.

In her book *You Can't Make Me*, Cynthia Tobias also expresses her reservations with prescribing medication to mellow behavior. She brings up this point: "What if the very traits and characteristics [your child] gets in trouble for are the ones that could potentially change the world? Not long ago, Dr. Peter Breggin quoted *Newsweek* magazine in his book *The War Against Children*. Dr. Breggin said that *Newsweek* had asked the questions: 'Where are the great thinkers of the 90s? Where are the Freuds, the Einsteins, the

Picassos?' Dr. Breggin then responded with a sobering thought: 'What if we're medicating them?'"[21]

Before agreeing to medicate your child, make sure that there is a legitimate health problem. These medical issues cannot be diagnosed accurately with a short conversation in your pediatrician's office. A complete evaluation should include reports from you, your child's teachers, child-care providers, and your pediatrician. Get multiple opinions. Above all, pray about it. Medication should be the last resort, not the first option. Medication can help those with real medical issues, but beware the seduction of using it just to smooth out your Ephraim's Child's temperament. Try working with his temperament first. Some informed parenting may help more than a pill.

## Stay Positive

You know that parenting the Ephraim's Child is not always a negative experience. There are those positive, joyous times when your feelings are so different. Realize that your child's temperament presents challenges, but you can feel proud as these traits blossom into exciting personality features and strengths. As you work with your child's temperament you will feel less helpless. As your relationship with your Ephraim's Child improves you will feel more confident and comfortable. You will also have those times when you feel connected with your child. Keep using your new and improved everyday names. Soon you will begin to see your child as the bright, enthusiastic, tenacious, caring, aware leader that she is. You can enjoy your Ephraim's Child. Then your real child—the one who can bring you moments of dazzling delight—will be your dream child, not because she has changed into one, but because you now have the vision to see her that way.

# 15

# The Special Occasion Nightmare

Ah . . . the holidays. Time off from work and school to be filled with memorable family traditions and gatherings with friends and family. It sounds peaceful, right? But if you have an Ephraim's Child, a special occasion can be anything but peaceful. A more appropriate description may be: the time your child becomes possessed by a wild alien that makes the Terrible Two's a breeze in comparison.

Many special occasions seem to bring the alien out. Holidays, reunions, birthday parties, and vacations are all culprits. It is difficult for parents to understand why these times do not bring the tender memories that they are hoping for, but rather herald a nightmare that one hopes to psychologically block. Why does your child's behavior worsen with every Christmas present unwrapped? Why must you spend the family reunion shadowing your child because she has suddenly gone berserk? And why must the birthday party you lovingly planned for your child usually end in fights and tears?

Now that you understand your child's temperament, you can begin to see why special occasions often become nightmares. Many times they involve situations and surroundings where a slow-to-adapt and sensitive Ephraim's Child may become overwhelmed. Parents are often stressed or distracted and unable to give as much attention to a demanding child who is feeding off their stress. Schedules and routines are commonly thrown to the wind and Ephraim's Children lose some of their predictability and control. Above all, Ephraim's Children often eat and sleep less at these times, making their energy levels low.

Special times do not have to be nightmarish situations, though. Some understanding and planning on your part can go a long way in making those hoped-for pleasant memories a reality. Take heart from the words of the Lord, "if ye are prepared ye shall not fear."[1] As with all aspects of parenting Ephraim's Children, navigating the land mines inherent in special occasions can be challenging, but not impossible. A little preparation and forethought can make special occasions just that . . . special.

## Be Realistic

We all have certain expectations for special occasions. Perhaps you envision Christmas Day going from one set of grandparents to the next and enjoying all the traditions and food from your childhood and from your spouse's childhood. Maybe a birthday feels special only when you have a big, elaborate, and wonderfully decorated party for your child. The point is, we all want something out of special occasions that will make memories for us and our children. Often that involves tangible things such as particular food or super special presents. And usually it takes more work than you realize to produce these special memories. How many of us feel our To-Do list growing longer the closer we get to Christmas, culminating in a late night Christmas Eve wrapping presents, assembling toys, or finishing that special handmade something for a loved one that you just couldn't quite get to?

The first step to reducing your special occasion nightmare is to be realistic. You have a child who is *more*. That usually means that you have a child who requires more energy on your part every day. Parenting an Ephraim's Child is draining. And parenting an Ephraim's Child through special occasions is twice as draining. You are already working hard. At these times your child will require more of your attention, energy, and help. Count on it. Plan for it.

Understanding this, look at all of your plans for these

occasions and downsize. Trying to do everything to have a Martha Stewart holiday is often going to end in the Nightmare Before Christmas. You will already be tired and stressed if you overextend yourself, and a challenging Ephraim's Child demanding more energy than you have will just make you both miserable. Trust us, realistic downsizing of your expectations will be a great help.

Reviewing your own expectations is important, but it is also a good idea to check your child's expectations as well. What you consider the most meaningful traditions may not be what your child remembers from last year. The intense Ephraim's Child can get extremely excited about upcoming events and holidays, and if they fall short of expectations there can be a wild blowup. Even if you cannot meet your child's expectations, you can try to avoid a surprise melt-down. Finding out in the middle of Thanksgiving dinner that the homemade pies you decided to forego this year were your child's favorite thing about the whole holiday is not a recipe for success. When you address your child's expectations ahead of time you increase the chances of success during the special occasion.

## Work With Others

Special occasions involving gatherings of family and friends may require some fast-talking on your part. To have a more enjoyable time, others need your help to understand and work with your Ephraim's Child. You want to avoid a similar scene as last year when all the cousins swarmed over your child when she walked in the door and she ran screaming from the room like she was being pursued by lions. Explain to them that your child needs some time to adapt before joining them. Your child detests fond kisses from relatives not because she does not like grandma and grandpa, but because she is sensitive. Others need to know that your child retreats into a quiet room periodically because she needs to take a break from all the activity, not because she does not like them.

For extended family to build a successful relationship with your Ephraim's Child, they need to understand him better. That will require explaining on your part. Tell them what you have discovered about your child and the techniques that are working for you. The challenge may be convincing them that in certain ways your child is different. And unless you have experience with an Ephraim's Child, the idea that one child can be so much *more* of everything may not be easy to grasp. Keep trying, keep explaining, and keep interceding until extended family can experience the rewards of a deeper relationship with your Ephraim's Child.

Special occasions require people to adapt to others in new situations. Your Ephraim's Child needs to learn how to do this, and others need to learn how to respect your child and let him learn. As the parent you may have to step in and help your child if others do not listen or are trying to force your child to transition quickly, or stop being so intense, or forcing a new food on him, etc. Use the moment as a time to teach them about your child. When everyone is watching a movie that is too upsetting for your child, explain that your son is not being a baby but that he feels things deeply and is too distressed by what is happening in the movie. Then suggest another activity for your child instead that others may join if they want.

If others are not listening to your suggestions and your child is having a rough time, you may need to change the situation. Perhaps you may choose to shorten visits in the future. Maybe you could suggest another location like a park or your house, where you have more control. You may even decide to visit less frequently. Remember that as your child matures and learns how to manage his temperament he will be able to handle special occasions better.

**Prepare Your Child**

Just as forewarning your Ephraim's Child of upcoming transitions will help her adapt, preparing your child for a special occasion will help her be more successful. Show your child pictures of the relatives you do not see very often. A picture is a way to forewarn, and she will not feel that she is meeting total strangers. Arriving early is a good idea. That way your child is dealing with the newness of the surrounding before the pressure to be social is too heavy. Your child can then adapt to one thing at a time instead of everything all at once.

Let your child know your expectations and what is acceptable behavior in advance. If she doesn't like a food item on her plate, it is not appropriate to scream or throw the offending green bean on the floor. She can, however, say, "No, thank you" or merely put it on the side of her plate. Instead of tackling your friend's baby when he tumbles into your child's elaborate game, help her understand that babies cannot control their bodies very well. Let your child know that she is not allowed to blow out the candles on her friend's birthday cake, but she can help eat it.

Prepare your child for patterns or procedures of the event. Explain to him that birthday presents will be opened after the cake and ice cream. If dinner will be later then your child's accustomed eating time, bring a snack or feed him beforehand. If it is a special adult occasion let your child know that the adults will not be giving him as much attention as he is accustomed to. Later you will be able to devote time to him.

You can also help your child learn how to handle enthusiastic greetings. When greeting people for the first time be there with your child, letting her know she has your support. If she hides behind you, explain to the great-aunt and uncle that she will give hugs in five minutes and don't force her. Sit on the floor with her or be near her as people arrive so that she can always run to you if she needs to. Older children can learn how to be gracious. You can practice saying hello, shaking hands, and then finding a place to retreat until she is comfortable joining in. Teach her how to tell others that she will join them in a few minutes or that she needs a little quiet for a while, but will be back.

When your child does behave, praise and reward her. Let her know that you noticed how well she handled herself. Give her positive feedback. This will help your child see that she can handle the situation. Bring up past successes to remind her that she can do this. This will also help you remember the times your child behaved like an angel rather than zinging around the room like a wild animal. When you praise your child in front of others, you will draw their attention to the times your child shows acceptable behavior instead of when she threw her cup across the room because she was given orange juice instead of apple juice.

## Beware of Crowds

Holidays are often synonymous with crowds, and crowds can be disastrous for the sensitive Ephraim's Child. Shopping before the crowd hits is always a good idea, but if you can't get all your Christmas purchases completed by September then go early in the morning. We know one woman that shops at four in the morning, and swears by it. You don't have to go before dawn, but crowds will be less at 9:00 a.m. than at 7:00 p.m. If you must brave the crowds, then shorten the shopping trips. If your child can only handle an hour being bombarded by sensation before turning into a whimpering heap at your feet, then do your shopping in one-hour segments.

Crowds not only occur in stores, but at gatherings as well. Find a place for your child to retreat or bring some calming activities to use. Planning for crowds can help reduce the nightmare of special occasions. Whatever approach you choose, decide on it beforehand and help your child cope with the crowds inherent in special occasions.

## Travel Plans

When special occasions involve travel, things will go smoother if you take some time to plan. When planning a family vacation, for example, take into account the temperamental traits of your Ephraim's Child. This does not mean that you completely cater all your plans to this child, but there are certain ways to travel that will be more successful than others.

We have already discussed arriving early for family gatherings to give your child time to adjust. It will also help if you give your Ephraim's Child time when traveling as well. Don't just drop your luggage in the hotel room and run out the door immediately to get in half a day at Disneyland. Give your child some time to adapt to the hotel first—go swimming, watch some television, or just hang out for a while. This will slow down the transitions and new sensations bombarding your child. Then you can begin your vacation in earnest with a calmer child. Plus, you would rather have your child getting used to the hotel in the afternoon than when you drag in late and try to get him in bed.

Another effective tactic is to avoid trips that involve sleeping at a different place every night for days on end. Pick a centralized location from which you base your activities for a couple of days. For a while you can return to the same location after seeing sights or doing things. Then you can move on to a new location for the next few days. The Ephraim's Child will have more time to adapt to new places and sensations and will be more successful.

It is all well and good to be prepared once you get to your destination, but without proper thought you may have a nightmare trip getting there. Spending a long time strapped to a car seat is difficult for any child. For an active Ephraim's Child it may be nearly impossible. Plan extra time for stops to stretch little legs, like picnic lunches at a park with a little time to play. You can play favorite music to help occupy your child. Definitely bring toys and activities like paper, crayons, coloring books, etc. for the car. Expect to interact with your child. Talk about things that you see as you travel. Play word games. Sing songs. With the right preparation the journey can actually be enjoyable.

## Essential Sleep

When your Ephraim's Child is tired, she will be less able to handle everything associated with a special occasion. Therefore it is imperative that you do everything in your power to keep your child well rested so that she has the energy to cope. However, getting an Ephraim's Child to sleep in an unfamiliar place or in the middle of all the holiday or vacation excitement can be a challenge in itself.

Ephraim's Children already have a hard time sleeping in new or different situations, and they usually need extra time to unwind. Your child may need to read or rock quietly to calm down from her excitement. Even though all you want is for her to go to sleep so that you can crash or visit, you must draw on extra reserves of patience. If you get mad and upset, you will just be adding extra stimulation and emotion to a child who may already be overwhelmed. You may need to stay with your child until she falls asleep, which may very well take longer than normal, no matter how tired she is or how late the hour. Just expect that bedtime will take more time and effort.

Try to stick to your regular bedtime routine and schedule as much as possible. Bring along familiar items like pillows, blankets, or books that will help your child feel more comfortable. Avoid irregular bedtimes and try not to skip naps. At this time your child needs more sleep than usual because of the extra energy needed to cope with new surroundings. It is not fair asking your Ephraim's Child to be on his best behavior with less energy, so try to fit in regular naps when possible.

## The Gift Trap

Does the idea of an occasion involving gifts make you want to crawl in bed and pull the covers over your head? Have you seriously considered foregoing presents at Christmas or birthdays to avoid another scene like last year? Is your Ephraim's Child an ungrateful brat because she is so poor at handling gifts? Others may think so, but the answer is a resounding no! However, your child does need to learn how to handle gifts gracefully.

Remember that the Ephraim's Child is intense and sensitive. Every emotion is felt very strongly and very deeply. Gifts can be exciting or disappointing, and for your child gifts either make his year or send his life crashing in ruins. These kids can get into trouble because they are unable to wait to open gifts; they want their presents NOW! They are so excited that they can hardly contain themselves. With this knowledge, do you wonder why a Christmas tree surrounded for a week by a pile of brightly wrapped presents is just asking for disaster? The area under our tree looks desolate until Christmas morning, but we no longer have fights over the presents that our child couldn't help but open. Help your child understand what to expect and find ways to help diffuse the excitement. Perhaps opening a present or two early would help your child calm down a little. At a birthday party you may want to open gifts first, then have the games and cake.

The slow-to-adapt Ephraim's Child also must deal with the element of surprise inherent in gift giving. You can help him prepare for it, however. Give him little hints or let him see glimpses of what may be coming. If you are not giving him the video game his heart is set on, let him know. When he has time to deal with the disappointment beforehand you will have less meltdowns when the presents are all opened and the coveted video game is not there. If you are giving him the gift of his dreams, don't tell him that you are not just so that it will be a surprise. Slow-to-adapt Ephraim's Children hate surprises. It may backfire on you.

When you don't know what the presents will be, like at a birthday party, you can still help your child prepare. Go through possible situations with your child so that she understands what behavior would be acceptable. What do you do if you don't like the gift? What if you already have one? What if your sister gets a gift you wanted? How would you feel? What could you do? This way your child is more prepared for disappointment.

Another way to prepare the older Ephraim's Child for gifts is to ask him to compile a list of things that he would like to receive. Be prepared for a long list. Then have him mark the ones he wants the most. Then you can use this list for your own shopping as well as gift ideas for others. That way your child has some control over what he receives and will have fewer disappointments in receiving something he doesn't like.

Give gifts wisely. Choose ones that facilitate the behavior you want. If you do not want your child destroying your house with a football in December, then don't give him one at Christmas. Squirt guns given in cold weather are grounds for a battle. Make sure that you like any books or music you give, because you will probably hear them over and over and over again. Toys that employ imagination are often good gifts, especially ones that can be used many different ways. One Ephraim's Child used a card game not to play Go Fish, but spread the cards out on the floor as roads, used them as soldiers in a battlefield, or pretended they were money or movie tickets. Your alternative thinker will be frustrated if he is pigeonholed into using a toy "the right way." Building blocks, toy people, dress up items, and play houses or buildings allow Ephraim's Children the freedom to play their own way.

Active Ephraim's Children do like active toys, but they cannot wait to use them. You need to have a place for your child to use the slide, trampoline, or bicycle. These toys need to be monitored when in use. You will sometimes need to step in and move to a calming activity when your child starts to wind up.

Instruct your child on proper gift etiquette. A more serious child will most likely not dance around with delight after opening a gift. She may not say thank you or even express interest in the present, which can be a major letdown for the gift-giver. Teach your Ephraim's Child that instead of yelling that she wanted pink instead of yellow, she needs to still thank her aunt for the gift and maybe later you can exchange it for a pink one. Let her know that she needs to express gratitude despite her feelings about the gift. Together you can find appropriate things to say beforehand. This requires planning on your part to sit with your child previous to the big day, but can save a lot of embarrassment.

You may also need to prepare your child for gift giving. When let your child choose a gift for someone else, he can get caught up in the thrill and excitement of choosing something cool. Watching that cool thing go into the hands of another child can be very difficult. Buying gifts for others and not getting anything for himself can be an emotional trigger for your intense child. Walk your child through possible situations, like when the one receiving the gift may not be gracious. When your child's best friend exclaims, "Yuck!" over the present your child agonized over, it can destroy your child. Help him find ways to deal with his emotion in these type of situations. Your child will need to learn how to handle giving gifts as well as receiving them.

Everyone likes to receive gifts. Presents are supposed to be a joyful event for both those giving and receiving. Participating in giving gifts to others can help your child learn the joy of giving to others, as well as give him more understanding of those who have gone to effort to give him presents. You don't need to give up gift giving completely. Some preparation on your part can help you avoid the gift trap.

**After the Occasion**

After a big event, life does not immediately return to normal for the Ephraim's Child. As an adult you may want nothing more than to get back to normal after a vacation, but your child is still riding on a wave of leftover emotions and excitement. She will need time to adjust back to normal life, whether that is getting used to less attention, fewer playmates, or less exciting activities. Playing in the backyard may seem boring after a vacation to Disneyland.

Leave yourself enough energy to help your child transition

back to normal life. Ephraim's Children often go to extremes and may crash after riding high. It will take time for your child to get over the special occasion and she may be more demanding than usual. A little forewarning when special occasions are coming to an end will help your child begin the transition. Help her understand that special occasions are special because they only happen once in a while. Be with her to help her deal with the let down.

Don't forget to allow yourself crash time too. These special times require more planning and energy on your part to successfully manage with your Ephraim's Child. Reward yourself and tuck away the successes to pull out next time to remind yourself and your child that you *can* do this. When you understand, plan, and prepare well, these special times can be joyful and full of those special memories.

# 16

# Grandparenting the Ephraim's Child

*"Perfect love sometimes does not come until grandchildren are born."*[1]
—Welsh Proverb

Being a grandparent is always a joy, but there can be some tricky moments to being the grandparent of an Ephraim's Child. It can be difficult watching your children struggle with their own little ones. It is going to take a large family effort to raise these children. Grandparents need to understand the Ephraim's Child as well.

However, there may be times when you as a grandparent will feel left out, like those times when only the parent can handle a situation, or when your presence sometimes overwhelms an over-stimulated Ephraim's Child. When your attempts to help result in rejection or a worsening of the situation, it can be upsetting. But do not despair. Grandparents are important people in a child's life. President Ezra Taft Benson said, "Grandparents can have a profound influence on their grandchildren."[2]

A grandparent fills a special niche in a child's life. In the book *Parents & Grandparents as Spiritual Guides*, author Betty Shannon Cloyd chooses five main roles that grandparents fulfill: to be present in the lives of grandchildren, to love them unconditionally, to connect the generations, to provide emotional, physical and spiritual support for their grandchildren's parents (their own children), and to be a strong spiritual guide.[3]

## Be Present

In order to have an impact on the life of your grand-child, you must first be involved in his life. This requires your presence, your interest, and your time. It is easier to do if you live close, as long as you don't keep putting off vis-its until tomorrow. Sometimes older adults feel that they have put in their parenting time and that once their own children have left the nest it is time to catch up on all the fun that was missed in earlier years. While this is true to some degree, realize that you still have a responsibility to your grandchildren. It will be difficult to be present in their lives if you are too busy catching up on all that you "missed" when raising your own children.

Many grandparents do not live close to their grandchil-dren. However, they can still be present in their grandchil-dren's lives. Through letters, telephone calls, and email you can know what is going on with your grandchildren. What child is not excited to get her very own letter or email? You can still have a strong relationship, even though you do not see each other every day or every week. Visits are still impor-tant and should be made as often as possible. The grandpar-ents and the family with children need to be willing to make some sacrifices in order to see each other on a regular basis.

Being present in the lives of grandchildren requires inter-est on your part. Find out what they are doing, who their friends are, and what they are struggling with. Show your grandchildren that you know what's going on in their lives by asking specific questions. Let them know that you care. If you have consistently been interested in their lives then your grandchildren will feel more comfortable sharing their joys and troubles with you. Grandparents need to make an effort to be an ongoing part of their grandchildren's lives.

## Love Them Unconditionally

Allan Frome once said, "Being grandparents sufficiently removes us from the responsibilities so that we can be friends."4 As a grandparent it is as if you are given a second chance to love unconditionally. Not that you are given a second chance as a parent—that is your children's job now—but a chance to love your grandchildren and love them unconditionally. Often parents are so caught up in the responsibilities and maintenance that is inherent in taking care of young children that they can forget to express their love adequately. In being removed from the cleaning, the cooking, and the daily hassles, grandparents are given a unique opportunity to practice loving their grandchildren unconditionally. Betty Cloyd gives the advice to not be timid about showing unconditional love for grandchildren "because this love will remain with them even after we are gone."5

Ephraim's Children can be challenging to love at times. One minute they seem to be golden children with intelligence and understanding much older than their years, and the next minute they can be rude and rebellious. It will be easier to love the Ephraim's Child if you understand her temperament. Then you can realize that your grandchild is telling you to go home because your visit is a transition, not because she doesn't love you. When you understand why this Ephraim's Child behaves the way she does, you no longer need to take things personally and can free up your emotions to love her with everything you've got, even when she is being difficult. Show her your love *especially* when she is being difficult.

### Connect the Generations

Cloyd remarks that grandparents stand in an unusual position because they have knowledge of at least five generations. They have information about their own grandparents and parents, knowledge about their children and themselves, and now knowledge about their grandchildren.6 They are a living bridge across generations. Grandparents can help grandchildren know more about their family and feel their place in their family history. Grandparents can help "turn the heart of the children to their fathers."7

One important thing that grandparents can do for their grandchildren is to share family stories with them. Often when families gather together someone will tell a favorite story and start a round of storytelling. This is a good practice to keep and is fun for children as well as adults. Another way to share stories is to invest in a little tape recorder and record stories a little at a time. Or you could simply get a notebook and write them down for your grandchildren. Writing things down is a practice that we as a church have been counseled to do time and time again.

President Ezra Taft Benson said: "We call on you to pursue vigorously the gathering and writing of personal and family histories. In so many instances, you alone have within you the history, the memory of loved ones, the dates and events. In some situations you are the family history. In few ways will your heritage be better preserved than by your collecting and writing your histories."8

Keeping a journal, either a personal journal or one specifically to grandchildren is a good way to connect the generations. President Spencer W. Kimball emphasized the importance of journal keeping. He said:

> We may think [there] is little interest or [no] importance in what we personally say or do—but it is remarkable how many of our families, as we pass on down the line, are interested in all that we do and all that we say. Any Latter-day Saint family that has searched genealogical and historical records has fervently wished their ancestors had kept better and more complete records. On the other hand, some families possess some spiritual treasures because ancestors have recorded the events surrounding their conversion to the gospel and other happenings of interest, including many miraculous blessings and spiritual experiences. People often use the excuse that their lives are uneventful and nobody would be interested in what they have done. But I promise you that if you will keep your journals and records, they will indeed be a source of

great inspiration to your families, to your children, your grandchildren, and others, on through the generations.9

Don't get hung up on the specifics of journal writing: what to write about, where to start, how exactly to say what you want, or whether your writing is boring. Sometimes all you need to do is grab a notebook and start writing. President Kimball also said that "your private journal should record the way you face up to challenges that beset you . . . . Your journal, like most others, will tell of problems as old as the world and how you dealt with them . . . . What could you do better for your children and your children's children than to record the story of your life, your triumphs over adversity, your recovery after a fall, your progress when all seemed black, your rejoicing when you had finally achieved?"10

The scriptures are a source of spiritual understanding to all people of this world. But the there is a special spirit invoked through the hearing or reading of experiences of someone that you personally know. Grandparents can record experiences and insights they have gained through years of living and learning. Their writings can help grandchildren in later years, giving them added strength and insight. If you think of your journal as directed to your posterity, you will find that there are many important lessons that you have learned that you want to pass on. Words of encouragement, words of insight, words of inspiration, and words of instruction can be written in the pages of your journal to help a grandchild even if you are not there.

## Provide Support for the Parents

If you are the parent of an Ephraim's Child you know the stress of trying to please Mom and Dad, especially if they aren't familiar with the intensity of your son or daughter. It is important that grandparents respect the parents and understand issues in raising a child who is *more*.

It is natural for a grandparent to give advice. However, even good advice is not very helpful if you do not understand the specific issues involved in raising an Ephraim's Child. Sometimes grandparents may feel disregarded because their good advice is not heeded. Unfortunately, what worked with their own children may not work with this grandchild. A grandparent's style of raising children will most likely be very different than the way grandchildren may have to be raised.

These beleaguered parents do not need criticism. They do need your support. Often all that is needed is a listening ear; someone to remind them that these difficulties are temporary, life will go on, and that they are refining characteristics that will be great strengths. Words of encouragement and hope will have extra meaning coming from you. You can give suggestions too, but only after you understand the Ephraim's Child. Then not only can you be a sounding board but can be a consultant to help parents find techniques that will make home a better place. Understanding and informed grandparents can be a great source of support, comfort, and strength.

Informed grandparents can also make visits much more enjoyable. They understand the rules and routines of the home and know that transitions and changes in routine can upset their grandchild. They can be aware of temperamental triggers and realize that the intense Ephraim's Child is not screaming at them because he doesn't like them. Informed and understanding grandparents can make their visits less chaotic and demanding on both the Ephraim's Child and his parents.

Another thing that grandparents can do for their adult children is to share some of the physical challenges of raising Ephraim's Children. If possible, babysitting for a few hours can give parents a much-needed break and time to rejuvenate. However, caring for an Ephraim's Child usually requires a great deal of physical strength and stamina. If this is beyond your capabilities, there are still other ways to help.

## Prayer

Fasting and prayer by loving grandparents can be a great source of strength for the parents of the Ephraim's Child.

Sometimes all a grandparent can do to help is fast and pray. The prayers of family can have great weight. In the case of Alma the younger and Mosiah's sons, the prayers of their fathers resulted in divine intervention. In Mosiah 27:14 an angel appeared to the rebellious boys and said: "Behold, the Lord hath heard the prayers of his people, and also the prayers of his servant, Alma, who is thy father, for he has prayed with much faith concerning thee . . . therefore, for this purpose have I come to convince thee of the power and authority of God, that the prayers of his servants might be answered according to their faith."

The probability of an angelic visitation as a result of our prayers is not likely, but dramatic things can happen from our prayers. The family of an Ephraim's Child often feels ill prepared for the challenges that many times seem singular to their child. The Lord has said, "If any of you lack wisdom, let him ask of God, that giveth to all men liberally, and upbraideth not; and it shall be given him."[11] This promise is not merely extended to the young Joseph Smith, but to all of us who have no idea what to do. As grandparents, pray for your family, and encourage the parents of your grandchildren to pray as well. Ask the Lord for wisdom in how to raise these Ephraim's Children. He sent them to your family and He knows how to parent—and grandparent—them.

## To Be a Strong Spiritual Guide

Grandparents are also role models for their grandchildren. Observant children, particularly Ephraim's Children, watcj wjat upi dp wjem upi are together. "Grandparents . . . can show children by word and by example how to treat others. The kindness and courtesy practiced in our homes can help teach our [grand]children how to deal lovingly and maturely with [other] family members."[12] Grandparents want their lives and examples to reflect the kind of life they want their grandchildren to emulate.

Grandparents can also be strong sources of spiritual support and guidance for their Ephraim's Grandchild. With their own children out of the home, many grandparents have more time to devote to spiritual matters. They can share insights and spiritual experiences with their grandchildren. They can help answer questions and provide extra guidance.

There are numerous little ways grandparents can be spiritual guides. Bear your testimony to your grandchildren. Share stories from the scriptures. Talk about the prophets. Share favorite scripture verses. Sing hymns or children's songs together. Talk about Jesus. Talk about God's love. One grandmother ends all of her weekly letters to her grandchildren with the words, "Remember Heavenly Father and Jesus love you, and so do I." Her grandchildren *know* she loves them, and every time they get a letter they are reminded that Heavenly Father and Jesus love them, just like their grandmother.

The presence of grandparents (whether in person, on the phone, through the mail, or via email) is important to grandchildren. Grandparents come to the role of grandparenthood with knowledge and wisdom gained from their years of living. They have already weathered many stages of life and begin to understand the important things of life and what makes life meaningful. This wisdom can be passed on to grandchildren. "What a wonderful contribution our grandmothers and grandfathers can make if they will share some of the rich experiences and their testimonies with their children and grandchildren."[13] Betty Shannon Cloyd says: "To tell of God's steadfast love and God's wondrous deeds to the generations to come is not only our challenge [as grandparents], it is our sacred responsibility."[14]

## 17

# Being Equal to the Task

**Raise the Bar**

In the book of Alma, the people of Ammon had covenanted to never again take up weapons for the shedding of blood.[1] However, when they saw the hardships of the Nephites in the war with the Lamanites, they wanted to join in the defense of their country, which would mean breaking their covenant.[2] Seeing this, the sons of the people of Ammon, who had not covenanted like their fathers, took up arms to fight with the Nephites.[3]

Thus we are introduced to 2,000 remarkable young men—often called the 2,000 Stripling Warriors. The scriptures record that "they were exceedingly valiant for courage, and also for strength and activity; but behold, this was not all—they were men who were true at all times in whatsoever thing they were entrusted. Yea, they were men of truth and soberness, but they had been taught to keep the commandments of God and to walk uprightly before him."[4] These young men faced danger and possible death as they fought valiantly against the much older and more experienced Lamanite army.

And yet as daunting as their challenge was, in the October 2002 General Conference, M. Russell Ballard said the following: "Today we are fighting a battle that in many ways is more perilous, more fraught with danger than the battle between the Nephites and the Lamanites. Our enemy is cunning and resourceful. We fight against Lucifer, the father of all lies, the enemy of all that is good and right and holy."5 In February of 1832, Joseph Smith and Sidney Rigdon received the vision recorded in D&C 76, in which they were shown the reality of Satan and were told that "he maketh war with the saints of God, and encompasseth them round about."6 That was true in 1832. It was true in the times of the Stripling Warriors. And it is still true today. The Adversary is not half-heartedly trying to lead God's children away from the truth. He has declared an all-out war and is waging it with everything he's got.

Elder Ballard talked about what is going to be required of our young people in this war. He used the expression "Raising the Bar," which has since become a catch-phrase referring to the raised expectations that these latter days will require for youth to survive spiritually. He tells us that there is no longer time for spiritually weak and semicommitted young people. No longer will it be sufficient to just fill a position. Your whole heart and soul will be required as faithful, thinking, and passionate people who know how to listen to and respond to the whisperings of the Holy Spirit.7

And as we learn in the story of the Stripling Warriors, this spiritual strength is possible for the young. "Now this was the faith of these of whom I have spoken; they are young, and their minds are firm, and they do put their trust in God continually . . . . They stand fast in the liberty wherewith God has made them free; and they are strict to remember the Lord their God from day to day; yea, they do observe to keep his statues, and his judgments, and his commandments continually."8 Not only is this spiritual maturity possible for youth, but it is what is needed for the times in which we live.

M. Russell Ballard also said:

These are "perilous times." We battle literally for the souls of men. The enemy is unforgiving and relentless. He is taking eternal prisoners at an alarming rate. And he shows no sign of letting up. While we are profoundly grateful for the many members of the Church who are doing great things in the battle for truth and right, I must honestly tell you it still is not enough. We need much more help. And so, as the people of Ammon looked to their sons for reinforcement in the war against the Lamanites, we look to you . . . . We need you. Like Helaman's 2,000 stripling warriors, you also are the spirit [children] of God, and you too can be endowed with power to build up and defend His kingdom. We need you to make sacred covenants, just as they did. We need you to be meticulously obedient and faithful, just as they were.9

The Lord's servants have called upon the youth "to rise up, to measure up, and to be fully prepared to serve the Lord."10

Parenting an Ephraim's Child who is already *more* requires more from parents, but the call has gone forth for all parents to do more to spiritually prepare their children. Elder Ballard said: "Consequently, if we are 'raising the bar' for your sons to serve as missionaries, that means we are also 'raising the bar' for you. If we expect more of them, that means we expect more of . . . [parents] as well. Remember, Helaman's 2,000 stripling warriors were faithful because 'they had been taught to keep the commandments of God and to walk uprightly before him' (Alma 53:21)—and that instruction came in their homes."11

In talking about the special spirits coming into the world in the last days, Neal A. Maxwell said, "We have long heard, and believed, that the Lord has reserved special spirits to come forth in the last days of the last dispensation. The Church's rising generation of young men and women are a part of that vanguard. Reserved by the Lord for this time, they must now be preserved by parents and prepared for their special moment in human history! They have been held back to come forth at this time, but now they need to be pushed forward to meet their rendezvous."12

It is the parents' job to push these special spirits forward. "What our youth need to know about their 'noble birth right,' we must teach them."13 Elder Maxwell also reminds parents that "just as the rising generation is here, now, by divine design—so are we who have been placed just ahead of them. Our lives and theirs have and will intersect many times before it is all over, and not by accident."[14] These children were purposefully given to us to teach and prepare to go forth into the world and do the work of the Lord.

The world is filled with things that take up time, attention, and energy. Many of them are important things, but none of them are as important as the things of eternity. Our family is the most eternally important thing to dedicate our time, attention, and energy to. Many of the Lord's messengers have stressed the importance of the work that we do at home. President Harold B. Lee said, "The greatest of the Lord's work you brethren will ever do as fathers will be within the walls of your own home."[15] And don't forget President David O. McKay's warning: "No other success can compensate for failure in the home. The poorest shack in which love prevails over a united family is of greater value to God and future humanity than any other riches. In such a home God can work miracles and will work miracles."[16] Parents need to give their children and family top priority.

As parents you can help your Ephraim's Child realize his full potential. It may feel like an overwhelming task, but you can do it. Heavenly Father has entrusted the care and the training of that child to you and you have your own unique abilities and talents to help you. When we struggle through the sometimes difficult task of raising an Ephraim's Child to fulfill his potential, Jeffrey R. Holland assures us that power from the Lord is available to help us. He says: "Keep praying. Those prayers will be heard and answered in the most unexpected hour. God will send aid to no one more readily than He will sent it to a child—and to the parent of a child."[17]

## Teach Truth

Brigham Young once stated that "we are the guardians of our children; their training and education are committed to our care, and if we do not ourselves pursue a course which will save them from the influence of evil, when we are weighed in the balance we shall be found wanting."[18] These are the covenant children of Abraham, his birthright sons and daughters. Great is *their* responsibility. They are given to us to teach and prepare to go forth into the world. We should not send them out unprepared.

Ephraim's Children may understand more than we think that they can. They will recognize truth when they hear it and can understand truth when it is taught to them. We do our children a disservice by being vague in our teachings. They are going into a world that is filled with dangers far greater than any generation before. We have to arm them with the gospel, and we cannot do that unless we teach the powerful truths of the gospel.

In a General Conference address in 1995, Dallin H. Oaks states that some knowledge is more important than others. He suggests that we should be constantly concerned with teaching and emphasizing the important knowledge—or what he called "powerful ideas." The most vital of these powerful ideas are eternal truths that will help us find our way back to the presence of our Heavenly Father.[19] The knowledge that we are all children of God, that mortal life has a purpose, and that Heavenly Father hears and answers prayers are examples of powerful ideas.

The view that today's children can understand more powerful ideas is apparent in the songs being chosen each year for children to learn for the Primary Program. Some adults may have noticed that children are no longer singing the "golden oldies," and may never have heard some of the songs that we grew up with. Just as all knowledge is not equal, all primary songs are not equal. Rather than missing out on fun songs, the Primary General Board has decided to help children learn powerful ideas. For example, the song "I Belong to the Church of Jesus Christ of Latter Day Saints"[20] teaches more about basic gospel fundamentals than "Give Said the Little Stream"[21] teaches about being generous.

Through music children are internalizing eternal truths that can help build a strong spiritual foundation needed to see them through troubled times.

Perhaps as important as teaching eternal truths is making sure that our children see us living them. Elder Holland gives parents this important counsel: "Live the gospel as conspicuously as you can. Keep the covenants your children know you have made. Give priesthood blessings. And bear your testimony! Don't just assume your children will somehow get the drift of your beliefs on their own."22 We can also follow the advice of Nephi who wrote: "We talk of Christ, we rejoice in Christ, we preach of Christ, we prophesy of Christ, and we write according to our prophecies, that our children may know to what source they may look for a remission of their sins."23

The job of a parent is so important. In what other area of life can we have so much impact on another human being as when raising a child? Elder Holland leaves us with this image:

> "Brothers and sisters, our children take their flight into the future with our thrust and with our aim. And even as we anxiously watch that arrow in flight and know all the evils that can deflect its course after it has left our hand, nevertheless we take courage in remembering that the most important mortal factor in determining that arrow's destination will be the stability, strength, and unwavering certainty of the holder of the bow."24

The important task of training these strong-willed Ephraim's Children and setting them on the correct path has been given to parents. And once these tenacious spirits are launched in a direction little can be done to turn them away from it. Envision what they can do in the Lord's hands, and then imagine what they can also become if they fall to the other path. Their persistence and intensity can be directed towards righteousness, or it can be set in doing harm and evil. Ours is such a vital mission. Who would suppose that the most important task to be assigned is that of the parent? It is not the command of armies or the ruling of a country, but the quiet task of parenthood.

This great task comes with great responsibility, and parents will be called upon to give an accounting of their stewardship of these choice spirits. James E. Talmadge said:

> See to it that while [your children] are young and plastic they are properly shaped, that they may become vessels fit to be used in the service of God. This is to me an all important subject, I trust it will appeal to every one, for remember that we are answerable to the Lord for these spirits that have come to us, and when we stand before the bar of God to answer for the deeds that we have done and to receive the reward or the condemnation that will follow, I believe that among other questions, these will be put to you, "Where are those choice spirits that were given to you? Where are my sons and daughters that were held back in my providence until the day of the great dispensation of the fullness of times, and then were sent forth with all the powers and elements of leadership and mastership within them? What have you done with them? Have you guarded and attended them until they became fit to walk alone, or have you exposed them to all the temptations of a false civilization?25

## Enjoy Your Ephraim's Child

We would like to say that parenting an Ephraim's Child will be smooth sailing after reading this book. Unfortunately that is not the case. Parenting an Ephraim's Child will probably never be easy, but many situations will be easier once you understand and work with your child's temperament. Just remember that you are foreordained to parent your Ephraim's Child. You can be equal to the task of raising him.

By understanding and working with your Ephraim's Child, you can magnify your calling as a parent of one of these special spirits. You do not need to be scared of intensity. You can enjoy and direct your child's persistence. Working together you can help her adapt to change. You can refine awareness and sensitivity into charity. You can direct your child's activity, intelligence, and independence towards building the Kingdom of God, and you can do all this without relinquishing parental authority or stripping your child of her control. With the Lord's help these temperamental traits can be molded into a latter day stripling warrior.

Ezra Taft Benson reminded us that we are dealing with "choice spirits among many that have been created. I am persuaded that in the veins of these boys and girls . . . flows some of the best blood that this world has ever known."[26] Ephraim's Children possess character traits that can be refined into weapons and tools that the Lord needs to build and defend His kingdom. Just remember that building a good relationship with your child takes time, as does molding and refining raw characteristics, but it is worth it. You *can* enjoy your Ephraim's Child.

# ENDNOTES

## Preface by The Authors

1. *Journal of Discourses.* Vol. 10, 188.
2. See note 1 above.

## Chapter One: Why ANOTHER Parenting Book

1. Kurcinka, Mary Sheedy. *Raising Your Spirited Child,* 13.
2. James 1:5.
3. Kimball, Spencer W. *Faith Precedes the Miracle,* 323.
4. D&C 133:58-59.
5. *Journal of Discourses.* Vol. 10, 188.
6. Brown, Hugh B. *The Abundant Life,* 203.
7. 1 Nephi 3:7.
8. D&C 68:28.

## Chapter Two: What Is an Ephraim's Child?

1. McConkie, Joseph Fielding, and Millet, Robert L. *Doctrinal Commentary on the Book of Mormon.* Vol. 3, 142.
2. Dobson, James. *The Strong-Willed Child.*
3. Budd, Linda S. *Living with the Active Alert Child,* 6.
4. Smith, Joseph Fielding. *The Way To Perfection,* 122.
5. Smith Jr., Joseph Fielding. *Doctrines of Salvation.* Vol.3, 252.
6. Bennett, Archibald F. *Saviours on Mount Zion,* 70.
7. *Bible Dictionary.* "Ephraim," 666.
8. See note 5 above.
9. See note 5 above.
10. Benson, Ezra Taft. *The Teachings of Ezra Taft Benson,* 104-105.
11. Smith, Hyrum G. *Conference Report,* (April 1929), 123.

12. Kurcinka, Mary Sheedy. *Raising Your Spirited Child*, 20.

13. Tobias, Cynthia Ulrich. *You Can't Make Me*, 11.

## Chapter Three: Do You Have an Ephraim's Child?

1. Goethe, Johann Wolfgang von. *Quotationary*. CD-ROM.

2. Foreman, Rex Ph.D., and Long, Nicholas Ph.D. *Parenting the Strong-Willed Child*, 11.

3. D&C 93:40.

4. 3 Nephi 11:29.

5. Kurcinka, Mary Sheedy. *Raising Your Spirited Child*, 8.

6. Kurcinka, Mary Sheedy. *Raising Your Spirited Child*, 52.

## Chapter Four: Intensity

1. Kurcinka, Mary Sheedy. *Raising Your Spirited Child*, 28.

2. Kurcinka, Mary Sheedy. *Raising Your Spirited Child*, 77-82.

3. Kurcinka, Mary Sheedy. *Raising Your Spirited Child*, 78.

4. Borge, Victor. *Quotationary*. CD-ROM.

5. "Q&A: Questions and Answers." *New Era* (Jan.1997), 17.

6. Matthew 22:37.

7. D&C 4:2.

8. See note 7 above.

9. D&C 58:27.

10. D&C 58:27-28.

11. Maxwell, Neal A. *For the Power is in Them*, Intro.

12. 1 Nephi 2:16.

13. Ludlow, Daniel H., ed. *Encyclopedia of Mormonism*. Vol. 2, "Jacob, Son of Lehi."

14. Ludlow, Daniel H., ed. *Encyclopedia of Mormonism*.

Vol. 2, "Mormon."

15. Joseph Smith—History 1:22.

16. Roberts, B.H. *The Seventy's Course in Theology, Third Year*, 182.

17. JST Luke 2:49.

18. Smith, Joseph F. *Gospel Doctrine*, 13.

19. Revelation 3:19.

20. Alma 21:23.

21. Alma 27:27.

22. Alma 27:30.

23. McConkie, Bruce R. *Mormon Doctrine.* 2nd ed., 854.

## Chapter Five: Persistence

1. Abraham 3:25.

2. D&C 56:3.

3. Genesis 39:10.

4. Genesis 39:12.

5. Edwards. Tryon, et.al. *The New Dictionary of Thoughts: A Cyclopedia of Quotations*, 478.

6. Edwards. Tryon, et.al. *The New Dictionary of Thoughts: A Cyclopedia of Quotations*, 477.

7. Cameron, Roderick L., and Lawrence R. Flack. *BYU Speeches of the Year*, Grant Oratorical Contest, Dec. 1, 1964.

8. Packer, Boyd K. "Begin Where You Are—At Home." *Ensign* (Feb. 1972), 69.

9. Wirthlin, Joseph B. "Never Give Up." *Ensign* (Nov. 1987), 9.

10. See note 9 above.

11. Avant, Gerry. "Mule Rides Filled with Thrills for Isle's Tourists." *LDS Church News* Feb. 8 1997, Z9.

12. Wilcox, S. Michael. *Don't Leap with the Sheep*, 15.

13. Moses 3:16-17.

14. See note 12 above.

15. Oaks, Dallin H. "Weightier Matters." *Ensign* (Jan. 2001), 13.

16. D&C 46:7.
17. "negotiate." *Random House Webster's College Dictionary.*
18. Fisher, Roger, et.al. *Getting to Yes, Negotiating Agreement Without Giving In.* 2nd ed., 13.
19. Fisher, Roger, et.al. *Getting to Yes, Negotiating Agreement Without Giving In.* 2nd ed., 12.
20. Kurcinka, Mary Sheedy. *Raising Your Spirited Child,* 99-100.
21. Coolidge, John Calvin. *Quotationary.* CD-ROM.
22. Benson, Ezra Taft. "The Gift of Modern Revelation." *Ensign* (Nov. 1986), 79 .
23. See note 9 above.
24. 1 Nephi 22:31; D&C 18:22; 20:25; 53:7.
25. See note 9 above.

## Chapter Six: Adaptability

1. Ashton, Marvin J. "Who's Losing?" *Ensign* (Nov. 1974), 42.
2. Nibley, Hugh. *Teachings of the Book of Mormon, Semester 4,* 209.
3. Mosiah 1:5.
4. Ashton, Marvin O. *Conference Report* (Oct. 1942), 53.
5. *Bible Dictionary.* "Jeremiah," 711.
6. Jeremiah 18:1-2.
7. Jeremiah 18:6.
8. Tefan, Jean A. "Jeremiah: As Potter's Clay." *Ensign* (Oct. 2002), 12.
9. Young, Brigham. *Journal of Discourses.* Vol. 2, 152.
10. *History of the Church of Latter-day Saints, The.* 2nd ed. Vol. 4, 478.
11. Tefan, Jean A. "Jeremiah: As Potter's Clay." *Ensign* (Oct. 2002), 12.
12. 1 Nephi 17:45.
13. Helaman 12:4.

## Chapter Seven: Awareness

1. *Diagnostic and Statistical Manual of Mental Disorders, The.* 4th ed., 84.
2. *Diagnostic and Statistical Manual of Mental Disorders, The.* 4th ed., 83.
3. Palladino, Lucy Jo, Ph.D. *The Edison Trait: Saving the Spirit of Your Nonconforming Child*, 200.
4. Foreman, Rex PhD., and Nicholas Long, Ph.D. *Parenting the Strong-Willed Child*, 104.
5. Foreman, Rex PhD., and Nicholas Long, Ph.D. *Parenting the Strong-Willed Child*, 105.
6. Foreman, Rex PhD., and Nicholas Long, Ph.D. *Parenting the Strong-Willed Child*, 106.
7. Foreman, Rex PhD., and Nicholas Long, Ph.D. *Parenting the Strong-Willed Child*, 111.
8. Maxwell, Neal A. *The Smallest Part*, 72.
9. 2 Timothy 3:7.
10. See note 8 above.
11. Clarke, J. Richard. "Love Extends Beyond Convenience." *Ensign* (Nov. 1981), 79.
12. Matthew 9:20-22; Mark 5:25-34; Luke 8:43-48.
13. Brown, Hugh B. *The Abundant Life*, 43.
14. Brown, Hugh B. *The Abundant Life*, 255-256.

## Chapter Eight: Sensitivity

1. Greenspan, Stanley I., M.D. and Jacqueline Salmon. *The Challenging Child*, 36.
2. See note 1 above.
3. Greenspan, Stanley I., M.D. and Jacqueline Salmon. *The Challenging Child*, 29.
4. Greenspan, Stanley I., M.D. and Jacqueline Salmon. *The Challenging Child*, 42.
5. Greenspan, Stanley I., M.D. and Jacqueline Salmon. *The Challenging Child*, 46.
6. Budd, Linda S. *Living with the Active Alert Child*, 144.
7. Budd, Linda S. *Living with the Active Alert Child*, 141.

8. Weissbluth, Marc, M.D. *Healthy Sleep Habits, Happy Child (revised edition)*, 5.

9. Weissbluth, Marc, M.D. *Healthy Sleep Habits, Happy Child (revised edition)*, 40.

10. Weissbluth, Marc, M.D. *Healthy Sleep Habits, Happy Child (revised edition)*, 72.

11. Weissbluth, Marc, M.D. *Healthy Sleep Habits, Happy Child (revised edition)*, 65.

12. Moroni 7:47; Ether 12:34; 2 Nephi 26:30.

13. 1 Corinthians 13:5.

14. 1 Timothy 1:5.

15. 1 Corinthians 13:4-7.

16. D&C 121:45.

17. Oaks, Dallin H. "The Challenge to Become." *Ensign* (Nov. 2000), 32.

18. 3 Nephi 27:27.

19. Smith, Joseph Fielding, comp. *Teachings of the Prophet Joseph Smith*, 174.

20. Ludlow, Daniel H., ed. *Encyclopedia of Mormonism*, Vol. 1, "Compassionate Service."

21. Richards, Stephen L. *Conference Report* (April 1950), 162.

## Chapter Nine: Activity

1. Numeroff, Laura Joffe. *If You Give a Mouse a Cookie.*

2. Kurcinka, Mary Sheedy. *Raising Your Spirited Child*, 154.

3. Young, Brigham. *Journal of Discourses*, vol. 19, 70-72.

4. Turecki, Stanley, M.D. and Leslie Tonner. *The Difficult Child*, 66-67.

5. Budd, Linda S. "Chapter Eight: How Your Child Learns," *Living with the Active Alert Child.*

6. Budd, Linda S. *Living with the Active Alert Child*, 170.

7. Budd, Linda S. *Living with the Active Alert Child*, 171.

8. See note 7 above.

9. Budd, Linda S. *Living with the Active Alert Child*, 176.

10. Budd, Linda S. *Living with the Active Alert Child,* 170-176.
11. James 1:22.
12. McConkie, Bruce R. *The Mortal Messiah.* Vol 1, 25.
13. D&C 58:27.
14. Peterson. Mark E. *BYU Speeches of the Year.* Grant Oratorical Contest, 1962.
15. John 5:17.
16. Clarke, J. Richard. "The Value of Work." *Ensign* (May 1982), 77.
17. Maxwell, Neal A.. "The Man of Christ." *Ensign* (May 1975), 101.
18. Richards, Franklin D. "The Gospel of Work." *Improvement Era* (Dec. 1969), 103.
19. *Gospel Principles,* 173.

## Chapter Ten: Intelligence

1. Budd, Linda S. *Living with the Active Alert Child,* 21.
2. Armstrong, Thomas. *Seven Kinds of Smart,* 8.
3. Armstrong, Thomas. "Chapter One: Many Kinds of Minds" *Seven Kinds of Smart,* 9-11.
4. Goleman, Daniel. *Emotional Intelligence,* xii.
5. Goleman, Daniel. *Ibid,* 43.
6. Goleman, Daniel. *Ibid,* 36.
7. Goleman, Daniel. *Ibid,* 189.
8. Goleman, Daniel. *Ibid,* 100.
9. Goleman, Daniel. *Ibid,* 101.
10. Goleman, Daniel. *Ibid,* 190.
11. Vance, Barbara. "How Children Learn to Behave." *Ensign* (May 1973), 37.
12. Kurcinka, Mary Sheedy. *Kids, Parents, and Power Struggles,* 37.
13. D&C 8:2.
14. Mosiah 2:9.
15. Mosiah 12:27.
16. 1 Nephi 17:45.

17. Romans 10:10.

18. D&C 64:22.

19. 1 Samuel 16:7.

20. Ashton, Marvin J. "The Measure of Our Hearts." *Ensign* (Nov. 1988), 15.

21. Alma 5.

22. "intelligence." *Random House Webster's College Dictionary.*

23. McConkie, Bruce R. *Mormon Doctrine.* 2nd ed., 386.

24. 2 Nephi 9:29.

25. Brown, Hugh B. *The Abundant Life*, 35.

26. Smith Jr., Joseph Fielding. *Doctrines of Salvation*, Vol. 1, 29.

27. Smith, Joseph F. *Answers to Gospel Questions*. Vol. 2, 89.

28. 3 Nephi 26:14,16.

29. Stuy, Brian ed. *Collected Discourses*, Vol.1, June 2, 1888.

30. Nibley, Hugh. *The Collected Works of Hugh Nibley: Approaching Zion* (Vol. 9), 281.

## Chapter Eleven: Control

1. *The Quotations Page,* <http://www.quotationspage.com/quotes/King_Edward_VIII/>.

2. Talmage, James E. *Articles of Faith*, 172-174.

3. Cline, Foster W. and Jim Fay. *Parenting with Love and Logic: Teaching Children Responsibility*, 72.

4. Kurcinka, Mary Sheedy. *Kids, Parents, and Power Struggles*, 4.

5. "Lesson 29: Developing Leadership," *The Latter-day Saint Woman*, Part B, 247.

6. Sill, Sterling W. "The Problem Is Always the Same." *Ensign* (Mar. 1973), 34.

7. See note 6 above.

8. 3 Nephi 18:16.

9. Kimball, Spencer W. " Jesus: The Perfect Leader." *Ensign* (Aug. 1979), 5.

10. Leadership qualities adapted from Maxwell, Neal A. *A More Excellent Way*, 53-54, and from Kimball, Spencer W. "Jesus: The Perfect Leader." *Ensign* (Aug. 1979), 5.

11. Matthew 19:21; Luke 18:22.

12. See note 9 above.

13. John 13:34.

14. Maxwell, Neal A. *A More Excellent Way*, 44.

15. See note 9 above.

16. D&C 88:118-119.

17. Quoted by Tanner, N. Eldon. "Leading As the Savior Led." *New Era* (June 1977), 6.

18. Luke 7:1-10; John 8:1-11.

19. Matthew 16:13-19; Matthew 19:16-22; John 21:15-17.

20. See note 5 above.

21. Ashton, Wendell J. "Unchanging Principles of Leadership." *Ensign* (June 1971), 57.

22. See note 21 above.

## Chapter Twelve: Independence

1. Ether 12:27.

2. 2 Nephi 4:34.

3. D&C 58:26.

4. Maxwell, Neal A. "Swallowed Up in the Will of the Father." *Ensign* (Nov. 1995), 23.

5. See note 4 above.

6. 2 Nephi 2:14.

7. 2 Nephi 2:16.

8. 2 Nephi 2:26.

9. Dyer, William G. "Interdependence: A Family and Church Goal." *Ensign* (Feb. 1971), 36.

10. Jarvis, Donald K. "Leaving Eden: A Lesson for Parents." *Ensign* (Feb. 1991), 39.

11. Smith, Joseph F. *Conference Report*, (October 1903), 2.

12. See note 9 above.
13. See note 9 above.
14. See note 9 above.
15. Taylor, John. "The Organization of the Church." *Millennial Star* (15 Nov. 1851), 339.
16. See note 9 above.
17. Bennion, Lowell L. *An Introduction to the Gospel*, 146.
18. Bennion, Lowell L. *An Introduction to the Gospel*, 147.

## Chapter Thirteen: Disciplining the Ephraim's Child
1. D&C 68:28.
2. Faust, James E. "The Greatest Challenge in the World—Good Parenting." *Ensign* (Nov. 1990), 34 .
3. Curwin, Richard L., and Allen N. Mendler. *Discipline with Dignity*, 23.
4. Packer, Boyd K. "Agency and Control." *Ensign* (May 1983), 89.
5. Romney, Marion G. "The Perfect Law of Liberty." *Ensign* (Nov. 1981), 43.
6. D&C 130:20-21.
7. D&C 121:37.
8. http://allthingswilliam.com/greatness.html.
9. Faust, James E. "Obedience: The Path to Freedom." *Ensign* (May 1999), 46.
10. MacKenzie, Robert J. *Setting Limits with Your Strong-Willed Child: Eliminating Conflict by Establishing Firm, Clear, and Respectful Boundaries*, 36.
11. MacKenzie, Robert J. *Setting Limits . . .* , 25.
12. MacKenzie, Robert J. *Setting Limits . . .* , 21.
13. MacKenzie, Robert J. *Setting Limits . . .* , 6.
14. Flake, Layne E. and Jana Squires. "Punishment—or Discipline." *Ensign* (Oct. 1983), 39.
15. "Disciplining with Love: Handbook for Families."

*Ensign* (Sept. 1985), 32.

16. Hinckley, Gordon B. "First Presidency Message: The Environment of Our Homes." *Ensign* (June 1985), 6.

17. Mead, Eugene. "Reward Them, and Teach Responsibility." *Ensign* (April 1974), 45.

18. Latham, Glenn I. *Parenting With Love: Making a Difference in a Day*, 13.

19. Latham, Glenn I. *Parenting With Love* . . . , 15.

20. Rehme, Carol McAdoo. "The Truth of Consequences." *Ensign* (April 2000), 32.

21. Latham, Glenn I. "Chapter Two: What To Do When Children Behave Well" *Parenting With Love* . . . , 23-35.

22. D&C 132:8.

23. See note 14 above.

24. Oaks, Dallin H. "Parental Leadership in the Family." *Ensign* (June 1985), 7.

25. See note 14 above.

26. MacKenzie, Robert J. *Setting Limits* . . . , 77.

27. See note 26 above.

28. MacKenzie, Robert J. *Setting Limits* . . . , 76-95.

29. MacKenzie, Robert J. *Setting Limits* . . . , 83.

30. MacKenzie, Robert J. *Setting Limits* . . . , 95.

31. Tobias, Cynthia Ulrich. *You Can't Make Me*, 95.

32. Proverbs 3:12.

33. See note 14 above.

34. "Teaching Children to Govern Themselves." *Ensign* (June 1986), 36.

35. Brown, Hugh B. *The Abundant Life*, 312.

36. "Combating Drugs: Building Self-worth in Youths Helps Them Survive." *LDS Church News*, May 6, 1989, 5.

37. Curwin, Richard L., and Allen N. Mendler. *Discipline with Dignity*, 70.

38. See note 15 above.

39. See note 15 above.

40. Proverbs 22:6.

## Chapter Fourteen: When You Don't Like Your Ephraim's Child

1. Sears, William, M.D. and Martha Sears, R.N. *Parenting the Fussy Baby and High-Need Child*, 71-85.

2. MacKenzie, Robert J. *Setting Limits . . .* , 3.

3. *Teachings of the Presidents of the Church: Brigham Young*, 338.

4. See note 2 above.

5. Mosiah 23:21.

6. Cloyd, Betty Shannon. *Parents & Grandparents as Spiritual Guides*, 91.

7. Scott, Richard G. "The Power of Correct Principles." *Ensign* (May 1993), 32.

8. Maxwell, Neal A. "Patience." *Ensign* (Oct. 1980), 28.

9. Maxwell, Neal A. *Men and Women of Christ*, 69.

10. Maxwell, Neal A. "Endure It Well." *Ensign* (May 1990), 34.

11. D&C 121:8.

12. Matthew 24:13.

13. Moroni 7:48.

14. Moroni 7:48.

15. Clegg, Gayle M., http://ce.byu.edu/cw/cwwomen's /archive/2001/clegg_gayle.html.

16. D&C 4:7.

17. Dunne, Diane Weaver. "Statistics Confirm Rise in Childhood ADHD and Medication Use." <http://www.educationworld.com/a_issues/ issues148a.shtml>

18. See note 17 above.

19. Diller, Lawrence M.D. "Just Say Yes to Ritalin." <http://dir.salon.com/mwt/feature/2000/09/ 25/medicate/index.html>.

20. See note 19 above.

21. Tobias, Cynthia Ulrich. *You Can't Make Me*, 81.

**Chapter Fifteen: The Special Occasion Nightmare**
1. D&C 38:30.

**Chapter Sixteen: Grandparenting the Ephraim's Child**
1. http://grammahugs.com/gp/poems/poems.html
2. Benson, Ezra Taft. "To the Elderly in the Church." *Ensign* (Nov. 1989), 7.
3. Cloyd, Betty Shannon. *Parents & Grandparents as Spiritual Guides*, 86.
4. http://www.quotegarden.com/grandparents.html
5. Cloyd, Betty Shannon. *Parents & Grandparents as Spiritual Guides*, 93.
6. Cloyd, Betty Shannon. *Parents & Grandparents as Spiritual Guides*, 92.
7. Malachi 4:6.
8. Benson, Ezra Taft. "To the Elderly in the Church." *Ensign* (Nov. 1989), 4.
9. Kimball, Spencer W. "President Kimball Speaks Out on Personal Journals." *Ensign* (Dec. 1980), 60.
10. Kimball, Spencer W. "President Kimball Speaks Out on Personal Journals." *Ensign* (Dec. 1980), 61.
11. James 1:5.
12. Curtis, LeGrand R. "Perfection: A Daily Process." *Ensign* (July 1995), 32.
13. Featherstone, Vaughn J. "The Savior's Program for the Care of the Aged." *Ensign* (Nov. 1974), 29.
14. Cloyd, Betty Shannon. *Parents & Grandparents as Spiritual Guides*, 106.

**Chapter Seventeen: Being Equal to the Task**
1. Alma 24:18.
2. Alma 53:13-14.
3. Alma 54:16-17.
4. Alma 53:20-21.
5. Ballard, M. Russell. "The Greatest Generation of Missionaries." *Ensign* (Nov. 2002), 46.

6. D&C 76:29.
7. See note 5 above.
8. Alma 58:27, 40.
9. See note 5 above.
10. See note 5 above.
11. See note 5 above.
12. Maxwell, Neal A. "Unto the Rising Generation." *Ensign* (Apr. 1985), 8.
13. See note 12 above.
14. See note 12 above.
15. Lee, Harold B. "Maintain Your Place As a Woman." *Ensign* (Feb. 1972), 51.
16. McKay, David O., quoting McCulloch, J. E. "Home: The Savior of Civilization." *Conference Report* (Apr. 1964), 5.
17. Holland, Jeffrey R. "A Prayer for the Children." *Ensign* (May 2003), 87.
18. *Teachings of the Presidents of the Church: Brigham Young*, 337.
19. Oaks, Dallin H. "Powerful Ideas." *Ensign* (Nov. 1995), 25.
20. *Children's Songbook*, 77.
21. *Children's Songbook*, 236.
22. Holland, Jeffrey R. "A Prayer for the Children." *Ensign* (May 2003), 86.
23. 2 Nephi 25:26.
24. See note 17 above.
25. Talmage, James E. *LDS Collector's Library '97*. General Conference, 6 April 1895.
26. Benson, Ezra Taft. *So Shall Ye Reap*, 27.

# BIBLIOGRAPHY

## The Scriptures of the Church

*Book of Mormon.*
*Doctrine and Covenants.*
*Holy Bible.*
*Pearl of Great Price.*


## Other Works

"All Things William." 12 April 2004. 12 April 2004
      <http://allthingswilliam.com/greatness.html>.

Armstrong, Thomas. *Seven Kinds of Smart.* New York:
      Plume, 1993.

Bennett, Archibald F. *Saviours on Mount Zion.* Salt Lake
      City: Deseret Sunday School Union Board, 1950.

Bennion, Lowell L. *An Introduction to the Gospel.* Salt Lake
      City: Deseret Sunday School Union Board, 1955.

Benson, Ezra Taft. *So Shall Ye Reap.* Salt Lake City: Deseret
      Book Company, 1960.

Benson, Ezra Taft. *The Teachings of Ezra Taft Benson.* Salt
      Lake City: Bookcraft, 1988.

Brown, Hugh B. *The Abundant Life.* Salt Lake City:
      Bookcraft, 1965.

Budd, Linda S. *Living with the Active Alert Child.* Seattle:
      Parenting Press, Inc., 1993.

"BYU Women's Conference, 2001." n.d. Brigham Young
      University. 12 Jan 2003 <http//ce.byu.edu/cw/
      cwwomen's/archive/2001/clegg_gayle.html>.

Cameron, Roderick L., and Lawrence R. Flack. *BYU
      Speeches of the Year.* Provo, Utah: Brigham Young
      University, 1964.

*Children's Songbook.* Salt Lake City: The Church of Jesus
      Christ of Latter-day Saints, 1993.

Cline, Foster W., and Jim Fay. *Parenting with Love and Logic: Teaching Children Responsibility*. Colorado Springs: Navpress, 1990.

Cloyd, Betty Shannon. *Parents & Grandparents as Spiritual Guides*. Nashville: Upper Room Books, 2000.

*Conference Report*. The Church of Jesus Christ of Latter-day Saints.

Curwin, Richard L., and Allen N. Mendler. *Discipline with Dignity*. Alexandria, Virginia: Association for Supervision and Curriculum Development, 1988.

*Diagnostic and Statistical Manual of Mental Disorders, The*. 4th ed. Washington, D.C.: American Psychiatric Association, 1994.

Diller, Lawrence M.D., "Salon.com. " 25 Sept. 2000. 12 April 2004 <http://dir.salon.com/mwt/feature/2000/09/25/medicate/index.html>.

Dobson, James. *The Strong-Willed Child*. Wheaton, Illinios: Living Books, 1978.

Dunne, Diane Weaver. "Education World." 12 Dec. 2000. Education World Inc. 22 March 2003 <http://www.education-world.com/a_issues/issues148a.shtml>.

Edwards, Tryon, et.al. *The New Dictionary of Thoughts: A Cyclopedia of Quotations*. United States of America: Standard Book Company, 1964.

*Ensign*. Salt Lake City: The Church of Jesus Christ of Latter-day Saints.

Fisher, Roger, et.al. *Getting to Yes, Negotiating Agreement Without Giving In*. 2nd ed. Boston: Houghton Mifflin Company, 1991.

Foreman, Rex Ph.D., and Nicholas Long, Ph.D. *Parenting the Strong-Willed Child*. Chicago: Contemporary Books, 1996.

Goleman, Daniel. *Emotional Intelligence*. New York: Bantam Books, 1995.

*Gospel Principles*. Salt Lake City: The Church of Jesus Christ of Latter-day Saints, 1985.

"Grammahugs Poems N' Quotes." 25 Feb. 2002. 12 April 2004 <http://grammahugs.com/gp/poems/poems.html>.

Greene, Ross W., Ph.D. *The Explosive Child: A New Approach For Understanding and Parenting Easily Frustrated, "Chronically Inflexible" Children.* New York: HarperCollins Publishers, 1998.

Greenspan,Stanley I., M.D. and Jacqueline Salmon. *The Challenging Child.* Reading, Massachusetts: Addison-Wesley Publishing Company, 1995.

*History of the Church of Latter-day Saints, The.* 2nd ed. 7 vols. Salt Lake City: Deseret Book Company, 1964.

*Improvement Era.* Salt Lake City: The Church of Jesus Christ of Latter-day Saints.

Kimball, Spencer W. *Faith Precedes the Miracle.* Salt Lake City: Deseret Book Company, 1972.

Kurcinka, Mary Sheedy. *Kids, Parents, and Power Struggles.* New York: HarperCollins Publishers, 2000.

Kurcinka, Mary Sheedy. *Raising Your Spirited Child.* New York: HarperCollins Publishers, 1991.

*LDS Church News*, Deseret News, published weekly.

*LDS Collector's Library '97.* CD-ROM. Infobases, Inc., 1996.

Latham, Glenn I. *Parenting With Love: Making a Difference in a Day.* Salt Lake City: Bookcraft, 1999.

*Latter-day Saint Woman, The, Part B.* Salt Lake City: Intellectual Reserve, Inc., 2000.

Ludlow, Daniel H., ed. *Encyclopedia of Mormonism.* 4 vols. New York: Macmillan Publishing Company, 1992.

MacKenzie, Robert J. *Setting Limits with Your Strong-Willed Child: Eliminating Conflict by Establishing Firm, Clear, and Respectful Boundaries.* Roseville, CA: Prima Communications Inc., 2001.

Maxwell, Neal A. *A More Excellent Way.* Salt Lake City: Deseret Book, 1973.

Maxwell, Neal A. *For the Power is in Them.* Salt Lake City: Deseret Book, 1970.

Maxwell, Neal A. *Men and Women of Christ*. Salt Lake City: Bookcraft, 1991.

Maxwell, Neal A. *The Smallest Part*. Salt Lake City: Deseret Book, 1976.

McConkie, Bruce R. *Mormon Doctrine*. 2nd ed. Salt Lake City: Bookcraft, 1966.

McConkie, Bruce R. *The Mortal Messiah*. 4 vols. Salt Lake City: Deseret Book Company, 1979-1981.

McConkie, Joseph Fielding, and Robert L. Millet. *Doctrinal Commentary on the Book of Mormon*. 3 vols. Salt Lake City: Bookcraft, 1988.

*Millennial Star*. The Church of Jesus Christ of Latter-day Saints.

*New Era*. Salt Lake City: The Church of Jesus Christ of Latter-day Saints.

Nibley, Hugh. *Teachings of the Book of Mormon, Semester 4*. Provo, Utah: Foundation for Ancient Research & Mormon Studies (F.A.R.M.S.), 1998-1990.

Nibley, Hugh. *The Collected Works of Hugh Nibley: Approaching Zion* (Vol. 9). Salt Lake City: Deseret Book Company, 1989.

Numeroff, Laura Joffe, *If You Give a Mouse a Cookie*, Mexico: HarperCollins Publishers, 1985.

Palladino, Lucy Jo, Ph.D. *The Edison Trait: Saving the Spirit of Your Nonconforming Child*. New York: Times Books, 1997.

"Quote Garden, The." n.d. 12 April 2004 <http://www.quotegarden.com/grandparents.html>.

Quotationary. CD-ROM. Midway, Utah: NovaSoft, LLC., 1999.

"Quotations Page, The." n.d. 9 April 2004 <http://www.quotationspage.com>.

*Random House Webster's College Dictionary*. New York: Random House, Inc., 1996.

Roberts, B.H. *The Seventy's Course in Theology, Third Year*. Salt Lake City: The Deseret News, 1907.

Sears, William, M.D. and Martha Sears, R.N. *Parenting the

*Fussy Baby and High-Need Child.* Boston: Little, Brown and Company, 1996.

Smith, Hyrum G. *Conference Report*, April 1929.

Smith, Joseph F. *Answers to Gospel Questions.* 5 Vols. Salt Lake City: Deseret Book Company, 1957-66.

Smith, Joseph F. *Gospel Doctrine.* Salt Lake City: Deseret Book Company, 1939.

Smith, Joseph Fielding, comp. *Teachings of the Prophet Joseph Smith.* Salt Lake City: Deseret Book Company, 1976.

Smith, Joseph Fielding. *The Way To Perfection.* Salt Lake City: Genealogical Society of Utah, 1940.

Smith Jr., Joseph Fielding. *Doctrines of Salvation.* 3 vols. Salt Lake City: Bookcraft, 1954-56.

Stuy, Brian ed. *Collected Discourses*, 5 Vols. 1886-1909.

Talmage, James E. *Articles of Faith.* Salt Lake City: Deseret Book Company, 1988.

*Teachings of the Presidents of the Church: Brigham Young.* Salt Lake City: The Church of Jesus Christ of Latter-day Saints, 1997.

Tobias, Cynthia Ulrich. *You Can't Make Me.* Colorado Springs: Random House, 1999.

Turecki, Stanley, M.D. and Leslie Tonner. *The Difficult Child.* New York: Bantam Books, 1985.

Weissbluth, Marc, M.D. *Healthy Sleep Habits, Happy Child (revised edition).* New York: Fawcett Books, 1999.

Widtsoe, John A. *Evidences and Reconciliations.* Ed. G. Homer Durham. 3 vols. Salt Lake City: Bookcraft, 1960.

Wilcox, S. Michael. *Don't Leap with the Sheep.* Salt Lake City: Deseret Book, 2001.

Young, Brigham. *Journal of Discourses.* 26 vols. Liverpool: Asa Calkin, 1854-56.

# APPENDIX

## Play Dough (not edible)
1 cup flour
1 cup water
1/2 cup salt
2 Tbls Cream of Tartar
1 Tbls oil
food coloring

Cook ingredients until they clump together in a pan. Pour it out onto wax paper and knead when cool. Store in an airtight container.

## Kool-Aid Play Dough (not edible)
2 1/2 cups flour
1/2 cup salt
3 Tbls. corn oil
1 Tbls. alum
1 3/4 cups boiling water
1 package Unsweetened Kool-Aid

Mix the dry ingredients in a bowl. In a separate pan bring the water and oil to a boil. Add to the dry ingredients. Mix, then knead as you would bread. Store in a airtight container.

## Peanut Butter Play Dough (edible)
1 cup Smooth Peanut Butter
1/2 cup Honey
2 cup Nonfat Dry Milk

Mix together the peanut butter and honey first. Add half of the dry milk and mix; then continue to add a little at a time until it feels soft. Use less than 2 cups of dry milk if the clay seems to be getting dry. You can add raisins, coconut, chocolate chips, etc. to decorate.

## Silly Putty #1

1/4 cup white glue
1/4 cup liquid starch

Mix together and work with your hands until it is the consistency of putty. You may need to add more glue if the texture doesn't act like silly putty in its elasticity.

## Silly Putty #2

1 Zip Lock Bag
1 Tbls. Glue
2 Tbls. Liquid Starch

Put glue into the Zip Lock Bag, then add starch. Zip the bag closed. Press and squeeze the bag until the glue and starch mix together.

## Puffy Paint

Equal parts of flour, salt, and water
Food Coloring
Cardboard squares or heavy paper
Plastic squeeze bottles

Mix equal parts of flour, salt, and water in a bowl. Add the food coloring to get the desired color. Pour into the empty plastic squeeze bottles (empty mustard or ketchup bottles). Squeeze out onto cardboard or heavy paper. Mixture will harden in a puffy shape. Colors will pool together without mixing together.

## Finger Paint
1 cup flour
1 tsp. salt
1 cup plus 2 Tbls. cold water
1 cup hot water
food coloring

Mix flour and salt and gradually add 1 cup plus 2 Tbls. cold water. Add 1 cup hot water and boil it until it comes clear. Beat until smooth and mix in food coloring.

## Applesauce Cinnamon Dough Recipe
1 cup Applesauce
1 cup Cinnamon

Mix the applesauce and the cinnamon until it gets to be a nice clay consistency. If it is too sticky, add a bit more cinnamon or even a touch of flour. You can make shapes and designs or even use cookie cutters. Put the shapes in a warm, dry spot to dry (this takes a few days). You can make sweet-smelling sculptures to decorate and/or paint.

## Bread Clay
7 pieces of white bread
7 tsp School Glue
1/2 tsp water
1/2 tsp dish soap

Cut the crusts off the pieces of bread. Break the bread into small pieces and put them a medium sized bowl. Add the glue and mix thoroughly. Add the water and dish soap and mix until you get a nice clay consistency. If your mixture is too dry, add a bit more water. You can make shapes and let air dry, which takes about 24 hours.

## Goop/Gak (not edible)

4 ounces of "White School Glue"
1 teaspoon Borax
Assortment of Liquid Food Coloring
One cup plain water

In a small mixing bowl mix together glue and 1/2 cup of the water. Add a few drops of food coloring. In a second bowl mix together 1 tsp of Borax and the remaining water. Mix this solution well. Pour the Borax mixture into the glue mixture, making a very thick liquid mix. Once they are mixed the Goop should form. Remove the Goop from the bowl knead it a little.

# RECOMMENDED ADDITIONAL RESOURCES

Budd, Linda S. *Living with the Active Alert Child*. Seattle: Parenting Press, Inc., 1993.

Cline, Foster W., and Jim Fay. *Parenting with Love and Logic: Teaching Children Responsibility*. Colorado Springs: Navpress, 1990.

Foreman, Rex Ph.D., and Nicholas Long, Ph.D. *Parenting the Strong-Willed Child*. Chicago: Contemporary Books, 1996.

Greenspan,Stanley I., M.D. and Jacqueline Salmon. *The Challenging Child*. Reading, Massachusetts: Addison-Wesley Publishing Company, 1995.

Kurcinka, Mary Sheedy. *Kids, Parents, and Power Struggles*. New York: HarperCollins Publishers, 2000.

Kurcinka, Mary Sheedy. *Raising Your Spirited Child*. New York: HarperCollins Publishers, 1991.

Latham, Glenn I. *Parenting With Love: Making a Difference in a Day*. Salt Lake City: Bookcraft, 1999.

MacKenzie, Robert J. *Setting Limits with Your Strong-Willed Child: Eliminating Conflict by Establishing Firm, Clear, and Respectful Boundaries*. Roseville, CA: Prima Communications Inc., 2001.

Phelan, Thomas W. Ph.D. *1-2-3 Magic*. Glen Ellyn, Illinois: Child Management Inc. 1995.

Sears, William, M.D. and Martha Sears, R.N. *Parenting the Fussy Baby and High-Need Child*. Boston: Little, Brown and Company, 1996.

Tobias, Cynthia Ulrich. *You Can't Make Me*. Colorado Springs: Random House, 1999.

Turecki, Stanley, M.D. and Leslie Tonner. *The Difficult Child*. New York: Bantam Books, 1985.

# About the Authors

Deborah Talmadge is a native of western Colorado and is the mother of three and the grandmother of five. Deborah is proficient at the piano and studied Piano Performance and Geology at Mesa State College. She even had the opportunity to stay for a month in Italy to study under piano masters there. She now teaches piano lessons around her writing schedule and has published two fiction novels. Deborah has served in numerous church callings including Primary Chorister, Ward Organist and Chorister, Music Chairman, Relief Society Teacher, Ward Activity Director, and eight years as a Gospel Doctrine teacher. She is currently serving as the Relief Society Nursery Leader and Sunday School teacher for ages 14-16. Deborah is very involved in the lives of her children and grandchildren and got a first-hand look at daily life with Ephraim's Children while caring for one Ephraim's Child grandson while his mom was on four months of bed rest. After taking care of him all day, she would then stay in the evenings with her other daughter and her two Ephraim's Children. Deborah enjoys early morning walks and hiking in the desert mountains and canyons of western Colorado.

Jaime Theler lives in American Fork, Utah, but grew up in Colorado. She attended Brigham Young University, where she met and married her husband Jason. She graduated from BYU with a Bachelor's degree in Physical Therapy. Following graduation, their first child was born, and thus began the quest to find parenting counsel that would actually work with this child. Two more children later, she finally feels like she has a general idea on what to do. Jaime is a stay-at-home mom with the full-time job of keeping up with her extremely active kids. She fits writing around naps, bedtime, and daily crises. Jaime's first two kids are very much Ephraim's Children, and her baby girl is showing definite tendencies of being one too. Jaime has served for years in the primary organization in three different wards and has ample experience with methods and techniques that do—and do not—work with super intense kids. She loves to play tennis, scrapbook, read anything she can get her hands on, and home decorate whenever she has a spare minute and dime.